AUGUSTIN IOAN

# POWER, PLAY AND NATIONAL IDENTITY

Politics of Modernization
in Central and East-European Architecture.
The Romanian File

D1250052

Cover by EUGEN ALEXANDRU GUSTEA

© EDITURA  FUNDAȚIEI  CULTURALE  ROMÂNE
Aleea Alexandru, nr. 38, sectorul 1
71273 București
ROMÂNIA
Tel.: 230.25.43
Fax: 230.75.59
EMAIL = fcr @ algoritma.ro


ISBN  973–577–203–5

# AUGUSTIN IOAN

# POWER, PLAY AND NATIONAL IDENTITY

## Politics of Modernization in Central and East-European Architecture. The Romanian File

Translated from Romanian by STELA TINNEY

THE ROMANIAN CULTURAL FOUNDATION
PUBLISHING HOUSE
Bucharest • 1999

# CONTENTS

5

# INTRODUCTION

The book at hand is the result of an older preoccupation with putting the problems of Romanian architecture in their proper context from a two-fold perspective. First, the book is about projecting them against the ampler backdrop of the architecture of their own time and place; secondly, it is about infusing contemporary methods of research in an area which, more than others, shows the wear of traditional modes of interrogating the object. A few epistemological paradigms have come and gone since the studies in Romanian architecture belonging to such venerable foregoers as Grigore Ionescu and Gh. Curinschi Verona. Having honed their nibs and tempered them in the flame of new theories, the young generations have now the duty to revisit the well-known, perennial (obsessive?) themes. Historians and theoreticians of all generations have already undertaken, with considerable effort, the methodological renewal and updating of the main arguments in their respective fields, with often spectacular results. Let me mention here only a handful: the late Dana Harhoiu's risky book about *Bucharest Between Orient and Occident* (1997), whose impact is far from having been evaluated yet, or the elevated discourse of recent studies belonging to Professors Sanda Voiculescu, Ana-Maria Zahariade, Anca Brătulescu, Nicolae Lascu — in Bucharest — or Teodor Gheorghiu, from Timișoara.

For some time now I've been busy looking at some controversial aspects of Romanian architecture in the past century. Within the context of the relationship between architecture and political power, examined in my first book (1992), I've given ample room to the manner in which Romanian architecture — its edifices and its "actors" — have developed in the twentieth century. Because many of those assertions still seem valid, I've restated them here; others are riskier, so I've qualified them. For instance, the problem of the Civic Center has been examined again and again in magazine articles and essays, and also in the 1992, 1996 and 1997 films shot with Nicolae Mărgineanu, Sorin Ilieșiu and Doru Segal. I've lectured on this theme in Cambridge, in Dundee, in Cincinnati, and the entire issue of **Baumwelt** featuring Bucharest was placed under the heading I've suggested as equally representative of the city and our way of interacting with it: "the unfinished project". And yet I still consider the idea submitted as a theoretical text to the contest of projects and ideas for the House of the Republic — that of "terraforming" the devastated area in a post-modern style — a useful exercise even for those who continue to shape urban policy, especially since, in the meantime, various investment projects have crystallized exactly along the lines of the vision I then proposed — from the Dracula/Transylvania Theme Park, suggested by the America's Partners Group in 1998, to the proposal of the ex-mayor Halaicu to sell the House of the Republic in order to have it turned into a casino.

Invited by Mrs. Mariana Celac and Mrs. Carmen Popescu to participate in the exhibition and, respectively, the catalogue on the Neo-Romanian style, I came to the consideration of Christian Orthodox architecture and its "entelechy" under the specter of collective identity. The problem seemed, both to the distinguished organizers and myself, larger than the too-narrow aesthetic frame. Thus we've extended this to include the latest significant gesture in the domain of rethinking Orthodox architecture: the 1942 contest for a never-built cathedral in Odessa. The results of this investigation appear to cast light on the entire theme of collective identity, on programmatic "Romanian-ness" in architecture. Moreover, on the metalevel, a theory can be derived, I believe, from the study of these paradigmatic examples — a theory about the manner in which any identity-conscious architecture is produced, including all national pavilions at international exhibitions, Houses of the Republic, cathedrals of the nation and so forth. Orthodox architecture, primarily because it is exemplary, has a rich potential for generalization. In addition, viewing old gestures through new criteria, whether supplied by post-modernism or by critical regionalism, may cancel the tension of the relationship with the object of study and, by way of consequence, lead to this object's escape from underneath the oppressive lid of all kinds of identitary ideologies. To obtain more generally valid results, is is more productive to talk about combinedness and ludic spirit than about Romanian-ness; the former discussion allows the comparison with other places and other times; the latter restricts itself to the particular, the accidental, the unique, leading very quickly, as we witness too often even today, to a theoretical blockage, to irrelevance.

The study of Khrushchev's 1954 speech is a consequence of the enduring interest in the too-oft neglected political influences controlling architecture — its institutions, personalities, and, above all, the significant sum of its buildings. It is an application of my theory, amply explained in the volume *Khora*, on the relevance of the **escorting discourses** which accompany buildings — from laws to political speeches to "petites histoires" — to the understanding of architecture as a whole-in-process, unexplained by the reification of buildings, by their isolation from the context which first produced them. Armed with the notion of **escorting discourse**, we could discover the connection between, on the one hand, the obsessive linoleum of the social dwelling and the prefab platform in Militari, and, on the other hand, a 1954 Soviet political speech.

A study about post-modernism — owing its publication in *Eurèsis-Cahiers Roumains des Etudes Littéraires* to Professor Mircea Martin — concludes the survey of the "historical" zone of my theme. This text is written in the style of a memoir because I possess the immediate, intimate knowledge of the period, during which I was an architectural student, when our school shuddered with red columns, broken gables and cynicism — the form taken here by the meek irony of a Venturi, Krier or Portoghesi. The contest for Tête Défense in Paris, in which Romanians took part with a mysterious frenzy, the incredible visit of Kisho Kurokawa, and the La Villette Park were all events more shattering to me than the iron ball that demolished the churches of St. Vineri and Văcăreşti; for me all these events eventually settled into their correct perspective only after 1989. Back then, however, I was innocently frequenting the American Library, sketching a presidential work visit à la Kim Ir Sen on a "complex project" which the school had assigned us, in complicity with the on-going demolitions in the city, since this project implied the razing of an entire historical district of Bucharest (The Gemeni Galatzi Marketplace), and sneaking in alternative projects to face the glacial judgment of our modernist professors.

Finally, after the subjective memoir, I've chosen the journalistic idiom in order to present the contemporary moment in architecture. It is the idiom I've been using for over two years in „Libertatea" (1995-1998) and, sporadically, in *Dilema* and *Românul Liber*. Here can be found both the article which singles out one problem and the pamphlet, since we are too close to a given phenomenon to judge it otherwise than ad hoc, with the instruments of the "greeting" criticism. I know I will be letting down those who, like my professor Cezar Radu, await my emergence from the provisional state inherent to all criticism and into a permanent residence placed under the nobler and more generous sign of advanced research. However, I think that the exceptional situation of Romanian architecture — among many other Romanian aspects — does require a minimum personal sacrifice. For me, this consists in postponing the withdrawal into the rarefied atmosphere of strictly academical research.

10

Besides, myself a child of post-modernism, I don't find such a perspective to be the only one adequate to fully understand the phenomenon unfolding before our very eyes. We have been too deprived of critical discourse to pretend to deny it citizenship. There have been no pens to promote this discourse, either before or after 1989. Before 1989, political reasons, and after 1989 also economical ones combine to stifle critical attitudes, with the result that there is no single example of an architectural masterpiece created in Romania since the Revolution. I am not deluding myself, though; certainly I have not stirred up any civic instincts within the readers of my column, nor have I won any supporters; quite the contrary, I've taken ironies and punches from those who bewailed by association with a "popular quotidian", while on the other side of the fence I've angered a couple of mayors as well as some unexpected "great of the day", some mayfly of a single season. Still it's a weekly effort which I do not regret and which, carried on by others, younger and no doubt stormier than I, could make a breach in the wall of indifference between society and the architecture in which it lives.

This volume is not at all intended as a single complete history of Romanian architecture over the past hundred years. If, however, it draws attention to several great themes; if it revises a few commonplaces; and, above all, if it proves that contemporary means can be used to write about perennial obsessions appertaining to the culture I belong to, then my goal, more modest than writing erudite but sterile treatises, will have been achieved. And for the effort to follow me, with understanding, in this intellectual journey, I thank my readers from the very beginning.

11

# ACKNOWLEDGEMENTS

*Some of the studies in this book were written as a result of my association with the New Europe College in Bucharest and, also, as a result of a research project supported by the Research Support Scheme of the Central European University in Prague. With the kind permission of these two institutions, those texts could be included in this volume. In addition, the article about Romanian post-modernism was published in French in the special issue of the literary magazine* Euresis — Cahiers Roumains des Etudes Littéraires *(Univers Press) dedicated to this theme, through the good will of its director, Prof. Mircea Martin, Ph. D.*

*The critical texts were published either in my column in the daily newspaper* Libertatea, *to which I contributed between 1995-1998, through the good will of the writer Bedros Horasangian, or in several prestigious cultural publications such as* Dilema, Românul Liber, Secolul XX, *or, above all,* Transilvania *(I owe the constancy of my being published in Sibiu to the poet Ion Mircea and to my very old friend Claudia Tița). The text about the pre-World War II Orthodox architecture in Romania was written for the catalogue of the exhibition on Neo-Romanian architecture, organized by the Romanian Architects Union in care of Ms. Mariana Celac and Ms. Carmen Popescu.*

*Finally, I am honored to address my thanks to the Romanian Cultural Foundation, and especially to the director of this prestigious institution, Academician Augustin Buzura, who made possible the publication of the English version of this book.*

*The Author*

# I

# ORTHODOX ARCHITECTURE
# AND THE THEME OF IDENTITY

## 1. Overview

*Christian Orthodox religious architecture, which coincides with the Neo-Romanian style in its period and, often, in its authors, is still insufficiently studied. The two major studies of the history of architecture in Romania signed by Grigore Ionescu and Gh. Curinschi-Verona make no mention of the most important examples of the period, let alone raise questions about the phenomenon, which is akin to the current of Neo-Romanianism and, in a broader sense, to the very birth, childhood ills and maturity of the national idea. About the role of parish churches in a period of coagulation and, then, of reformulation of the urban tissues in the Kingdom of Romania, two architects have written pertinently in recent years — Dana Harhoiu, with an explicit focus on Bucharest (1977) and Sanda Voiculescu (1977, 146-53) — as well as, from the ranks of theologians, Theodor Baconsky (1977, 61-3). The subject belongs, though, to a couple of domains — that of the sacred and that of national identity — which have been so grossly disfigured by the atheistic nationalistic ideologies of the communist regime that many researchers still find it unpalatable.*

\*\*\*

There are at least two distinct steps in the affirmation of sacred architecture in Romania in the last hundred years, and both steps are linked to the national idea. The Orthodox churches built in

15

Dobrogea (after the adjudication of this territory in 1877 when Romania won its independence from the Ottoman Empire) were the visible signs of the new Romanian power in an ethnically and denominationally mixed region. The Cathedral of Constanța, authored by Ion Mincu, belongs in this category. Taking possession of Dobrogea by means of religious buildings was a gesture somewhat facilitated by the leniency of the former Turkish administration which had been quite tolerant here, on the *limes**, of non-Moslems, who had been able to build churches and synagogues in relative autonomy. In Tulcea for instance (where every Christian community — the Greeks, Bulgarians, Lipovans, Russians and Romanians — had already built at least one church of its own in the XIXth century) the turn of the century brings only an upgrading — supported by the local administration — of the St. Nicholas Church in the center of the city (the church was redone on a larger scale and columns were added, calqued from the Casino in Constanța). Villages, where the Romanian ethnic component grew considerably through the post-1877 colonization of Dobrogea, were also stimulated to erect Orthodox churches, an activity pursued until World War II. Nevertheless, rural churches in Dobrogea are in very small degree ethnic architectural manifestos; on the contrary, neoclassic elements, such as engaged columns ending in concise capitals, decorate the exterior. Some can be recognized as having been influenced by the urban architecture seen in Constanța or Tulcea. Possibly a great many of these churches belong to the vernacular, as they were produced by teams of artisans who cut, pasted and cloned elements which, through systematic repetition, had already become the property of the entire region.

Such Orthodox churches were being simultaneously raised throughout the rest of the country. Combinatory techniques were used to create a rhetoric of the unity of the two territories brought

---

* *Border*, in Latin (t.n.)

together under the name of Romania; for instance, the defining elements of the places of worship in Wallachia and Moldavia were used side by side in a single edifice, such as the main church of the Sinaia Monastery.[1] The idea was to synthesize the fundamentally different modes of creating religious architecture in the Romanian provinces which had been united under the crown of Carol I*. Such a synthesis couldn't help being akin to the eclectic style dominating the official architecture of the period, culled by architects from their "beaux arts" studies in Paris. Here is why the fusion takes place only horizontally, for the time being, as scattered and dissimilar elements, lifted right off the prestigious mediaeval precursors found in the historical regions of the new state, were brought together. Only in a second phase, in the first decades on the new century, did the study of the "mothers" begin — be they Byzantine (when the slogan claimed the Romanian people were born Orthodox) or Latin (when history required the exclamation of the ethnic origin) — which begot the churches in Wallachia (via the Serbian connection) as well as those in Moldavia (irrigated by the Caucasian and Slavic decorative craft). This new perspective was founded on the stability of the newly-formed ideology of the national state, an idea which was once again in a state of flux after the 1918 Union with Transylvania.

At the same time, within the Romanian kingdom, the research and discovery of mediaeval vestiges, even when practiced by French architects using methods that rather brutalized the integrity of the "restored" (i.e. reconstructed) monuments, were also part of the larger work of imagining, horizontally, through assembly and collage, an identity for the abstract notion called the Romanian national state. The Romanian communities in Transylvania, at the end of the XIXth century and the beginning of the XXth, were also building urban religious edifices, free, however, of any question of making an ethnic statement. The model followed here was the

---

* The first Romanian King, of German origins, from the House of Hohenzollern (t.n.).

17

church it serves. We may also recall one of the projects for a "municipal hospice" in Bucharest which also included a traditionalist "bell tower" as a sort of campanile over one building of the eclectic compound, or Mincu's project, hovering between the French-school Neo-Gothic style he had just used for the Palace of Justice and the "national" elements.

Historically speaking, this manner of assembling a national style is strictly contemporary with the **"pilgrimage" to the sources** that is, with a first phase of this pilgrimage to the mediaeval sources of religion and power in the Balkans: Constantinople. Thus, instead of calling upon precedents in the "Byzantium after Byzantium"*, the original Byzantine models were consulted, with the advantage that these offered an immediately comfortable urban scale. Thus the anamorphoses suffered in the intervening five centuries without Constantinople's spiritual and political patronage are placed between parantheses[2]. "We are the descendants — i.e. heirs and defenders — of the genuine Orthodox tradition, of Constantinople," could be the slogan of this other direction.

Before and during the war the "pilgrimage to the sources" replaced Constantinople with Rome, as its goal was ethnic identity rather than the religious one. The works of sacred architecture belonging to Legionnaire architects would show precisely this change of paradigm, after Marcu, Creangă, Miclescu and Cantacuzino tested it within the civil programs associated with Carol II's regime, under the specter of the so-called "Carol II style". "Above all, we are Latin, heirs to the glory of the Roman Empire", would ring the slogan of this direction, which, even more than modernism, ranked us with the equivalent orientations of the quondam super-powers: Germany, of course, but especially our cousin, Italy. This is the case of the Cathedral of the Nation in 1940, but also, in a far more nuanced form, of the 1940 projects belonging to the same two architects — Constantin Joja and Nicolae Goga

---

* **i.e.,** Romanian Provinces, cf. N. Iorga (t.n.).

— evincing entirely new rhetorics vis à vis Orthodox precedents; their projects for the Odessa Cathedral no longer relied on memory and recognition in order to be appropriated by their users (virtual Romanians). Even their detractor, Spiridon Cegăneanu, couldn't help noticing the **striking modernity** of the two, when he was scolding Joja's project, akin to Goga's (and to the one they realized together in 1940), for being a "factory whose religious-maniac owner had decorated its exterior with the decorative panels of the Metropolitan Cathedral in Bucharest" (*Arhitectura* 3-4/1942, 38). The two architects had a relaxed attitude toward the Byzantine tradition, as we shall explain further on; suffice it to say, for the time being, that they committed an act of **hybris** toward the tradition: they modified the plans to the point where a second axis of symmetry emerged, perpendicular to the normal east-west axis; they modified the reciprocal ratios of the elevation elements and their ratios to the whole (registers, number and height of steeples); they brought panels of basso rilievo and alto rilievo — of Art Deco origin, which can be found elsewhere in the distinguished architecture of the time — to the façades of their projects.

Also in the forties, P. Antonescu conducted his experiments, which surpassed the conventions of the autochthonous discourse in the direction of a **positivist approach** using new techniques and materials (reinforced concrete) which promoted their own formal logic. "Being the product of the innovations we provoke, we change as we build," could be the almost-modern slogan to accompany the "New Churches"*.

These two latter attitudes, the most radical yet, closed the cycle of the modernization of Romanian Orthodox religious architecture, a cycle which was to stay closed for many decades. Not even in the most recent years have any projects appeared that could match the conceptual depth of the ones above. The Joja-Goga churches

* An Antonescu extended project (t.n.)

21

and Antonescu's studies were in architecture the crowning response to many decades of searching for a Romanian national identity, a problem which had already received a few consistent **philosophical answers** by then. Lucian Blaga's "sophianic", "mioritic" space was such an answer, which would take decades to permeate the arts, arriving there only after the poet and philosopher's death. On one of the rare occasions when he touched upon architecture, Blaga foresaw the difficulty of a "future architectural style of high class" (1925, 1), which would be based exclusively on traditional rural architecture. Even more, Blaga himself felt constrained to define the Romanian village only by comparison with the Saxon village of Transylvania; the attributes of individual houses and of the entire village are thus relative to another referent, rather than seen as intrinsic values. Reduced to the strictly functional, the houses of the Saxon folk — "reserved people, bearing the categorical imperative on their foreheads" as Blaga defines them with gratuitous irony — differ considerably from the disorderly, poverty-stricken, but unusefully-decorated Romanian houses, consequences of "architectonic whims". Was Blaga regarding these attributes as positive, or was he speaking tongue-in-cheek? Today, they appear to us as things mostly in need of correction, rather than principles of the above-mentioned high class style, especially if we corroborate some other views the same philosopher expressed about houses and also about the churches of the ethnic majority[3]. Here Blaga placed himself at a careful distance, as he observed that, "in urban architecture, this style has only vague and approximate successes", and, "only decorations, hardly any architectonic essentials" that are Romanian. Blaga's concepts, though quoted and invoked as elevated alternatives to the lowly nationalistic discourse of the 70's and 80's, couldn't become "operational" in the architecture of the communist era; nor are there any signs that after 1989 such a philosophy, now outdated both in local context and within the discipline to which it properly

22

belongs, could still serve as the foundation of yet another identity-conscious architecture.

＊

## 2. The Neo-Romanian Style of the Second Generation

Most of the pre-war authors of churches — especially those preoccupied with designing large urban churches (cathedrals) and those emerging in the 30's — were those who redefined "de facto" the "Neo-Romanian" style of the second generation, energized as they were by the impressive momentum this program gathered after the 1918 Unification. Even more than after 1877, there was a pressing need to signify the presence of the unitary state in the newly-acquired regions — Transylvania, Banat, Bukovina, Bassarabia. Consequently, the Neo-Romanian style carried a much more explicit political weight at this moment than it had before the war. The imperious demand was not now to **define** a "national" spirit in architecture as much as to **promote** this national spirit which had already been given concrete expression in the works of the first generation of architects of the national-romantic direction, extant in the territory.

The combinatory methods of the former generation were now rejoined by the latter's need of monumentalization — not only because of the urban central positioning but also and above all because of the political denotation of any such chosen site. Cathedrals of large dimensions in all "sensitive" cities — Alba Iulia, Timișoara, Satu Mare, Tîrgu Mureș[4]: here was a major national political problem (the administrative and symbolic appropriation of the national territory) going far beyond the merely aesthetic question. The cathedral would show who had taken possession of and governed a given region. Thus, through the sacred building, the region would become part of the map of Orthodox Romania; and it was this Romanian Orthodoxy, attested by the overwhelming numbers of its representatives on the national scale, that defined the identity of the new country after the 1918 Unification. Up until King Carol II's abdication, this programmatic monumentalization of Orthodox architecture, especially in those regions where Orthodoxy had been previously pushed aside or where it was numerically insignificant (in the cities of Transylvania and Banat primarily but also in the midst of Hungarian communities) was dilligently pursued, even if some of the projects remained unfinished because of WW II.

Churches built before the First World War were, as a rule, parish churches relatively small in size (Bradu-Boteanu, 1909; E. Doneaud's St. Visarion, 1912). The problem of monumentality, of their being representative, as "holographic fragments", of all Orthodox Romania had not yet arisen. Such picturesque churches would continue to appear even after WW I, but larger in scale (St. Spiridon/Spirea Veche, 1928, Bucharest), as expressions of individual parishes (territorial criterion) and/or of guilds, corporations or large firms (professional criterion), which, as the city grew, had ceased to belong to a professional neighborhood, as if happened before (see for instance the Belvedere/CAM Church, 1932, Bucharest). However, these churches can be considered marginal projects by comparison with the goals of the other (major) project to build "Romanianizing" cathedrals (i.e. cathedrals that would signify the appropriation of the newly-Romanian territory, where Orthodox Christianity appeared as an essential ingredient of the national identity).

## a. "The Byzantines"

However, the very problem of large-scale sacred architecture is the absence of prestigious models, comparable in size, other than the Byzantine. Since many of the preferred objects of reference in Wallachia — Cozia, Curtea de Argeș — had already been inoculated with the Byzantine model, it seemed only logical, to the architects of later, larger churches, to seek a fusion between their projects and the "original" models.

To some church architects, this option to short-circuit the anamorphic series of sacred spaces all the way to the "first cause" was not only a way to glorify the common origin of "national" precedents and newly-built churches, but also an elegant way to avoid the impasse faced by lay programs, and mainly by the large administrative buildings. Lacking urban-scale precedents, these had to resort to the same sacred models (the monastery cloister[5] for the Girls' School, the Tower of Dionisie for the Cotroceni Palace) or to the immeasured amplification of the details of a single historical style, for instance Brâncoveanu's (Capital City Hall). Sacred architecture alone had the under-exploited chance to circumvent the pressure of the as-yet-unsure national imagery, while remaining within the bounds of the familiar and even stressing the recognizably traditional as such.

Often, even the floor-plans were changed, abandoning the consecrated typologies of the Middle Ages in the two large and predominantly Orthodox Romanian provinces, in favor of less- or even un-characteristic ones. Architect Ionescu Berechet is one among those who used the centered Greek cross, even adding plainly Byzantine mosaics, as stylistical reference, to the interior of the Caşin Monastery (1937). Architect G. Cristinel in Cluj or V. Vlad in Tg. Mureş had already done likewise. The cathedrals proposed by Antonescu in "New Churches", studies which will be examined further on, are also commentaries in a Byzantine mode and on a monumental scale; here can be found, for example, the octagonal plan of Constantinopole and Ravenna. Antonescu had already built a cathedral in Galatzi (1912) but the studies submitted to the Academy in 1942 were "contaminated" by a properly modern simplicity, which he used freely in order to elaborate on the basis of planimetric types and formal vocabularies more or less alien to the Romanian sphere.

The New St. Elefterie Church in Bucharest (still under construction when it was featured in *Arhitectura* 3-4/1942), a project of architect C. Iotzu — one of the most elegant urban churches in Romania — is also an eclectic study in a Byzantine mode, cleared, however, of too many decorations, by the decades of modernism preceding its construction. Thus the interior space — which is centered — is especially roomy and simple. The façades toward the city (of which, for reasons of location, the most important is the northern one, including therefore a monumental and, for Orthodox churches, atypical entrance) are also decorated only with brick layers which frame the "stone" blocks, a mediaeval device found in religious architecture south of the Danube (Serbia) and north (possibly built by the same teams of master masons); the alternating white wall/red brick layers, seen in Romania predominantly in the Sub-Carpathian regions of Argeș and Vâlcea[6] "ties" the urban church to its native ground. The brickwork becomes ornament. Thus the play of white and red warms up the considerable size of the monument, crowned as it is by five Wallachian steeples, ending in perfect semi-calottes.

## b. "The Regionalists"

As is known, a radical — and, for this very reason, questionable — form of celebrating the spirit of place was apparent in the activity of Lecomte de Nouy. The St. Dumitru Church in Craiova and the one in Curtea de Argeș somehow represent applications of Viollet le Duc's theories on restoration; thus, the "restored" building was supposed to have become more faithful to both the original and the ideal model of the edifice than the real, surviving vestiges ever could be. In fact, this manner of piecing together an epoch by sweeping aside (as gangrene and ballast) everything that time and, often, the wisdom of ulterior users had added, was as much an act of creation as the project of a "new" church.

Ionescu Berechet can also be found — whether by intuition or design — among the promotors of a "regional" direction in sacred architecture. In Constanţa, far from the Orthodox architecture prevalent in Wallachia, he designed a bell tower in front of the St. Emperors Constantin and Elena Church (1935), a tower which immediately recalls the equivalent construction in front of the Constanţa Mosque but could also be an homage to the Italian campanile. The use of rough stone in the main register of the façade is also of local inspiration. The device had been used locally as attested by a precursor built before 1878, namely the church-on-the-cliff built by the Greek community. This church, made of limestone and adorned with vaguely neoclassic columns, resembles more closely, in its architecture, the mosques extant in the area than the Orthodox churches of the Kingdom. Nevertheless, if the Ottoman presence before 1878 would explain such a phenomenon, in 1935 it could only be a remarkable gesture of flattery addressed to the tomitan "genius loci". This method is conceptually more consistent than Socolescu's, used at the end of the XIXth century, at the old Neo-Romanian City Hall. Here, typically Oriental archways and details appear although Constanţa is not an Oriental city, but rather, like all harbors, a cosmopolitan one. In this city, even a Roman Catholic church of Italian descent, (akin to the Italian Church on Magheru Boulevard in Bucharest), such as Stoppa designed and built near Mincu's cathedral and the large mosque, fits in easily. Too explicit a reference to a single tradition — be it Oriental or "Romanian" — would have transformed these edifices into manifestos of an ethnic identity, into strange, exotic objects indifferent to their context. Rather than being natural, harmonious dwellings inscribed within a similar historical, physical and cultural context, these would have become celebrations of alterity, not identity.

Ionescu Berechet is not the only inter-bellum architect who, for some of his works, would be called a "critical regionalist" by Kenneth Frampton. In Mediaş, Gh. Liteanu espoused clearly non-

Orthodox models (but poignanty local ones) when he designed the main façade of the Orthodox church, which is flanked by two slim towers after the fashion of German or Hungarian Protestant churches. Nor is the austere white simplicity of the St. Nicholas Church in Cluj (1930) unrelated to Lutheran puritanism: the entrance is surmounted by a bell tower; in a larger sense, though, the church is tailored both inside and out according to Byzantine models.

The churches along the Prahova Valley, erected between the two world wars from local stone in accordance with an also local method of "mise en oeuvre" are rather exotic exemples in the context of the Orthodox architecture of the time. They illustrate the conformity to the vernacular architecture in the vicinity rather than introduce "foreign", (post) imperial models (See for example the Church of St. Elijah of Tesvita, built between 1933-1939 from plans donated by Paul Smărăndescu, and consecrated on December 17, 1939, by the Patriarch Nicodim Munteanu). Here we are at the other extreme of Neo-Romanian sacred architecture. This church was "cloned" later on, in smaller versions, all along the Prahova Valley, although it is more Byzantine than "Romanian". Its popularity was owed perhaps to its resemblance to such local landmarks as the Royal Railway in Sinaia, Villa Bebe in Cumpătu* or the trafo posts spread throughout the city, all of which had been designed by architect Duiliu Marcu practically at the same time, rather than to the large church at the Sinaia Monastery.

This Orthodox church celebrates no pre-existing Romanian model, either in aspect, which is reminiscent of the basilicas in Ravenna, or in materials. Nevertheless, the architecture of this church, carefully inscribed within its specific site, built with local materials, and alluding to the spirit of both its time and its place, is "more real" (in Gadamer's sense regarding "the optimum solution" in architecture) than the identitary manifestos predating

---

* High-life district of this resort town (t.n.)

it in the Neo-Romanian style. The church is built primarily of stone, while reinforced concrete was used for its structure. The roof is made of "Turkish tiles"[7] and the painting belongs to Nina Arbore. An interesting detail is that its "iconostasis" (the icon screen in front of the Orthodox altar) is made of masonry and the icons are painted directly on the wall. The main dome is multifaceted and it has many windows, with the result that the naos is far better lit than is customary in an Orthodox church. The departure from "tradition" is obvious here; we can almost hear the architect's commentary, that "overshadowing" should not be an immanent attribute of Orthodox spaces, being only a side effect of mediaeval construction techniques; in contrast, the reinforced concrete of his time, also used later on by Petre Antonescu in his "New Churches", allows the increase of divine light within the sacred space.

### c. "The Cosmopolitans"

Another, more prolific tendency manifested itself at the same time as the previous two. This eclectic tendency, running counter to the regionalists' was capable of removing mediaeval Moldavian models to Timișoara, for example, (I. Traianescu, Timișoara Cathedral, 1935) where typically north-eastern Romanian steeples surmount a building decorated with alternating layers of stone and brick, a mostly Wallachian device. The Coronation Cathedral pile in Alba Iulia (1924, architect V. Ștefănescu), using a perimetric colonnade, tried to broaden the expressiveness of the Orthodox monastery cloister as its destination was changed to that of a representative public space. The Seniorial House here belongs to the Brâncoveanu idiom as spoken by the Horezu Monastery, for example, but the ensemble appears more vigorous precisely in order to "tell" the story which Horezu, on its modest scale, could not have told had it been transplanted as such into an urban environment.

N. Liteanu used the same device in his project for an Odessan cathedral, whose motto "The Three Hierarchs" explicitely suggested its source* to be transplanted to Crimea. So did I. Traianescu when he proposed a replica of his own Timişoara project, also with a great many spires, for Odessa. This device of transplanting models can be encountered in Bucharest, too, in the Belvedere/CAM Church (1932) and the Spirea Veche Church (1928). The cosmopolitans already had a tradition behind them. Ghika-Budeşti had built (Cuţitul de Argint, 1910) a stone replica of a Bukovinian church, with three registers of niches on the façade, while the Greek Catholics also had had in Bucharest since 1908 a Moldavian-like church with buttresses and white niches, designed by the same architect.

However, a more radical manner of transplanting types, forms or decorations than both the inter-regional exchange and the Byzantine loan was also in use. This manner recalled Tsar Peter the Great's reform of Russian Orthodox architecture, by an import of Western models even if they belonged to secular architecture. Thus Peter — through Trezzini — brought to Petersburg the dome of the Amsterdam Stock Exchange and turned it into church steeple. This implant is, in Pierre Chaunu's opinion, "to the Baltic capital what San Marco's campanile is to Venice" (1986, II, 166). Romania also imported such far-off cultural goods between the wars; for example, the colonnade around the cupola borrowed from the Parisian Panthéon or St. Paul' Cathedral in London (which appears in Cristinel & Pomponiu's Cluj Cathedral, 1925-1935, as well as in its replica, submitted by C. Pomponiu alone for Odessa; or in the Sts. Archangels Cathedral in Satu Mare, 1930, designed by V. Smighelschi); the Italian campanile, used to accentuate verticalities (in such projects as the Patriarchal Palace in Bucharest, 1937, designed by Gh. Simotta; or in the already mentioned Church of the Sts. Emperors Constantin and Elena in

---

* **I.e.** the cathedral of the same name in Iaşi, built under Vasile Lupu's reign in the XVIIth century (t.n.)

30

Constanța); the Egyptian gates borrowed from Memphis (at least so claimed the critics of the project, to be quoted "in extenso" further on) by Joja for the entrance to his Odessan cathedral; finally, the Romanic architecture of T. Niga's project, bearing the motto "… and defeating they the pagans, raised they a monastery", submitted to the same contest for a cathedral in Odessa.

## 3. A Failed Start?

For the purpose of this study, 1942 is an essential year. While in the previous decade the manner in which Orthodoxy, modern ideas, and national identity could all collaborate within the same architectural context had already taken a sharp turn, 1942 marked a fracture, a divorce from former ways of thinking. If the fourth decade had produced only a few examples of Orthodox architecture which were eminently new vis à vis their backdrop — St. Elijah of Tesvita Church and the other churches along the Prahova Valley within the same anamorphic series; the New St. Spiridon Church in Bucharest — 1942 suddenly offered solutions to the entire range of problems caused by the urge to renew. Some of these solutions were: a complete set of projects for practically any region in the country and on any scale, from the rural churchette to the cathedral (P. Antonescu's "New Churches"); the Joja, N. Goga, and, at some distance behind them, T. Niga's projects for large urban churches, drawing on the still fresh experience of the Legionnaire exhibition of 1940, projects submitted for the Odessa Cathedral contest.

On May 1st, 1942, at the Romanian Academy, Petre Antonescu delivered a speech on the imperative to transform a disaster (i.e. the 1940 earthquake) into a new beginning in Romanian Orthodox architecture. Antonescu argued that the recent experience of the earthquake should teach us that new Orthodox churches could no longer be built as they had been. This touched not only upon outdated construction methods and materials, but also on their dangerous consequences as they would hamper expression, a situation which was creating a growing gap between civil programs and sacred architecture. When churches crumble, some of the faith placed in them crumbles, too. Designing churches, the speaker implied, was more than designing common buildings[8].

Antonescu's arguments, endeavoring to establish a theoretical foundation for a technologically and aesthetically new architecture, still closely linked to the old Orthodox architecture, are worth looking into. To begin with, Antonescu had a modern view of history, whose motor was progress. To buttress his plea for renewal, he argued that renewal itself was the driving force behind architectural development. Not only must we act accordingly, he suggested; this is the very way that architecture had, since always, moved on.

The prime examples, to be sure, are the basilica and, before it, the Greek temple. In Antonescu's view, the struggle with its materials become the source of renewal in the idiom of the first Christian architecture. Here is the historical precedent, on which the contemporary argument is also founded: the moment when Christianity became the official religion, under Emperor Constantine. Although manifested with difficulty at first and then a martyr for three centuries, Christianity had had time to crystallize its rituals so that the imperial architects only needed to look among the models at hand to find the optimum space for this already-formed ritual; the basilica, that is "the type of building perfectly fitting the requirements of the new cult" (Antonescu 9), prepared to receive, in its capacious belly, the triumphant Christians having escaped persecution. Was it really a coincidence or, rather, the result of that "great ingenuity and remarkable luck" of the Emperor's men, who knew precisely what they were looking for?

We would never know, because, soon enough, the new places of worship, however well they may have been shaped, proved too frail to withstand both time and barbarian attacks, especially because of their highly flammable wooden ceilings. The architects and master masons of the time, however, took the (same) step as their Greek and Roman ancestors, as they began to use vaults and domes, which expressed formally the structural potential of brick and stone masonry. In other words, architecture was not modeled by the pressure to symbolize but by the need to find a suitable expression as new materials came into use. The vault would have appeared, first of all, out of structural reasons, and only afterwards acquired the familiar symbolic meanings. Consequently, ran the architect's argument, since shape was a property of the material, an optimum result of its use within the construction, it would necessarily follow that contemporary use of contemporary materials — this time, reinforced concrete — create contemporary shapes.

## Modernism vs. Tradition?

We confront here, obviously, a coherent discourse which no doubt would appear justified to a spirit raised at the flame of modernism. Had this argument been followed without deviation, it would have implied the duty, on the part of Orthodox architecture, to quickly match the formal revolution which new materials, in use for decades, had already caused in civil programs. However, Orthodoxy was no longer in the auroral circumstances of Constantine's age, when a secular space could be converted into a sacred one with minimal adjustments. The intervening centuries had raised tradition to the rank of primary term of reference in defining Orthodox Christianity, that of its raison d'être. The faithful safeguarding, in spirit and in letter, of the teachings handed down from olden times requires that architecture should also preserve in the memory of its new sites the being of those of long ago. Hence, Antonescu found himself here all too obviously at the heart of a logical difficulty. The materials must change and, therefore, their use and arrangement within the work; this process must immediately cause a visual change in church buildings; yet these cannot give up their traditional appearance without transgressing, committing in the process an act of hybris, an existential betrayal.

Thus the author renewed the argument of the Greek temple, this time to support the opposite of what he had stated before. For those in the know, the stone temple of the ancient Greek was only a "faithful transposition of the shapes of the old wooden temple, which had been built since time immemorial in the Dorian woodsfolk's Greece, and namely since a time when the art of stone building wasn't in common use there" (10). In other words, despite its transposition into superior materials, the old wooden temple would have remained forever inscribed in the flesh of the new one.

Whereas before, nothing seemed to impede the process of "adequation" of the forms to the material in which they would receive determinations, at this point Antonescu introduced a codicile to this "evolutionist" theory of architecture. Shapes did develop along with materials and methods of use, of course. However, not just any shape could be altered let alone "sacred" ones, which, being ideal forms, remained pure regardless of any updating they might have to undergo throughout history. Thus Greek art came to perfect its creative powers only "by strictly respecting the forms sanctified by tradition even when they no longer corresponded to the requirements of a completely different technology" (11).

The striking contradiction could be resolved, however, by introducing an already-mentioned third term: appearance. The architect was warning us that he would select those forms which owe the most to the technical causes having shaped them and would leave their appearance unchanged — those very forms "upon which immutable meanings of symbolic religious value are anchored" —

but would transpose them into the new material. The vault and the dome, according to the logic of Antonescu's positivist demonstration, should have come to the end of their historical period. To be consistent, we oughtn't (even though in practice we could) transpose vaults and domes into reinforced concrete, since these are not forms properly belonging to this material. A church built of reinforced concrete should strive, instead, for sharp frames and "firm" beams. However, Orthodox churches without cupolas were inconceivable, no matter how much progress and change we would accept, the architect conceded, feeling compelled to introduce nuances and qualifiers in the solid argument unfolded so far. As it happened, the cupola was "precisely one of the easiest to imagine (sic) to execute in the material which ensures today such large resistances in our new buildings" (13), that is, in concrete. But what traditional shape isn't easily imaginable in this resilient material?

Dwellings could thus be up-to-date (in framework or material used) and at the same time traditional (in overall silhouette, details applied to the structure and symbolic "discourse"). Antonescu would have preserved the general appearance of churches as being traditional — the silhouette, number or steeples, their cupolas reduced however to the minimum necessary regional decoration. In contrast, he would have used the reinforced concrete of the posts and beams not only for the walls of the church but also for the vaults and cupolettes lacking any structural/"functional" role (hence "useless" from a modernist viewpoint). Nevertheless, the architect had to temper his reforming elan.

Some possible analogies lent him support in his attempt. Thus, the wooden church could be updated in concrete as a result of some "analogies of use" as well as of the "proven similarities of structure between these two materials, however odd this may seem at first sight" (12). The oddity remarked here was, naturally, the logical one; what could be the benefit of translating the wooden church into concrete? This church (of wood) had long since crystallized its optimum material-to-expression ratio and, in any case, the translation into concrete could only destroy the optimum in this ratio. Antonescu answered softly that the wooden churches, like the basilicas of long ago, were "perishable" (12) and must, therefore, be translated into the more durable concrete.

Yet the architect seemed to require this new material rather when he desired to change the structure of the plan than when invoking tradition. He wished to optimize the shape of the narthex by eliminating the wall between pronaos and naos, which — in the architect's opinion — was there only for constructive reason (a false premise, since the wall in question or the few columns supplanting it marked two essentially different kinds of space, hence a qualitative rift inside the church). In addition, Antonescu believed that the hunger for space accounted for the presence of the apses (or of the transept in the Catholic church): he was wrong again; the apses (transept) served the purpose of inscribing as obviously as possible the sign of the cross on the floor plan, while at the same time allowing the largest possible number of worshippers as close as possible to the vertical/qualitative axis of the sacred space, leading to the Pantocrator.

The presence of concrete pillars in Antonescu's work is manifested at the exterior, where it subdivides the façade in both vertically and horizontally modulated registers (see his study for the Bicaz Monastery, shown in the book "New Churches" at Plate VII under the heading, however, of "simple church with skeleton of reinforced concrete"). Placed on the panels just below the roof are niches (Plate IV, the church of the "Mother of God of All Consolations" Monastery) or decorations suited to the region where the church would be built (the same area that determines the type of plan, number of steeples and silhouette of the roof). In addition, the pillars replace the columns of the porch (Plate XII, church with skeleton of reinforced concrete). In the interior, concrete beams replace the vaults, star-shaped frames — the cupola's support arches, and the cupola with concrete ribs — the masonry dome.

The most spectacular discrepancy between structure and appearance is shown in Plates XIX and XX, where the reinforced concrete skeleton is presented in an axonometric projection which looks like one of Mondrian's drawings, while in fact it is concealed within an enormous roof, such as a wooden church in the mountains might have.

## *Urban Churches*

Also truly remarkable in Antonescu's study is the inverse ratio of size to traditional appearance. In other words, the smaller the church the more it resembles its precursor, a resemblance which attains near-identity in the case of small wooden churches. In contrast, the larger they become, from the so-called "large churches" to the "cathedrals", Antonescu's projects drift farther and farther apart from their typological and formal sources. The floor plans and volumes become complicated; the cathedrals move on to an entirely different source of inspiration, which appears to be the Byzantine model, joined with the influence of Western styles (e.g. San Vitale is invoked as the source of the octagonal project of Plate XXXIV), but also open to the current of modern simplicity of both expression and technology (e.g. Plate XXXIII, or the parabola of the dome in Plate XXXVI). The paradox of Neo-Romanian architecture is edifyingly illustrated by Petre Antonescu's endeavours and also by Tiberiu Niga's in Odessa. As the scale of its edifices increases, so as to conquer the city, the Neo-Romanian style must forsake almost all reference to the vernacular architecture — of modest size and mostly rural — which grounded it.

Here we find the architect's strongest argument in favor of change: namely, when urban architecture is brought into discussion rather than the small-scale architecture isolated in the countryside; problems such as the silhouette and the "aura" of the city church are essential to the 1942 architect (as well as today's). His solution is two-fold: on the one hand, the height of secular buildings should be limited; on the other, churches need to be re-sized, overwhelmed as they've been by nearby construction, and, therefore, unable to play their signal role as "condensers" of the traditional communities to which they belong. Re-sizing would also mean "more capacious buildings to host and organize meetings", as well as "beautiful tall belfries to preside over the urban perspective" (Antonescu 12). Also, increasing the scale will have as necessary consequence the abandon of all commentary on a local tradition which offers no convenient precedent of scale and function — that of the urban church — in favor of subtler compositional processes than the mere amplification of size, and, moreover, in favor of "more genuine" precedents both from a historical and formal perspective.

## 4. The Cathedral of the Nation and the Odessa Contest

By 1942, the autochthonist discourse of the first four decades of our century had collapsed into redundancy. This indigenous eclecticism seemed so utterly devoid of perspective that C. Pomponiu's project "Victoria" for the Odessa Cathedral was in fact a repetition of the Cluj Cathedral, while I. Traianescu submitted the same project anywhere — be it Timișoara or Odessa — including the same inflammations and multiplications of Moldavian steeples. The materials and the scale of cities had changed; urban architecture already spoke the modern idiom; in spite of the war and the change of regime, buildings belonging to the "Carol II" style (elsewhere known as "stripped classicism") were being completed.

The Odessa Contest was in many ways an end of the road for Neo-Romanian architecture as well as a failed beginning. The end is attested by the above-mentioned projects, mere repetitions of already-built edifices, illustrating the limits of the cut-and-paste method used to re-size vernacular types to an ampler scale. The beginning can be discerned in Joja's project — the winner of the contest — and in its clone, N. Goga's, as both projects represent a radical break for the entire Romanian architecture and not just for the Orthodox one. Unfortunately, this direction remained unexplored for over two decades, and, in sacred architecture, until after 1989.[9]

## Speer Revisited

Joja's project (then signed C. Jojea) and, respectively, N. Goga's, are, in fact, more elaborate replicas of the project they designed together for a Church of the Nation[10], published in *Arhitectura* 3-4/1940, which featured the exhibition of **Legionnaire Work in the Arts** having opened on December 22, 1940. The avowed goal of the participants was to forsake individualism and embrace "in a team spirit goals of general interest to the entire nation" (45). In addition to the Church of the Nation, a House of the Captain (N. Goga) and a Palace of Culture (Joja, Goga, Puşchilă, Stănescu) were also exhibited. Any one of these projects could have been signed, with serenity, by Speer. The church itself is a triple peripteral series of pillars, whose registers are separated by highly profiled architraves. Not a trace of decoration. Not a trace of a roof[11]. Only the colossal, vertical accents of the main building, and, above all, the two extremely tall spires, of equal visual value, announcing a rigid symmetry determined by the N-S axis, untenable in the interior of an Orthodox church.

What can be remarked by comparing this to the 1942 moment? Most devoted to the common project of 1940 was Goga, signing along with I. Puşchilă and I. Ciupală. If in 1940 the pilasters stood alone as they surrounded the façade at some distance, in 1942 these pilasters are engaged, the wall predominates, and the biaxial symmetry is even more accute through the use of vertical registers of alto relievo. The ambiguity of this symmetry can be clearly seen here, though; the longitudinal section reveals that the steeple above the pronaos is hidden on the inside by a cupolette while the one above the naos opens up to a Pantocrator at a considerable height, although both steeples are of the same height and diameter. The floor plan is also composite. For similar reasons of biaxial symmetry, the naos and the pronaos are of the same amplitude; moreover, they are separated by two rows of lamellar posts.

But Joja's project, more ostentatious than in 1940, is at the same time less radical. To overcome the rigors of a jury headed by Horia Creangă but including many traditionalists, Joja multiplies the number of steeples from two to five and places them as follows: two above the porch, flanking the entrance; the same two as in 1940, though proportionally (to the church building itself) far more elongated; finally, complete surprise, one above the altar, an unheard-of thing in Orthodox architecture on Romanian territory. The project is also a symbiosis between a Moldavian floor plan and a Wallachian volume akin to the Patriarchal Cathedral's, a similarity so noted and criticized by those who dissociated themselves from the jury's decisions. Joja transmogrifies the Byzantinesque paradigm which dominated the first decades of the century into one more radically autochthonic. However, like N. Goga, Joja makes up new proportions for the element he takes over. His project is a subtle celebration of regional precursors, within a modern dicourse. The exaggerated heights of the steeples, clearly branding his cathedral as an urban object, and the use of panels of bas-relief, utterly atypical to the Orthodox church, round out the project's modernity.

The amplification of a Moldavian floor plan, peculiar to relatively small churches, brings with it an amplification of both its advantages and disadvantages. The jury[12], but mostly the detractors[13] of this project did remark the dilemma the architect thus faced. The jury accepted it as inherent to the source, but others deemed it a gaffe to opt for such a limited plan, without potential for monumentalization, in order to design a vast cathedral. In fact, by making this choice, Joja announced one of the theoretical themes of his later period: the potential of autochthonous vernacular architecture to produce a monument. Yet in time those who warned against the amplification of the scale of an object which had been conceived on a smaller scale appear to have been right, along with the inter-bellum "Byzantines". Joja himself refined the proportions of his edifice in later studies, which can be consulted at the Constantin Joja Memorial House.

These proportions and the number of registers were modified in any case between 1940 and 1942, but only to be further amplified; from two to three naves, with the two lateral naves markedly lower than the central nave. The vigorous pilasters of the former project have faded even more than in Goga's project, to the point where they merely suggest the "ropes", cable mouldings and other means of separating vertical registers in Wallachian architecture; but instead of ending in arches at the top, they end in right angles, just like Antonescu's "new churches". The same dichotomy between interior and exterior is manifested by the use of alto relievo.

Goga's project at the same contest is more faithful to the '42 version and consequently refines the intentions of the former. As before, the project is inventive and takes the liberty to reinterpret past models of great prestige. Thus Goga introduces the biaxial symmetry, absent from most Orthodox churches in Romania. Between the pronaos and the naos, both square and each crowned by a very tall tower (above the narthex a "false" one which on the inside is closed up by a cupolette), Goga introduces a dividing space akin to the floor ditch which marks the N-S symmetry axis. The classicizing tone is self-evident both in the 1940 project and in Goga's 1942 project, as is the almost playful liberty Goga and Joja both take in re-interpreting the vocabulary supplied by tradition.

To what extent can past models, which were built on a reduced scale, be re-sized to the scale required by urban churches? This is the very dilemma of the entire Neo-Romanian architecture, be it sacred or secular. It must be negotiated within the bounds of the concept of "absolute measure", which Michelis thought to be inherent to every creature and every architectural work. In an architectural object and/or program assumed to be of optimum size, this measure determines a certain ratio of volume to scale and amount of detail. Moreover, absolute measure ought to discourage any abrupt translations from one scale to another, movements which do, however, become feasible when the process takes place in a long enough time. But here is "in extenso" the passage from Michelis which should conclude any discussion of Neo-Romanian architecture, as well as ground all criticism of Joja's theoretical work:

> The cathedral cannot be merely the amplification of the village church, just as the tiny village church cannot hold on its façade, in miniature, the entire wealth of an immense basilica (…) Each shape has its necessary size and, if we insist that the village church have the conformation of the church of Pisa, it would appear ridiculous and would be anything but a church (…) The large church requires a structure which is an organic development in order to reach such dimension. (Michelis, 1982, 809)

The discussion of this aspect of Joja's work and, by extension, of the entire problem of a "national" architecture (including the Neo-Romanian one) is carried on with greater eloquence than the present study permits by Cezar Radu (1989, 241-260), the aesthetician who first employed the concept of absolute measure in Romania and used it along with other theoretically refined arguments to attack the uncritical use of rural architecture in monumental, urban projects. The reader is referred to the entire chapter in the book of our distinguished mentor and professor of aesthetics in order to follow his demonstration in full. At the time of its publication, this study was the only solid commentary of Joja's work, a work projected — unfortunately — against the backdrop of the nationalistic ideology of Ceaușescu's regime and associated with the abasement of Romanian architecture under the pressure of the obsession of the "national character".

## *Addenda: The Antimoderns*

Tiberiu Niga's project for Odessa, although the winner "ex-aequo" along with Joja's does not at all have the same potential as the three Speer-like projects of the Joja-Goga tandem. What it does have, however, is the quality of completely delivering his church from the "national" obsession. The floor plans call for a double edifice in two tiers; one below, perfectly symmetrical, of the ossuary; and the church proper on top, a Latin cross with apses (semicircular on the inside) which are barely visible in the façade. The expression of this façade is Romanic, entirely lacking any autochthonous references. It rather resembles the baptistery in Pisa. Nevertheless, here as in Joja's project, the jury saw the "traditional note". This is quite a remarkable conclusion drawn by a jury who, under the pressure of a nationalistic discourse and of the political range of the theme, saw traditional notes where today we see only the departure from tradition. But perhaps those of over fifty years ago were more open and unconstrained in their approach of the theme than we are.

However, we must note that the jury was by no means unanimous in its judgment. Today the difference in rank between Joja-Goga on the one hand and the rest of the proposals on the other stands out. Moreover, there were vehement dissidents among the jury, who formulated their opinions and conclusions separately. Thus the delegate of the Romanian Architects' College, I.C. Roșu, dissented from the jury's verdict and refused to accept the classification of Goga's church, on the grounds that "it has all the flaws of the Sts. Constantin and Elena project (i.e. Joja's) and none of its qualities, nor does it have any qualities of its own".

Spiridon Cegăneanu's separate opinion is even more interesting, since he was the most violent opponent of Joja's project. Part of his reproaches had to do with the manner in which the contest had unfolded, others addressed the very content of Joja's winning project. Whereas the former seem perfectly justified, the latter, coming as they did from ultra-traditionalistic positions, become in context a denunciation of the atypical and un-conservative attribute of the winning project (ex aequo). In his dissent, Cegăneanu revealed the enormous pressure exerted upon the jury to declare Joja's project a winner, allegedly because it was a manifesto of the young generation; but if "the secret of the contest had been its essential condition, I don't see how anybody could have known that the project belonged to the young generation" (35). Further on in his protest, he adds to the accusation of Joja's having broken the rules of anonymity of the contest that of the "project author's" having plagiarized. "This project is a reprint of the scale model of the Cathedral of the Nation (…) This strange apparition, having offended profoundly the logic of construction, the aesthetic sense and the Orthodox tradition, does not represent, however, a common property but is the personal work of an architect whose copyright is fully protected by the law of artistic property. Should the present author be different from the author of that project, we have on our hands a case of plagiarism which must be dealt with as such" (36).

If the architect should be one and the same, however, Cegăneanu goes on to say that he would stick to his original "estimation" of the 1940 project, adding but a few new observations concerning the 1942 project. The façade "strays into the domain of extravagance and lack of logic" (36); on the main façade are displayed "Egyptian gates" covered with decorations coming from "the Metropolitan Cathedral in Bucharest, surmounted by a series of factory chimneys (...) a tube one knows where it begins but neither when nor where it will end" (38). Had Joja been a modernist from Le Corbusier's family, he would have prized as war medals the accusations formulated here about his project's analogy to industrial architecture. Cegăneanu's conclusions were less honoring; "a monument of apocalyptic vision, inexplicable other than by either a major error or a tendency of another kind, seeking an official artistic success in order to obtain the support necessary elsewhere. A dangerous error in every way, but especially in the domain of aesthetics, at a moment when the young generation isn't yet sure of itself" (38).

# 5. Conclusions

What 1942 brought to Orthodox architecture, through the two above-mentioned events, was a remarkable freedom from both the autochthonistic discourse of the first generation of architects issued from Mincu's school and the "imperial" solution, which attempted the return to Byzantium, preferred by the inter-bellum generation. Despite the political discourse, driven to nationalistic hysteria by the war, architecture proved to be — through Antonescu, Joja & Goga, Niga — remarkably autonomous in its discourse vis à vis the sources it invoked. It manipulated widely varied scales and compositional methods, and it quoted from a series of foreign vocabularies — following atypical recipes which today we would label ludic-post-modernistic — belonging to diverse epochs, from the stripped classicism of the era to modernity.

The projects proposed by Petre Antonescu standardized, on the basis of principles shown above, Romanian Orthodox architecture in terms of possible size and site. The church had a greater degree of typological generality, in Antonescu's opinion, than the dwelling; and yet, only single examples of his work were ever built. Orthodox architecture shows no national character anywhere in Romania, but it does possess clear regional attributes. Antonescu's projects and Joja's proved the difficulty of identifying a national "quiddity" of sacred architecture on Romanian territory. Instead, both architects favored the regional aspects; the Moldavian floor plan, tripartite from west to east, with barely sketched apses in the interior; the vertical registers of the Wallachian churches; the slender silhouettes of the Northern wooden churches.

Just like the 1940 Church of the Nation, the projects of 1942 had a relaxed attitude toward the architectural tradition. They were, rather, commentaries on both vernacular themes (the structure of the plan, the vertical registers, the steeples) and classical ones (the pilasters and the architrave). These were not modernist projects. The exterior expression became essential and it conditioned the interior, the very opposite of what we may expect as we discuss the "introversion" and the "sophianic" character of the Orthodox space, or as we repeat the modern mantra of "form follows function". In other aspects, the exterior expression is not recalled by the configuration of the interior space. Without being strictly modern stylistically, the three projects discussed above are, to date, the most elaborate phases of the dialogue between the autochthonic tradition and Orthodoxy on the one hand, and modernity on the other. A road not taken either then or later, this direction strived for a symbiosis between two apparently conflicting attitudes about architecture. However, this direction has been forgotten today; what then seemed negotiable, has become a rift. Will it be permanent?

# II

# MAN-MADE ENVIRONMENT
# IN POST-STALINIST EUROPE*

## II.1. Socialist Realism Revisited

*For the first time in many centuries, reality and artistic ideal
are no longer contradictory (...) because never before did such an
epoch exist, where the very grounds of historic reality are
beautiful.*

I.V. Stalin

The way official edifices were built between the two World
Wars and — as far as socialist realism is concerned — after World
War Two, cannot be dissociated from the general context of their
respective epochs: economic and moral crisis, social restlessness
and radicalism, the threat of an emerging war. We discuss
*Zeitgeist*, yet we should not forget the self-commitment of its actors.
Gone was the utopianism of the early 1920's, with technology and
the myth of progress as universal panacea. Gone was the Russian
constructivist "disurbanism", and the aesthetic-political project of
the avant-garde to reshape reality was finally fulfilled; yet not by
the avant-garde itself, and not in the way it had envisioned the
process, but by a new political elite. This elite believed itself to
be far more entitled to implement the project than a bunch of radical
and untrustworthy artists.

Such a pessimistic (realistic?) abandon of the critical edge of
the avant-garde in architecture as well as in other arts, explained

* The publication of this chapter is possible thanks to the New Europe
College Bucharest (a.n.)

by Kenneth Frampton in his text on critical regionalism*, boosted the "conservative" discourse and its promoters, who had been ostracized for a while by the avant-garde architects. Academic and/or ethnocentric, always populist, such discourse produced the official architecture of the totalitarian regimes that governed during the inter-bellum period and, half a century later, post-modern architecture.

The first five-year plan in the USSR, the economic crisis in the West and in U.S. replaced overnight the fantasies of their early days with "realist" projects: utopias were replaced by short deadlines within which existing cities were supposed to be reshaped by implanting monumental edifices and by inflicting the absent "rational" (i.e. straight) axes upon the "irrational" (i.e. mediaeval) textures, while new communities were also being developed and ample public works — bridges, canals, highways — undertaken. What emerged was a new kind of utopianism**: anti-mediaeval, populist, focused on rewriting the cities, "heroic" and, like every utopianism, based upon an "archetypal", primal and "pure" architecture, arrived at by replacing the War Communism in Russia and its small utopias, convincingly described by R. Stites in his excellent book on the "revolutionary dreams" of that epoch.

Re-designing the existing, corrupt reality, accompanied by rapid and radical building programs for a society in crisis might constitute the grounds for an apparent paradox. In fact, building was the soundest evidence of how strong and stable a given regime was, since it enacted the myth of the salvation-by-state and its willingness to control the shaky social reality. Weak states and societies in crisis build massively. Architecture offered the

---

* K. Frampton in Hal Foster, p. 16 sqq. (a.n.)

** The utopian nature of that epoch was further analyzed by this author in the research journal *Simetria-Caiete de Artă şi Critică* of the Institute for Architecture Bucharest (Summer 1995), as well as in my thesis *The Other Modernism*, Cincinnati University, 1994, published in Romania in 1995. (a.n.)

antidote against the mistrust with which its subjects regarded a certain regime. Yet this was Architecture with capital A (i.e. monumental edifices, ample urban schemes aimed at entirely reshaping capital cities), one which favored stability over the other two attributes in the Vitruvian definition. As for styles, the mixing of various languages from modernism to eclecticism* to Art Deco was the envisioned method of using the best in each style while avoiding the dangers implicit in any one: the alleged lack of monumental potential** in the case of modernism, redundance in that of eclecticism or any of the national variants of historical styles (vernacular gothic in Völkisch, "Aryan" doric in Heimatstil, Russian baroque, Neo-Romanian), and an overstated penchant for decor in Art Deco.

The result? An architecture with antique references, centered, symmetrical, experienced frontally, solemn, "heroic" and orderly, best suited for an epoch in which control over society, often exercised in a totalitarian manner, was seen as the answer to crisis. The emergence of such a discourse was refreshed by the modern attribute: fewer or no ornaments at all, structural sincerity, rational expression of the façades and interior spaces, and most important, the free-standing, high-rise building, autonomous from the urban tissue.

Here one must ask two fundamental questions regarding this fusion vocabulary: a) How can the same style — "purged classicism" or "conservative modernism" bear witness to two apparently self-styled opposed ideologic discourses? and b) How can the nationalist rhetoric, centered on the question of identity,

---

* With a special mark for Soviet architecture, where this word entails several 'Classical' stages: Greek architecture, Renaissance, as well as Russian baroque and neo-classicism. (a.n.)

** In fact there was probably just the absence of major works. The competition for the Smithsonian Institution, won by Eliel Saarien, as well as the edifices built by European modernists such as Van der Rohe and Gropius would soon prove otherwise. (a.n.)

be expressed by divergent formulas? The first such formula was to exhibit the very same architecture, as it happened in Paris at the 1937 *Exposition Universelle* with the Soviet, German, Romanian, Italian, and British national pavilions; the second formula was to put forth replicas of certain heritage edifices, pertaining to a given national historical myth or event, to a regional/local idiom expanded to a "national style" ("sentimental regionalism", as Frampton called it), as had happened in Paris in 1900.*

There is an immediate answer to the first question: the idioms of the 1930's emerged from relatively similar conditions, regardless of the ideologies in each of the above-mentioned states. The solutions given to reshaping reality covered evenly the entire range, from left to right. I shall not comment here why Stalinist ideology was inherently "rightist", and thus "conservative", or why Roosevelt's New Deal, allegedly democratic and placed at the left of classical liberalism, needed its "conservative" edifices.

Yet one can propose the following hypothesis: the way those buildings looked was relatively independent of aesthetic criteria. Their expression was the result, not the cause. Only a discourse on the former's origins might illuminate the differences between, say, the "democratic" and the "totalitarian" architectures of that epoch. The "progressive" attitude toward reality condemns it as inescapably corrupt and proposes alternative utopian communities, combined with a total condemnation of the sinful cities. Only radical and violent changes, achieved by the revolutionary purification of the environment, could change the latter's essence.

What followed? Environmental revolutions: the Volga-Don Canal, Tennessee Valley Authority's terraformations, disurbanistic and experimental communities in early Soviet Russia (described by R. Stites), the United States and Italy (comparatively

---

* The Austro-Hungarian pavilion at that exhibition was a replica of the Vajda-Hunyad Castle; that of Belgium was the replica of a famous city hall, whereas the eclectic one of Russia was somewhat reminiscent of the Vassilii Blajenii Cathedral in Moscow. (a.n.)

investigated by Diane Ghirardo), or — on a smaller scale — in Germany. According to the other, "conservative", approach, the city was not to be abolished, but healed by implanting authority, and thereby formal order, within the wounded tissue. This perspective was centered on negotiating with the past and with its formal anamorphosis; one had to create new Jerusalems, ideal cities or city centers which, by empathy, would replace the existing, often mediaeval structure. This perspective was based on private ownership, traditional values in society and the family. "Conservatives" treasured the white, European, male culture, founded on issues of identity and authority. In the 1930's such edifices and urban schemes could be found in Washington, D.C., where they followed L'Enfant's rigorous/rational axes of the Enlightenment. Yet the Zeppelinfeld as well as the Stalinist plan for Moscow (1935), Hitler's and Speer's Berlin, as well as the 1935 plan for Bucharest looked precisely the same.

One can thus undestand why the architectural processes of the thirties cannot be confined exclusively to one or another of the above-mentioned categories. In fact, the official attitude toward the built environment was rather problem-solving, "pragmatic", pursuing the adequate answer to a given challenge, beyond ideologies. The attitude of the authority with regard to transforming reality was "leftist", "progressive", as well as "rightist", "conservative", according to the context and the nature of the problem.

One can even forward the hypothesis that there are clear similarities between the projects of the avant-garde and the official rhetoric on the arts in the 1930's and 1940's; this may well raise the question whether, despite opposite appearances, avant-garde and modernism as a whole did not, perhaps, outlive their time frame as totalitarian projects; in other words, whether at last parts of the edifices and mass architecture built under totalitarian regimes did not employ concepts proposed by modernism. Thus bottom line lies in the following question: was modernism a totalitarian project?

There are at least three perspectives on this topic. The first and the most radical, advanced by Boris Groys in his book *The Total Art of Stalin* (Princeton: 1992), argues that the aesthetic/political plan of the avant-garde to fundamentally reshape reality was in fact over-fulfilled by the Stalinist regime. Both plans dwell on the fact that society as well as its built environment should be highly controlled. Furthermore, the idea could be extended to post-Stalinist Eastern Europe, where hard-core modern concepts such as 'prefabrication', 'standardization' and 'urban control' became deliriously successful from 1954 onward, as well as to Romania in the 1980's, sliding backward to the "Neo-Stalinist" architecture of the so-called "new Civic Center" of Bucharest, spiced as it was with a modernist rhetoric of "national specificity" and of "upgrading" the capital city.

If socialist realism could change the style of a nearly-erected constructivist building (Moskva Hotel), the reverse example is equally at hand: Ceciulin's "White House" (Russia's House of the Soviets), built as late as 1981, was in fact a Stalinist design stripped of its ornaments, Palladian statues and other ingredients that made it desirable before 1953. "Modern" edifices erected after 1954, such as the Palace Hall and the Radio House in Bucharest, are stripped versions of classicism (or "conservative" variants of modernism, for that matter), as well as remakes of pre-war edifices. Even committed modern architects could dance the socialist-realist polka perfectly (Duiliu Marcu, Octav Doicescu in Romania, Rimanockzy in Hungary, as well as the Vesnin brothers in the U.S.S.R. a decade earlier), only to serenely return to their betrayed "first love" after 1954.

According to this interpretation, the apparently least modern of all, that is the Stalinist regime, in fact did the most to reshape Soviet reality in its entirety, thus implementing the project of the avant-garde beyond its original expectations, albeit distorted in its aesthetic appearance and without the original "road-fellows" — the modern architects who were left behind by the rapid changes they had first designed.

The second viewpoint is in fact a milder form of the previous one, in saying that totalitarian regimes reserved the most relevant official edifices for themselves. These were to be designed in a rather traditional, classicizing manner (for instance the Führer's Third Reich buildings, the Royal Palace and the Victoria Palace in Bucharest, the Palace of the Soviets in Moscow and so on). Thus they could remain rather detached from the mass production of architecture and second-rate edifices, which could in fact continue to be "modern" (i.e. driven by efficiency rather than expression). It was there, at the periphery of official discourses, in industrial architecture, collective dwelling quarters as well as upper class residences, that marginal modernists could still employ their previously acquired skills.

Finally, the third is the healthy modern tradition, represented by C. Cooke, Khan-Magomedov, Ikkonikov, A. Kopp, which acknowledged the definitive break between avant-garde and modernism on the one hand and totalitarianism on the other hand. Its arguments? Avant-garde artists were marginalized, constructivism and other "degenerated" and "decadent" styles were ridiculed as "formalist" (U.S.S.R.), "Judaic/Masonic" and "Bolshevik" (Germany, Italy). A huge amount of literature supports this line of reasoning, so I shall only add that the first, two-fold hypothesis — modernism as a totalitarian project, and its reverse, European totalitarianism as heir of the aesthetic-political plan of the avant-garde to redesign reality — has recently taken the fast lane, particularly since 1989, and is well-represented in the Eastern European literature  published so far on the topic. Scholars in architecture as well as other various art and cultural fields (often) representing the younger generation are currently investigating the modern project and its embodiments in Eastern Europe from that perspective, with solid results. Mention should be made here of Tatiana Pereliaeva from Russia, Mart Kalm from Estonia, the German Boris Groys, the first to advance this concept, as well as of the Romanians Caius Dobrescu, and myself.

Starting from the above-mentioned arguments one can infer that the interest of the Soviet elite lay in controlling the arts by controlling those who produced them, rather than a particular aesthetic. The so-called Edifice Committee, *de facto* jury of the Palace of the Soviets Competition, was a short list of the Politburo itself, albeit without Stalin. What the jury expected from this competition was not the emergence of some esoteric new artistic ideas. The outcome, i.e. Iofan's design as well as the clues as to what the architectural expression of something called socialist realism would have to be, were mere by-products, side effects of the political agenda underlying the competition. This was: *a)* the "socialism in one's country" architectural variant, i.e. no "gringos" working in the U.S.S.R.; *b)* the limitation of avant-garde influence within the artistic field and its organizations; *c)* a grand replica of the building resulting from the Palais des Nations competitions, which was to be — what else when it comes to Moscow? *d)* the largest building in the world.

We know now that the competition was rather useless, since the difference between Iofan's original tower, topped with the statue of an anonymous worker, and the winning entry is only a minor one. Both designs reflect the principle of subordinating architecture (the building is seen as a mere pedestal for a gigantic statue); the statue of the worker went out as Lenin made his grandiose appearance. Yet the worker did not disappear for good; he returned in 1937 on top of the Soviet national pavilion (coupled with the Kolhoz Girl), and once more in 1939, to mimic the Statue of Liberty in New York by grabbing a star from the Queens sky. This was really cynical: the resemblance to the "Lady with the Torch" was precisely the reason why Iofan's entry for the Palace of the Soviets had been rejected in the first place!

However, during this competition, much of what the Bolshevik elite had wanted was fulfilled: *a)* foreign architects — most of them committed Modernists — disappeared from the very beginning with the sole exception of Oscar Hamilton, a co-winner, who was eventually also eliminated; *b)* apart from the Vesnin brothers, who made it to the final stage of the competition only by disfiguring (i.e. classicizing) their design beyond any constructivist recognition, all the other avant-garde architects were eliminated, including the proletarian architects from VOPRA, who were then closest to the party line; *c)* the importance of this competition already surpassed that which the Palais des Nations competition had had; *d)* the design finally bred was indeed that of the largest and tallest building in the world, a result arrived at by revising the design several times so that it would become taller than any of its contemporary American challengers. Furthermore, the decree of April 23, 1932 (i.e. issued during the competition) had dissolved the existing organizations and forged the controlled Union of Architects and the Academy of Architecture, namely the very institutional grounds for an abrupt change in the way in which socialist realist architecture would eventually be designed.

## II.2. A Post-Modern Critic's Kit for Interpreting Socialist Realism

When discussing Soviet socialist realism of, roughly, the period between 1932 and 1954*, and post-modernism, which flourished and then faded away in the 1980's, one has to address several points which can shed light on possible aesthetic solutions to common, or rather comparable tasks. Here I shall address the adverse reaction to avant-garde and modernism respectively, as a plausible "primordial cause" for both "styles", centered on the question of identity. Thus the anti-modern matrix, the use of the classicist idiom in architecture, and of realist representation in the fine arts will be analyzed as the major tools in the resuscitation of a populist adherence to certain value and power systems induced by the two discourses. As there is a large amount of contemporary literature on post-modernism, and the primary interest of this paper is socialist realism, the "reading" here given will use the lenses/concepts usually associated with post-modernism. Therefore the comparison is rather indirect and perhaps unbalanced. Inevitably and by way of consequence, there will be more room for socialist realism than for post-modernism.

The issue of identity underlines both Reaganism in the United States, and Thatcherism in the United Kingdom, as a way of reacting against a dissolving, corrosive lack of ideology. By reactivating the ideological rhetoric in the dry veins of the power system, "conservative revolutions" have awakened the latter's dormant inner strength, reaffirming values associated with tradition, and, implicitly, approaching an aesthetic different from that of the exhausted, redundant modernism, already drained of its last drop of expressiveness.

---

* Although Stalin died in 1953, several projects were not finished until as late as 1956, when the process of "de-Stalinization" actually began. (a.n.)

## Fragmentation — Pastiche — Collage

In looking at the aesthetic discourses of socialist realism and (historical) post-modernism, one has to note that both were cultures of fragments, collating and pastiche, though for different reasons. Post-modernism rejected the unified set of values promoted by modernity, in saying that there were many more systems, equally valid, and that its aesthetic should include as many as possible, no matter how contradictory or even opposed. It was not recommendable to repress any virtual chance a building might have to please the masses. As a way of enhancing the meaning of a certain edifice, it was desirable to address the diversity of possible options by bringing into the text, (and thereby enriching it), multiple references which could allude to the cultural plurality the text stood for. Pastiche was a way of "quoting" other texts, and therefore a tool in expanding the horizon of meanings, references, sources, and related layers of interpreting a given text.

Socialist realism used pastiche, collage and fragmentation in the appearance of its architecture as yet another way of reaffirming its identity. What sort of identity, though? One defined by contrast, and by Manichean dichotomies; inclusivist, yes, but only after the target answered positively to the friend-or-foe message launched toward the history of art (architecture) by socialist-realist censors. History was divided into "revolutionary", "progressive" episodes, which fought against "retrograde", "conservative" ones. The criterion used in "dividing" history was the Bolshevik one: according to Marxist theory*, there were epochs in which the most

---

*Lunacearsky delivered several speeches on the appropriate use of historical styles in socialist realist arts on many occasions, of which the meetings of the Orgburo of the Writers' Union between 1932 and 1934 are only the most important. At the 1934 Writers' Congress, Maxim Gorky delivered the official address, presenting an annotated version of 'good' and 'bad' sides of history. Since Gorky was then celebrated as the father figure of Stalinist literature and was a close friend of Stalin, his speech can be seen as the manifesto of socialist realism. (a.n.)

advanced social forces expressed their political agenda through the arts. For socialist realism, Greek classicism was "progressive" because it belonged to a "democratic" society. The Italian Renaissance was admitted into the post-apocalyptic, members-only club of Stalinist culture, because it was responsible for promotion of the bourgeoisie, then an "advanced" social force. In the fine arts, the Peredvizhniky realist movement of nineteenth-century Russia was yet another select guest, for both national and social reasons, whereas in architecture the Russian neoclassicism and baroque were reliable sources for the enrichment of the vocabulary. In playing inside this wide range of discourses, all of them "politically correct", an artist was not only allowed and entitled to select from its melange of historical forms, but was morally (i.e. ideologically) obliged to do so. Could it then be said that, once inside the "good" half of history, an architect could "play" at will? Not really. There were rules according to which one edifice had to be more severe than another. Furthermore, local and traditional ornaments were to be included, in compliance with the Stalinist thesis of a compulsory "socialist content and national form". A socialist realist edifice would therefore account for trans-historical class solidarity, being a living proof that history finally made justice for the "good", who now enjoyed the Bolshevik heaven. Since socialist realism inherited this treasure of "purified" discourses, its identity could best be expressed by association with the moral virtues encompassed within the "left" half of mankind's history.

Subsequently, all further research of "new" vocabularies had to stop. Communism was the happy end of history, and socialist realism had to be the ultimate style, which recycled, and, in so doing, dramatically improved the meaning of "the chosen ones". To search for new forms meant to reject the positive message encompassed by previous discourses, and to refuse the aura of continuity, legitimacy and, consequently, of identity that could be bestowed by using a "reliable" pool of rhetoric devices. For an ideology centered on historical Manicheism and social teleology, not to take advantage of such an opportunity was a capital mistake, a heresy which had to be severely punished. The aesthetic of the constructivist avant-garde served as an example in this respect. A joyous, eclectic play of fragments and pastiches of earlier edifices,* or of earlier vocabularies[9] unified the aesthetic of the avant-garde.

## *Decorum and Classicism*

A unique power grid expressed in a plurality of discourses, allowed to play, as in post-modernism, either at random, or according to implicit ideologic scenarios, seems to be a contradiction in terms. However, this contradiction is only apparent, since the play remains artificial and superficial. The edifices are decorated in rich, but nevertheless external skins. The decorum that enveloped both socialist realist and post-modernist edifices was meant to beautify an austere way to express power. It was meant to appropriate popular culture, to make the edifice "user-friendly" and theatrical, by apparently sharing with the average citizen the "secrets of the gods" which reside in Form. Consequently, populism came into the picture, and official propaganda advanced either the "Soviet people's right to columns" (Lunacearsky), the "popular capitalism" (Thatcherism), or the "Versailles for the people" (Boffil) slogans.

In erecting "palaces for the masses", the piano nobile moved outside/in front of the building (Arata Isozaki's Tsukuba Civic

---

* Tcentrosoyuz Building, designed by Zholtovsky and erected in Moscow in 1934, copied the Palladin Palazzo del Capitanato in Piazza dei Signori, Vicenza, Italy. (a.n.)

Center), or in the square (Piazza d'Italia). The socialist realist edifices, exhibiting their richness to the city, had squares for mass gatherings and marches in front of their main elevations (the Palace of the Soviets, Lenin's Mausoleum, all regional party headquarters), which also incorporated tribunes for leaders/orators. Since the masses could not enter, and were not to have access to the "Winter Palaces" of the Soviet regime ever again, sharing the meaning of the edifice by organizing gatherings in front of it was a minor concession aimed at maintaining a fascination in the masses by suggesting that it was sometimes possible to short-cut the hierarchy, and that the top leaders were somehow accessible, at least visually.* Conversely, by designing luxurious, rich, symbolic edifices such as supermarkets and company headquarters, the corporate world intended to suggest that consumerism and businesses were meaningful activities in today's society, and were to be celebrated as such.

In this context, the "popular places" of socialist realism and post-modernism were a means of rendering accessible and explicit that which allegedly was elitist and encoded: the modernist aesthetic. They were "decorated sheds" not "dead ducks". They simulated the grass-roots origins of the power system, which stood for and was an offspring of the people, and shared with them the richness of representation, by celebrating common values in a unanimous, allegedly classless society. The best way to assert and celebrate those values was through a classical language. Classicism could decorate the offices of the State Department, at the top of the pyramid, city halls and corporate headquarters, placed some-where at the interface between "masses" and power structures, as well as consumerist institutions, placed at the lower end of the

---

* The light which was always on in "Stalin's office" in the Kremlin was another Agitprop trick: the Father of the nation was ever without sleep, permanently caring for his people. (a.n.)

60

social hierarchy. Its language could be both elitist and populist; both utopian, and therefore projective, and "realist" and retrospective.

Both discourses addressed the question of origins. Whereas socialist realism "inherited", and consequently displayed its stylistic "ancestors" who were identified according to ideological criteria, post-modernism intended to recapture and appropriate tradition, from "the primitive hut" to the "golden", Classic Age. Graves' allusions to megaron-like structures on top of the proposed Portland building. Rossi's "types", Leon Krier's and HRH Prince Charles' nostalgic and retrospectivist attempts to recapture past values as if they were forever engraved within classic forms, all dealt with "primordial", "pure" architecture in a way which differed from that of modernism.

Classicism was not only delightful in both discourses, but was at the same time more meaningful for the community as compared to modernism. It inflicted order and hierarchy upon cities, granted edifices an accessible monumentalism, and, unlike modernism, could act as a "readable" and, therefore, "understandable" text.

The contradiction between post-modernist irony and the "seriousness" with which socialist realism made use of classicism dissolved into the concept of play. Post-modern architects were ironic and sarcastic about the values celebrated in their buildings. Nevertheless, they did not attempt to dissolve them. Unlike deconstruction, post-modernism acknowledged the centered grids of power while attempting to play with exterior appearance, the interface between power and society, in a sort of semiotic schizophrenia. It made no attempt to uproot or set free the inner contradictions within architecture which were only being camouflaged. Socialist realism was also allowed to play with synonymous languages within a unique frame of (ideological) meaning, without questioning it. It was a highly regulated game: the meaning was controlled by the party, as was the amount of toys involved. The artist had only to choose from among the officially approved portfolio the best (combination of) vocabularies in order to embellish and make the meaning more accessible to the masses.

Despite the global visions and degraded utopias of the Stalinist plan for Moscow (1935), and of successive post-war plans to reshape the most important Soviet cities, the implementation of socialist realism was only local and piecemeal. Retrograde heavens, those "Communist Jerusalems" were so highly present in posters, international exhibitions, maps and models set with precious stones, that there was little need to have them actually erected. Holograms and fragments of a larger discourse, the edifices, "cvartals" and squares which actually managed to become "real" allude to an immanent and imminent vision of total coherence. Socialist realism and post-modernism defined themselves by contrast to avant-garde and modernism, respectively. They were implemented as disjointed, yet ubiquitous epiphanies. It is hard to identify the same comprehensive approach in the case of post-modern urbanists. Rather, one can speak about a local and piecemeal kind of approach, as if, by implementing punctual works or ensembles, the corrupt environment would be healed through mutual sympathy. It was Cristopher Alexander's Architectural DIY Handbook for the "average citizen".

Both post-modernism and socialist realism attempted to embellish reality, and to transform the state into a work of art. Yet they remained fragmented, collated, epidermic and superficial. Playing with forms, having no deeper agenda of their own (because, allegedly, no such agenda could exist, or was not within the reach of the artist/architect, respectively) behind their "beautiful" façades, neither of these two styles changed the world. By 1953, socialist realism was a corpse. An embellished one, yet a corpse nevertheless. But was it really the "dead style walking"? Perhaps the strongest arguments against an untimely burial of socialist realism would be: 1) at least in name, socialist realism was the official Soviet style up to the Gorbachev era; 2) immediately after Stalin died, many designs which had been on the waiting list stripped off their theatrical décor, and were born anew as modern edifices.

## II. 3. Nikita Khrushchev's Speech of 1954: The Lost Manifesto of Modern Architecture?

*Is Khrushchev's discourse of December 7, 1954 at the* All-Union Conference of builders, architects and workers in the construction materials industry, and the machine-building industry, in design and research organizations *really the "lost manifesto of modern architecture"?*

### *Goals*

Before the speech delivered in 1956 at the party congress, widely regarded as marking the actual beginning of the de-Stalinization process in the U.S.S.R., the discourse Khrushchev gave in December 1954 — albeit a "gentle manifesto",* as Venturi's was to be twenty-two years later — was, arguably, his first major attack on Stalinism, though an oblique one. In it Khrushchev stood up against the previous official perspective on architecture — the socialist realist one — rather than against the ideology which had produced it. However, certain points can definitely be made with regard to the speech itself, from a modernist/functionalist perspective on architecture.

a) The speech proclaimed the urgency to modernize (i.e. to industrialize) construction techniques, and thus emphasized the standardization of building types, prefabrication and mass-

---

* Khrushchev's discourse opens with a *laudatio*: "The industrialization of the Soviet country has been accomplished thanks to the fact that our party has continuously put into practice the teachings of Lenin and Stalin". (a.n.)

production of structural elements, and eventually — derived from the above — the need to change the way architecture was designed in the U.S.S.R.

b) Khrushchev argued against monumentalism (unique monuments and church-like edifices), and favored instead social/common dwellings, which were to be judged on the grounds of the average building costs per square meter, rather than on the number of ornaments adorning their façades.

c) Although the speech did not explicitly bring forth constructivism as "good" architectural ideology, it identified the latter as a "false target", in saying that fighting constructivism was at that time merely a diversion to camouflage the poor architecture of the Stalinist era.

d) Finally and by way of consequence, by criticizing Mordvinov, the head of the Academy of Architecture, Khrushchev in fact violently attacked the institutional structures Stalinism had left behind.

## *The Industrialization — Prefabrication — Serial Homes: Line of Reasoning*

Khrushchev's speech was clearly structured as an attack against architecture as it had been conceived during Stalin's period. First of all, this was neither a conference of the Union of Architects, nor one of the Academy, although both institutions were present (and severely criticized) at the meeting. Rather, it was a meeting of the building industry, of which architects were just a tiny part, and certainly not the most important one, as they had been during the Stalinist era. Let it be remembered that architects were among those most favored by the previous *nomenklatura*: when had to be depicted the highest living standards in the U.S.S.R. in movies, the interiors featured were those in the homes of architects. The union had its own *dacha* outside Moscow, at Suchanov. The Academy used an old palace all by itself. Even Frank Lloyd Wright, who was on the American team attending the first Congress of the Union of Architects in 1937, was surprised and delighted by the luxurious standards architects enjoyed.*

The title of the discourse itself made no reference whatsoever to architecture ("On implementing on a large scale the industrial methods, on improving the quality and on reducing the cost of construction"); the profession itself was mentioned second to the builders in the subtitle. Furthermore, architecture was barely mentioned in the first part of the discourse.

The introduction claimed that heavy industry was the only one which could contribute to the proper development of the U.S.S.R. Khrushchev then took the idea one step further, saying that heavy industry meant: *a)* more cement and thus more reinforced concrete; *b)* "the large-scale industrialization of construction", and thus *c)* prefabricated, *not* monolith concrete,** and, in any case, definitely *not* bricks. For Khrushchev, "more progressive" meant "industrialized building methods"; thus a whole industry had to be created starting from the concept of progress:

> By decree of the C.C. of P.S.U. and of the Council of Ministers of the U.S.S.R., it is envisioned that in the next three years four hundred two new factories and two hundred platforms for the production of prefabricated elements and items of reinforced concrete will be built. In these three years, the production of reinforced concrete prefabricated units will increase five-fold; accordingly, the cement production will grow by more than one-hundred-and-fifty percent (...).

---

* See F.L. Wright: "Architecture and Life in U.S.S.R." in *Architectural Record*/Oct. 1937; trans. Augustin Ioan, *Simetria*, Bucharest (Spring, 1995): 137–44. (a.n.)

** "We'll indicate the names and we'll not accuse those who have directed the builders towards using monolith concrete. I think those comrades have themselves realized they were on the wrong track. Nowadays it is clear to everyone that we should follow *the more progressive* way, (which is) the way of using prefabricated elements and pieces" (italics mine, A.I.).

Within the realm of prefabrication, it was hard for the Soviet leader to choose between the existing systems — with prefabricated structure and panels, or just with large panels. Therefore he would rather have them compete in the future in a "democratic" fashion: "(...) it seems to me that for the time being one does not have to pass a certain verdict (...) We must offer both systems the chance to develop." Furthermore, everything that could be prefabricated out of reinforced concrete — not just walls and building elements — had to be done in this way: bridges, pipes, milestones, everything, in order to replace wood, bricks and metal: "In buildings, everything that can be replaced with concrete or reinforced concrete will be replaced." There was a shortage of wood in the U.S.S.R. at that time, allegedly; metal was used inappropriately and "unjustly"; yet when it came to bricks, Khrushchev's concern clearly regarded the backwardness in construction which was associated with their use: why use manual labor when machines and mechanisms were more efficient?

Backwardness is a key word in interpreting this speech, under-scored as it were by a "moral" dichotomy, very similar to that employed by socialist realism in the interpretation of history. Bricks and manual labor belonged to the past, therefore they were bad. Cement/reinforced concrete and industrial building techniques were 'progressive', therefore good. The same logic applied to design activity, the topic of the second chapter in Khrushchev's speech. The design process was lagging behind industry, in Khrushchev's opinion: "sometimes simple buildings are designed over a period of two years or more". If architects did not realize how slow they were, industry nevertheless would urge them to move forward more rapidly. What, then, was "progressive"? Typified designs — the simpler, the better. Even more: the fewer types, the better:

> Why are thirty-eight typified projects currently being used? Is this *rational?* (...) One must choose a limited number of type-designs for dwellings, schools, hospitals,

kindergartens, shops, as well as for other buildings and constructions; one must mass-build only according to these designs, for, say, five years. After this period we will discuss this issue, and, if there be no better proposals, the duration of using these will be extended by another five years. What's bad in this proposal, comrades? (italics mine, A.I.).

In Khrushchev's dual logic, there was no room for elaborate (his word is "exaggerated") finishings and adornments. Architects who designed individual buildings suddenly became "an obstacle against industrializing construction"; they were the reactionaries who did not like "building well and fast". Rather they were taught to build monuments (by which the Soviet leader meant "a building erected according to a personal project"), and probably the education they had received in school was also to blame. By no means less guilty was the Academy of Architecture, whose president "has changed after the war. He is no more the same comrade Mordvinov".

The speech sketched a definitely more "social" trend in the question of architecture than the previous socialist realist agenda. U.S.S.R. did not need monuments, at least not any more, but rather "humble" social housing projects, "useful" buildings like hospitals, *crèches*, schools. Unlike Stalinist architects, who had lost touch with reality, Khrushchev had empirical, grass-roots arguments from "out there" to prove his points. Here is one of his examples: in the industrial city Vatutenki (Moscow region) the kindergarten was oversized (91,9 sq.m./child instead of 24 sq.m./child, as the norms stated) and "overloaded with stucco ornaments"; it was a "palace", ironically claimed the speaker, which cost three times the "normal" building. Yet, the author of the design was awarded first prize. For what? For wasting funds.

If architects wanted to "walk in step with life", they had to learn not only to design forms, but rather to use new materials, techniques and — even more importantly — economy. One can see here a clear attack against the *beaux-arts* tradition of the Soviet architectural schools. By the same token, Khrushchev favored the polytechnical method of teaching architecture, closer perhaps to a Bauhaus curriculum, yet nevertheless strictly controlled by the Bolshevik party. By embellishing their architecture, the *beaux-arts*-ists hung tasteless and — a modern argument — useless decorations on their façades. They were difficult to build, expensive, time and energy-consuming. Instead, Khrushchev asserted that the only important criterion of effectiveness in construction was "the cost per square meter of building".

## *"Ornament Is Politically Incorrect": The Hidden Modern Agenda*

"Ornament is a crime", Adolf Loos once said. Khrushchev would have agreed with that, adding that it was the fault of an aberrant ("irrational") building program, which had favored high-rise buildings at which "we can look, but in which we cannot dwell or work". The argument against the Stalinist edifices ran eventually as a typically modern one. Why did Moscow need spires at all, price aside, since they looked like churches? "Do you like churches?" the Communist leader asked rhetorically. It was not just the spires, but the improper expression of the interior function: "One cannot transform a contemporary house, by means of forms, into some kind of church or museum. This bring no extra confort to its occupant, but complicates the use of the building and makes it more expensive."

But, unlike Loos, Khrushchev was sarcastic in criticizing the adornments of high-rise buildings in Moscow. "These are perversions in architecture", and whoever did not understand this had to be replaced ("He who will not understand must be brought on the right path"), as had happened to comrade Zaharov, who had been previously removed from leading a design studio. His fault, apart from belonging to the Stalinist nomenklatura? Allegedly, he had designed a tall building with Palladian statues on top, yet this was an apartment building with "a living room with five walls, with a corner window [which] was not comfortable, let alone that the occupants had to look at the backs of the statues all of their lives. One can understand that it is not very nice to live in such a room".

Yet Zaharov was not alone in this. He could have been inspired by the theories of the necessary monumental approach towards cities' skylines. A.G. Mordvinov himself, the president of the Academy of Architecture, quoted by Khrushchev from *Architektura SSSR 1/1945 (nota bene*: nine years before the speech), as well as professor A.V. Bunin, had both argued in favor of major, tall urban elements without an immediate purpose ("porticos, monumental halls, towers"); the city centers, believed Bunin, had to exclude prefabrication, and had to be individually designed, with domes and towers, that is with major vertical silhouettes. It is no wonder then that architects sacrificed comfort and cost, since came from the very top such examples of misunderstanding.


## *"Dead Style Walking": Nikita Khrushchev Promoting Constructivism?*

But was it really a misunderstanding, or worse, since, under the banner of anti-constructivism, Stalinist architects only "justified their wrong direction"? From this point onward, Khrushchev entered the most surprising and radical part of his discourse. He had to demolish both the Stalinist establishment in architecture, and the atheist ideology promoted in its name. He could deal with the former easily way, using a Trojan Horse named comrade Gradov, who had allegedly tried to criticize Mordvinov (i.e. the establishment itself) by using arguments similar to those used by Khrushchev on December 7, 1954. Yet Mordvinov had tried to prevent him from speaking at the meeting, which proved once again, according to the party leader, "that in the Academy of Architecture there are neither the necessary conditions for a free exchange of opinions regarding architectural work, nor criticism". It was not exclusively Mordvinov's fault: worse even, he shared it with the State Committee for Construction, which was supposed to oversee the work of the academy and to promote the "standardization activity, urban planning and city building", which they had hardly ever done before 1953.

As for the aesthetics of socialist realism, Khrushchev had to be subtler than just imposing another language by decree; rather, he preferred to build his argument on a more the-enemy-of-my-enemy-is-my-friend kind of approach. Which was the single most hated aesthetics for socialist realism? Constructivism. The avant-garde elite was gradually replaced even before 1925 by classicists as I. Zholtovsky, A. Schusev* and I. Fomin. How then to best subvert the socialist realist rhetoric other than by claiming that it was obsessed with fighting constructivism instead of concentrating on how to properly design the Soviet architecture? "Of course" one had to fight against constructivism (Khrushchev did not want to go all the way to surprising his audience), but it had to be done only by using "rational means". What does this key word in his speech really mean?

If constructivism meant formalism, and if that was bad, then perhaps the Stalinist architects were the real constructivists, since they themselves "slide towards the aesthetizing passion for a form

---

* "One of the fundamental contradictions of Schusev's work was that between his progressive stand — to reject eclecticism and to use the national forms — and the reactionary content of these buildings, often serving the anti-popular czarist church (...) Only after the Great Socialist Revolution in October Schusev could rise up to his own possibilities, his works gaining a proper social and ideological content, thus placing Schusev among the first and most important masters of Soviet architecture". "Alexei Victorovici Sciusev — The Great Master of Soviet Architecture" in *Arhitectura* 2/1953. Note the way Stalin's thesis on the dichotomy form/expression and its content is used in dissociating Schusev's churches before 1917 from his work after the Revolution.

disconnected from its content". They were probably blind — one can argue following Khrushchev's arguments — not to see that, well, there were good parts in constructivism after all. First of all, "the grey, sad box-style", as the *Great Soviet Encyclopaedia* called it*, would have been cheaper than building towers and colonnades. Then the interior distribution of its buildings, the way they could be used were obviously more "rational", as he liked to point out frequently during the speech, than the useless adornments of the façades. It was more of a negligent attitude toward "the ardent needs of the people" than was it efficient in fighting constructivism.

Khrushchev went on to stupefy his audience even more by proclaiming several aesthetic points dear to any modernist. a) First of all, a generic one: "We are not against beauty, but against useless things". Then, derived from this slogan, it followed that b) façades should be beautiful not because of their decoration, but due to "skilfull proportions of the whole building, a good proportion of the windows and doors (...), due to a proper use of finishing material", and, perhaps the clearest paraphrase of the "form follows function" modern mantra, c) façades had to be beautiful by "*vertically outlining* the wall pieces and elements in the block buildings with large panels".

## Bare-Naked Architecture and The Malignant City: Effects on Architectural Practice

Obviously, this speech was meant to be a manifesto *against* socialist realism as the most representative expression of Stalinism, more than a catalist *for* a specific aesthetic alternative. The agenda of modern architecture was used in order to define by contrast what Khrushchev was fighting against. However, it is obvious that its

---

* Edited in Russian in 1953, vol. 22, pag. 437, quoted in the text by Khrushchev himself, only to point to the ideological irrelevance of the way constructivism was actually defined there.

influence in reshaping the architectural discourse in the Soviet Union and its satellite countries was enormous. After 1954 several socialist realist buildings which were under construction in 1953 continued to be erected, yet not without harsh criticism for their costs and decoration. Mordvinov, author of the Ukraine Hotel in Moscow (one of the seven Stalinist sky-scrapers), had his share of party criticism on the spot, during the speech: the square meter was allegedly 17% more expensive here than at the Moskva Hotel*, due largely to the excessive decoration. Many other pavilions at the Agricultural All-Union Exhibition in Moscow (which was extensively described by its chief architect A. Jucov in *Arkitektura SSSR* 7/1954, as well as in *Arhitectura RPR* 9/1954) were completely finished after Stalin died**. D.N. Ceciulin's Soviet House of RFSSR on Krasnopresnenskaia was eventually built*** very much with the same outline as it had been designed before 1953, yet entirely stripped of its ornaments. Later edifices, such as Lenin Central Stadium in Lujniki (1956, A.V. Vlasov, who was in 1954 the chief architect of Moscow, "a good architect, but who sometimes does not manifest the right perseverance", Khrushchev argued in his speech), recall pre-war edifices such as B. Iofan's Dinamo Central Stadium: still

---

* The story, described by Tarkhanov and Kavtaradze, runs that Schusev had to redesign the façades joined along the symmetry axis instead of as two separate variants. As he was not allowed to see Stalin personally to explain the two options, the latter signed across the drawings, which thus became official. No one dared to explain the mistake to Stalin, and the hotel was built with two slightly different half-façades.

** Tarkhanov and Kavtaradze, in their 1992 *Stalinist Architecture*, wrote about Khrushchev's obsession to compete in making "his" pavilion the most flamboyant of the agricultural exhibition. While he was the party leader in Ukraine, he ordered that its pavilion should be the most decorated. Becoming eventually the party leader in Moscow, he ordered this next pavilion to be redesigned, to surpass the Ukrainian one.

*** And badly damaged during Eltsin's 1992 attack against the Russian parliament.

classicizing, yet without the emphasis on flamboyant decorations of the post-1949 ones.

In November 1955, the "useless stylistic elements" were officially and definitively eliminated from the architectural discourse. According to Ockman and Eigen, the first to mention this speech as a possible modernist text (1993:184), by 1958 almost 70% of the structural parts of a building were prefabricated, as opposed to 25% in 1950. While in 1948 the Academy of Architecture had to advance prototypes for various building types for five different regions in the country, typification was hardly the result — in Khrushchev's terms later on — since the outcome was: 50 different types of dwelling units and (nota bene) 200 types of public buildings, each with its own set of decorations and "traditional/local" details. After 1954 this was hardly the case anymore, although it did not mean that the Soviet modernism evolving from Khrushchev's speech was in any way a return to constructivist experiments. Exhibited at Brussels in the Soviet pavilion, prefabricated architecture tailored according to Khrushchev's speech meant in fact "a stripped-down façade treatment and fewer compulsory symmetries, but in rigidity of conception it remained very similar to the work carried out under Stalin" (ibidem).

Although it is clear that the first trend after the speech was to "look back" to bridge the gap socialist realism had inflicted upon the architectural discourses in East-European architecture, the sources of this retrospection may have varied from one country to another. In its major edifices before the war, Romania envisioned a hybrid, classicizing modernism and/or a stripped classicism (the so-called "Carol II" Style celebrated by promoters like Petre Antonescu or I.D. Enescu) indebted to Italian examples. And for good political reasons: Italy and Romania are both of Latin origin, while the German official architecture at the time was questionable, as was anything Nazi.

Estonia had its alternative modern tradition, while the Soviet Union could not quite return to the blamed constructivism wholeheartedly, despite Khrushchev's half-blessing. However, after 1960, Bauhaus and CIAM urban schemes became the norm in East European architecture, only to be somehow altered later on, at the top level of the discourse, by a late-Corbusierian aesthetics of rough concrete and spectacular, "poetic" forms.

Very much the same thing happened in Hungary, where architects like Rimanockzy worked before, during, and after Stalinism, only to return to his old tools again after 1956, when the revolution had abruptly switched the clock from socialist realism "back" to plain modernity. A similar trend can be seen in Estonia, which, largely exposed to pre-war Scandinavian/Aalto modernism, did precisely the same thing after 1954, that is a return to its modern pre-war sources before the war.

## Ideology as/instead of Aesthetics: Effects on The Critical Discourse

The real issue in interpreting East European architecture is that it lacked critical edge, self-reflexiveness. After the suppression of the avant-garde in the U.S.S.R., official discourses stood for — and thus replaced — any form of criticism. The leaders would "draw the official line", while architects would eventually strive to "implement" it within their discourse, embellishing the respective vague, superficial suggestions with an aesthetic/architectural parlance, attributing it to a line of reasoning allegedly deduced from the given speech. After becoming norm, no one but the party leader himself would dare criticize the "official line" in architecture, be it socialist realist or its opposite after 1954.

One must say that socialist realism itself was not the immediate result or certain elaborate aesthetics descending from Stalin, Jdanov or the like, but a by-product of their acts within the realm of architecture, as well as the "translation" of their rough discourses on architectural topics. Socialist realism was the offspring of many step-parents: the 23 April 1932 decree which had supressed the extant professional organizations, replacing them with a union and an academy; the Palace of the Soviets competition which rejected any straightforward modern as well as foreign designs, thus suppressing the European avant-garde-ists as well as the local ones; and finally, the method of interpreting history formulated by Lunacearsky and Gorky, who concluded that it was not only commendable to use historic precedents in the "new" Soviet architecture, but also compulsory, since Bolshevism was the intended end of historical "progress". After 1934, when V. Vesnin criticized the "Schusism" of Soviet architecture, (i.e. its complete abandon of any aesthetic set of principles in favor of "anything works", a sort of cowardness promoted, Vesnin believed, by Schusev), and some weak criticism at the first congress of the union in 1937, there was no critical agenda attached to Soviet architecture before Stalin died.

Which returns us to Khrushchev's speech. This was the first top-level official discourse in the communist world which focused upon specific aesthetic issues, drew the respective consequences derived from the theoretical approach and thus imposed practical tasks upon Soviet — as well as East European — architecture. My point is that its thoroughness was precisely what further suppressed the critical edge of East-European architecture. From then on, one could find merely buildings, and very little, if any, critical discourse. In contrast, it is extremely relevant to interpret not only the corpus of modern edifices in the West, but also that of theoretical discourses (criticism, utopian designs, "myths" and various *ars poetica*) the researcher of Soviet/East European architecture has to contend with reflections and traces of the official discourses in various how-to texts on architecture, as well as in the built environment.

Perhaps the most illuminating examples in that respect are: a) an article by I. Nikolaev, called "Questions of economy and aesthetics in Soviet architecture" (*Arhitectura RPR* 7/1955), an architect's digest of Khrushchev's speech, as well as b) the "table talk" at the Academy of Architecture "about the question of the nature and specific [task] of architecture" (*Arkhitektura SSSR* 6/1955), a deciphering session of the same discourse, now properly translated into professional jargon, justified with citations/interpretations of historical precedents, and rounded up with the envisioned consequences to architectural practice at the end of each talk.

Eloquent examples of such immediate fruits of Khrushchev's speech can be found in the architectural media, where discourse could be swiftly tuned to the pitch of the official hymns. Reading the 1955 summary of *Arhitectura*, the journal of the Union of Architects *and* of the (post-Stalinist) State Committee for Architecture and Construction of the Ministers Council, is tantamount to reading the abstract of Khrushchev's speech. First of all, industrial building methods took over the content: to theory and history — the last chapter — are devoted roughly only one seventh of the pages through out the year. The titles address anyting but building unique edifices; instead, dwelling units, social-cultural buildings, industrial and agricultural buildings are the norm. And — above all — standardization, prefabrication, and typification. *Type*-designs for social-cultural buildings in the countryside (issue 2/55), *type* designs for public buildings (5/55 — *horribile dictu*, would have said the Stalinist architect before 1953!), *type* designs for schools and kindergartens (10 and 11-12/55) are the key concepts.

Furthermore, the main concern of the third national conference of the Union of Architects in the People's Republic of Romania (December 10-11, 1954, covered in *Arhitectura* 3/1955, precisely in the aftermath of Khrushchev's speech), had, because of the blurred significance and consequences of the speech, a rather confused and remarkably low-key agenda, while the final conclusions resembled in a striking manner the way Khrushchev's speech (neither he nor it are in any way acknowledged in the text) was structured. But while the latter discussed the industrialization of building activities, followed by the consequences for architecture, former's conclusions addressed the agricultural architecture for the emerging collective farms (kolhozes).

Later, urbanism became again a key issue, as the so-called "systematization of the national territory" began to be looked at as a means to control the landscape/reality, as an early sketch of the *megastructure* concept that took over the discourse in the 1960's.

## *The "As If" Manifesto of East European Modernism*

Is Khrushchev's discourse really the lost manifesto of modern architecture? The answer is two-fold. Yes and no at the same time, depending on where the mirror stands.

Yes, because it entailed definitely modern consequences (a definite social agenda for its envisioned architectural program, prefabrication of buildings, the predominant use of concrete, as well as a remote yet recognizable "form-follows-function" approach); because it rejected the socialist realist aesthetics, used a "rational" parlance, and because it reversed the anti-constructivism trend in Soviet architecture.

No, because is was merely a political discourse, not to be critically scrutinized, perhaps opposed, but which was meant to be obediently "translated" and applied in practice as such, without further question. And no, because many of his aesthetic principles were not inherently modern, but rather the conclusions of Khrushchev's economic obsessions: price-per-square-meter, heavy industry, concrete and the industrialization of building techniques, mirroring a compulsory lack of alternatives to the worldwide trends socialist realism wanted to ignore for so long.

Perhaps a better way to characterize the discourse of December 7, 1954, is this: a) the beginning of the de-Stalinization process; b) the speech that *stood for* East-European Modern manifestos largely by replacing them and suppressing their eventual birth.

## II. 4. A Reading of Modern Architecture in the Fifties and Sixties

### *The Disappearing Body of Modern Architecture?*

Architecture in the fifties and sixties increasingly lost its corporeality. It was not just the disfigurement of its face. It was not just an *écorché*, a skinless mechanism, displaying (rarely in a glass window) every single organ to the outside; it emphasized its respective shape (brutalism), flexing rough concrete muscles (Paul Rudolph's Yale Faculty of Architecture, late Corbusier's La Tourette, Chandigarh and Notre Dame de Haute Ronchamp).

It was much more than all these: architecture after the war revolted against its integrity, completion, definitiveness, permanence, and inside coherence. It stood against internal measure (Michelis, 1982: 200-8) and ended up being anti-anthropomorphous — at one end the Hi-Tech wizardries, at the other end Kurokawa's "cyborg architecture". Architecture as a unique body exploded. Its internal, sustaining structures became interconnected and proliferated, leading to the megastructure concept, while its cells became autonomous, replaceable, moveable, only to evolve eventually toward Reiner Banham's "bubbles"\* to capsules (in metabolism) and to disposable (Cook called it "throw-away") architecture later on.

---

\* In "A Home is not a House" (1965, reprinted in *Design by Choice*, 1981) with drawings by Francois Dallegret (a.n.)

## Megastructures and East European Look-Alikes

*Megastructure had a great size: "was built of modular units; was capable of great, or even 'unlimited' extension; was a structural network into which smaller structural units (for example rooms, houses, or small buildings of other sorts) can be built — or even 'plugged in' or 'clipped on' after having been prefabricated elsewhere; a structural framework expected to have a useful life much longer than that of the smaller units which it might support"*
*Reiner Bahnam (1976:2)*

The part played by corporeal metaphors in post-war architecture has not been thoroughly researched. First of all, it may be looked at from the perspective of an analogy between the functional and the organic: among the ideologies of functionalism identified by Benjamin Handler (1970:5) organicism was by far the most radically encompassing. Sullivan's slogan is thus enhanced, since Handler looks at the perfect identity between form and function (Handler, 1970:9). Form was understood as the outcome, the external expression of an internal process of functioning. According to the theory of systems, form would be "the functioning of the whole" (ibidem).

Obviously, post-war modernism played with its body (or with what was left after dismembering it) in a rather peculiar way. Architecture as a single, internally and (thus, the modernists would say) externally coherent body had to disappear. Brutalism was an *écorché*: skinless architecture without its protecting envelope to keep together in a unique body the entire building, and to mask its interior from the outside. The house did not need to be draped by a unique façade anymore. Instead, each part of any given building should be exclaimed, displaced from its system/structure and loudly displayed toward the exterior, to be widely visible. For the Smithsons, "form follows function" became "every single function should be expressed in a separated exterior shape/volume".

By setting the parts free, brutalism pointed toward the internal mechanism of the (architectural) body, toward the vital systems sustaining it, which then became essential: circulation/transportation, water pipes and electrical wires in the city, structural and correspondents of the above in the building.

There was only one step left to the megastructure concept, which could be looked at as architectural structuralism. This step was taken by Archigram and Yona Friedman, by Japanese metabolists, Urbanisme Spatial in France and by Cittá Territorio in Italy. The body disappeared, only to be replaced by a two-fold alternative: on the one hand the mega/meta organisms that could spread over a whole city and even a national/world-wide territory; all that mattered was the "biological", internal functioning of the whole; how the "atoms" moved and were distributed within it was secondary. While the first modernists, like Le Corbusier, were fascinated by cars and hangars, architects of the so-called "second Machine Age" (Martin Pawley) looked at space forms and chemical plants instead, "all canned-in exposed lattice frames, NASA style" (Colquhoun, 1986:17), since those provided the kind of "dismembering" needed to prove their point.

Without bodies to contain them, the internal mechanisms could proliferate malignantly, from house to city to the whole environment. All of those were in fact systems of control and manipulation of the urban structure, which gradually evolved and took over the architectural discourse, and from which the Western environment was saved (except for the interesting Cumbernauld example), since they remained largely urban utopias rather than became realities. In the East "and in Cuba" (Banham, 1976:10), though, megastructure — as a macro-concept regarding a whole country as *the site* for heroically extending the central control over it — became increasingly popular since the sixties, only to devour its host — the city — in the late eighties in Romania.

For megastructure was not the "neutral grid" (Colquhoun, 1986: 121) designed by Yona Friedman for the University of Berlin, or by Le Corbusier for his hospital project in Venice — neither in its original understanding, nor in its East European counterparts. First of all, because the frame was dominant, permanent, fixed and structural. Secondly, because, given the above-mentioned inner qualities, it was supposed to be expressed in a monumental way, which eliminated definitively its neutrality. The frame was not the background against which the city projected its functioning, but the functioning mechanism turned into the very essence of the city/environment.

In late 1960's Romania, as well as in the West earlier, the community spirit was replaced by "civic centers" — monuments dedicated to it, best described, as were its West European counterparts, as "grotesque civic monuments with compulsory piazzas (...) an elephantine tendency" (Curtis, 1982: 349) inspired obviously by "the last" Le Corbusier*. It is where the frame/structure exists that the internality of the architecture exhibits its "heroic" part in sustaining the whole. The grids were metaphors of control displayed on the façades of major administrative buildings built since late 1960's in every county capital city. Although the structural/decorative frames did not become autonomous, as in megastructures, this exhibition of inflated concrete grids is perhaps the most important feature of East European official architecture in the 1960's and 1970's (see photos).

In the same "heroic" style, but closer to a brutalist disem-bodiment, several major edifices were built in the sixties and early seventies in Romania. The Polytechnic Institute in Bucharest (1962-1972, Octav Doicescu chief architect; P. Iubu, C. Hacker, S. Lungu, P. Swoboda, I. Podocea architects) was an early example of a monumental, brutalist approach toward a dramatic change in designing edifices after Stalinism. Grids and rough, plugged-in

---

* These buildings are described as "rough concrete piers, heavy crates of brise-soleil and rugged overhangs" (Curtis; 1982: 349). (a.n.)

volumes were nevertheless masked with superficial brick finishing, altering their "sincere expression" praised by Gheorghe Curinschi Vorona (1981: 344). A slightly similar approach was conveyed in designing the Academy "Ștefan Gheorghiu" (Ștefan Rulea chief architect): its auditoriums are huge masses detached from the concrete grid of the façade and individually exposed as "prima donnas" of the exterior composition (see photo).

Communist Eastern Europe, plagued by prefabrication and social housing after 1954 (i.e. exclusively common dwelling units, with very little ownership allowed until the 1970's), was the perfect playground for megastructures — an efficient way to control the environment and its inhabitants. During the sixties, vast areas of the environment and historical city centres were destroyed everywhere in Europe in the name of development (Curtis, 1982: 349). Tradition disappeared for modernism to take over and impose "a simple and architectonic order on the layout of human society and its equipment" (Banham, 1976: 199).


## Capsules and the (Re)Movable Home

*"Art. 1. The capsule is cyborg architecture. Man, machine and space build a new organic body which transcends confrontation (…). Art. 2. A capsule is a dwelling of Homo movens."*
*Kisho Kurokawa (1977: 75-6)*


A different aspect, also discussed, was the prime unit: a dwelling capsule — detachable, transferable, thus mobile. The body metaphor retreated inside the cell. Yet the cell was secondary, since it depended on the megastructure. Within a "permanent and dominating frame containing subordinate and transient accommodations"*,

---

* Reyner Banham in *Megastructure: Urban Futures of the Recent Past*, quoted by Colquhoun (1986: 120).

the capsule was just another function of the city "housed" in "a large frame"*. While the capsule celebrated by metabolism had its own roots in the Japanese tradition: *kago*, the individual transportation unit, and the *shoin* pavilions called *jiga* (Charles Jencks in his Foreword to Kurokawa, 1977: 11), in the West it was a clear mark of disembodying architecture.

Yet Kurokawa refined the concept, since the capsule was no longer exclusively biologic: he talked about "cyborg architecture" — an architectural body with prostheses. Architects should not look at the body for inspiration, bur rather to its technological alter-ego. And, with technology and the capsule, "[a h]ome is not a [h]ouse" any more, as claimed by Reiner Banham in 1965. Any of its internal functions could be supplied technologically, and thus their material expression became irrelevant: solid, permanent walls, windows, furniture with its bourgeois, monumental appearance criticized by Baudrillard (1968).

Despite their compulsory modernism, East European architecture and interior design have never questioned the alleged "conservative" nature of furniture, capable of subverting the "revolutionary" message conveyed by the social common dwelling. Moreover, after the war Romania produced outdated yet traditionally "bourgeois" furniture items, such as the enormously popular glass cases, in which household valuables could be displayed. Moreover, modern architecture was transformed and even repressed by vernacular ways of appropriating the internal home space: the "clean" room for guests took over the living room as a place with the best furniture and the most valuable possessions in the household, where children were not allowed to play; the kitchen, despite its small size in modern apartments, was still the "fire center" of the home, and arguably the most important place in any Romanian apartment and so on and so forth.

---

* Fumihiko Maki on megastructure (1964), quoted by Colquhoun (loc.cit).

Yet, as a consequence of their mobility, homes of post-war visionaries lack *oikos*, the site with qualities best described by the concept of *Raum* (Heidegger, 1995: 185). "Home of the *homo movens*" (Kurokawa, 1977: 76), the capsule is in fact the most elaborate consequence of previous concepts of the constructivist "disurbanists", who ought to allegedly give the Soviet citizen unlimited freedom to move across the Soviet Union without having to depend on a given, fixed "dwelling place". Placeless architecture was the alternative to the "bourgeois" city, envisioned by disurbanists who had been repressed since 1930 by Stalin and Jdanov who said that, since the Bolshevik revolution had won in the cities, it followed that those cities were revolutionary from that point onward. With capsule architecture plugged into megastructures, one dealt with generic human beings as opposed to individuals. Man became a social, anonymous being docked in a space without attributes, which he did not own, yet which he had to call home.

The question arises here whether standardization and prefabrication of homes in East European architecture was the ultimate encapsulation of dwelling, expressed on the façades as well. Architecture in the 1960's emphasized the structural frame, which then celebrated the repetitiveness of its internal units*. The actual limits of any given home (i.e. apartment within the building, even individual rooms) were not only left apparent, but also

---

* "Some architects around 1950 (…) identified endlessness as a particular aesthetic virtue of frame construction" (Banham, 1966: 91). Thus the structure was no longer "neutral". In fact, as Banham pointed out previously, for most of the works of modernism, technology has to be understood "as symbolic rather than actual technology" (ibidem). Modernists as Heinle and Max Bücher could believe though that structure is neutral as long as it is "sincere" and presents itself "to be contemplated in is entirety" (1971: 285), without noting that, by saying exactly this, they had in fact recited a stylistic, hard-core modern slogan. Curt Siegel went even further to say that "another important characteristic of structural form is its independence of all 'trends' and 'new directions' in architecture" (1961: 303). (a.n.)

emphasized toward the exterior. Façades as drapes that could veil and mask such details had already disappeared. One can look at it as a "brutalist" attitude: the box frame "expressed the actual physical limit of each dwelling; each unit reads" (Banham, 1966: 91). Poor craftmanship and mere economy induced this separation of each panel, rather than any conceptual attitude.

While in the West the common dwelling was rather the exception, in the East it was the norm: an artificial environment, liable of being manipulated, which could repress self-representations of individual egoes, favoring in exchange social indistinctiveness. With the skinless, paneled façades, home as a shelter/refuge/hiding space was gone from post-war modern architecture.


## CorpoReality: Organic vs. Technological or Architecture as Prosthesis

*"Naturalism does not fit well with modern trends, nor with the structures of today".*

E. Heinle & M. Bücher (1971: 284)

By the same token, "organic" meant something different in post-war modernism. While Gaudi's bone columns and visceral Guel chapel still refer to the body metaphor, for metabolists the organic was just the host for healing technologies. Modern organic architecture looked at how organisms worked; at systems, not at their shapes. It was fascinated by velocity, self-sustained processes, internal functioning — in a word metabolism. Bionic architecture itself was not about mimicking the complete plan of the animal body, but rather about why it worked so well. "Organicism" in later discourse was not a celebration of the Body as a whole, but of the way it worked as a *Mechanism* — the ultimate metaphor of modern architecture.

Banham's environmental bubble as well as Quarnby's "organic" forms and the fantastic shapes of W.E. Wedin's polyurethane houses have all both descended from and informed sci-fi/cosmic architecture, such as Barbarella's Sojo city (imagined by Mario Garbuglia in 1968) and fur-lined space ship in which Jane Fonda purred bare-naked — all are somewhat indebted to the organic metaphor, yet expressed in non-organic materials. Although Kurokawa did discuss "living" concepts, they scarcely addressed the body alone: movement (Kurokawa, 1977: 87), dynamic modulation (ibidem), growth and change (idem: 89-91), or even a possible "aesthetics of death" (Jencks in idem: 10) referred to mechanism, to cyborgs more than to beings.

Combining existing materials, inventing new, artificial building materials and building colors, eroding conventional ways of employing old and new materials in architecture were perhaps the most radical strategies in displacing the being from its nest of conventions regarding its urban/public as well as interior/private space after 1950. The most intimate archetypes, such as the trilitic arche-structure, had to be disrupted and dis/re/placed.

Unlike before the war, when architecture, albeit modern, still had still a sense of appropriateness in dealing with (building) matter, after 1950 one can see architects looking to find "new" ways of twisting, folding, packing, inflating, exposing and even making invisible the very same matter, or its "cyborg" mutants.

A look into the substance of architecture and how dealing with it changed the very nature of the architectural discourse in Western and Eastern Europe might illuminate fractures as well as continuities within this process, and their relevance to our understanding of the architecture of the fifties and sixties.

## Erotic vs. Heroic: Plastic/Soft Architecture

*"Architecture can be seen more related to the ambiguity of life."*

Peter Cook (1970: 67)

The most important quality of plastic, apart from its modernity, came from its versatility: by designing plastic furniture, one could invent items with multiple functions and, most important, with non-conventional colors. Even entire cities could be designed, plastic utopias such as the Spatial Housing Project (W. Doring), or the suspended Rendo Housing Project (Casoni & Casoni), or the 1966 utopian pneumatic town by Gernot Nalbach. A living capsule made entirely of the same material thus became reality, while inflatable furniture, with its erotic, soft and sometimes transparent shapes, was fashionable in the sixties (and has made a comeback in the mid-nineties).

There were clear references to attributes of the body, yet "embodied" by the most artificial, anti-organic material. Soft architecture is perhaps the best example.* Bionics and metaphors of life were clearly incorporated into this definitely modern material, which was more clearly related to the sixties, with its out-of-body experiences — mind-expanding drugs (H. Rucker: *Mind Expander*, 1968) — than with "classical" anthropomorphism as such. "Sculptectures": all these dialogues, distortions, frustrations have to do with corporeality, witnessing the impossible struggle of modernity to completely exile its traces from within the

---

* Quarnby gives (1984: 63) a thorough classification of spatial enclosures made out of plastic: shell assemblies (pure or frames filled with shells); on-site enclosures; folding structures; suspension structures; and pneumatics (with low and high pressure), such as the French Pavilion at Expo 1970, made by Birdair Structures Inc., or the Fuji Pavilion at the same exhibition. (a.n.)

architectural discourse. Finally, one can argue that the most striking similarity between the body and later modern architecture was their sheer temporality. Architecture was no longer eternal, but replaceable, disposable, and ready to die. Plastic does not die, however.

It has a pre-war history especially in Germany — which wanted to be independent from importing raw materials — and in the UK — with its 1941 Building Plastics Research Corporation in Glasgow. Eventually, it emerged as *the* alternative, up-to-date building material in the early fifties*, due to the dwelling crisis and to plastic's easy prefabrication. The first real structure did not come out until 1955, when, at the Paris Exhibition, Ionel Schein (with R.A. Coulon and Y. Magnart) exhibited a plastic house.

The plastic capsules appeared later on, designed by the same team: the motel cabin (1956) and exhibition units for a mobile library (1958). Plastic was so popular and "hip" in the sixties, that it was adopted instantly by pop culture, thus being present at Disneyland, as a crossed plastic home sitting on a pilaster (1957), shaping "the ideal home" designed by the Smithsons (1956), and envisaging future habitations (Monsanto House of the Future by Hamilton and Goody).

Plastics then offered unexpected ways to avoid traditional design strategies and conventional forms. There were details: curved window frames, probably alluding to (space)ships, or no window frames at all. Then it corroded the very nature of any architectural structure to date. As mentioned in the beginning of this chapter, Peter Cook thought that a revolution in architecture happened during the fifties and sixties, as new materials and structural techniques allowed architects to blow the trilitic system

---

* Quarnby gives a history of plastics, of which one can note: 1950 — mass scale Teflon; 1952 — MacDonald produced commercial polyformaldehyde; 1953 — Ziegler produced polyethylene; 1954 — Matta produced polypropylene (idem: 15).

up. By detaching the structure from the architectural skin after 1945, each component had its own eventual destiny. Without columns and beams, the skin became the structure by itself, due to Otto Frei and Buckminster Fuller: plastic structures*, pneumatics — with their erotic, "very exciting-looking shapes" (Cook, 1970: 62) — reinforced cables, as well as geodesic domes.

Finally, architecture could become really "new". And, more importantly, modern architecture found a way to be thrilling without employing strategies of visual heroism. Soft architecture, although inherently big, was regarded as a "gradual erosion of monumentality" (idem: 67). One must remember here that the lack of monumentality was by far the strongest argument against modernism before the war: it was seen as an unreliable aesthetic, since it was not capable of offering the heroic structures the elites of nation/states needed to convey their messages within city textures.

Modernism thus had to accept pollination with other idioms to accede to more important edifices than extravagant houses in the woods for the rich and the snob intellectual/art elite before the war. Rationalism, Art Deco and classical features negotiated together to offer a cocktail called either stripped classicism (as seen at the Paris Exhibition in 1937), or classical modernism (of the New York World Fair in 1939)**. This is why Cook's remark is highly important in a discussion of whether modern architecture was ever able or indeed really willing to produce monumental structures at all.

---

* For more details one can consult my book *The Other Modernism — Utopian Spaces, Decor and Virtual Discourse in the 1930's*.

** Cook quotes the 1962 Pascal Hausemann house, the 1964 housing project by W. Dring, and the 1965 W. Chalk, R. Heron and Gaskit homes.

## Glass and Concrete Playing Sight Against Touch

*"Glass (…) was, quite clearly, the ideal 'skin' (…) the purpose was to produce maximum invisibility for the wall and maximum visibility for the structural skeleton of the building"*

Peter Blake (1977: 72)

Perhaps the most striking development in modern architecture after the war was the steady disappearance of other senses but vision in experiencing the built matter. In fact, seeing became more and more the only possible way to experience architecture. Yet the more the visual took over, the more substanceless the façades became. Glass was used either as a mirror, or as a transparent "skin" whose primordial function was not to protect, but to unveil, even expose the structural skeleton.

How had it come to this? First of all, there was the separation between structure and façades, which was a product of the first modern generation: Gropius' Faguswerk, Le Corbusier's continuous glass windows, and especially Mies van der Rohe's triangular glass Friedrichstrasse tower competition entry which displaced the wall from its structural purpose, which was attributed to pillars retreated behind the glass façade. Then, in the fifties and sixties, even the pillar disappeared, as in Fuller's U.S.A. Pavilion and his "roof" for Manhattan, only to make room for a completely glass/transparent façade, regardless of how intimate the interior might have been — a home, as in Philip Johnson's New Canaan residence, or a sky-scraper, as in Lever House of Mies/Johnson.

As the façade was peeled off the structure, the former became just a way of negotiating the dichotomy between interior and exterior, and the latter was increasingly regarded as the essential part of the architectural organism; it was then only logical that the former should "disappear" in order to display/emphasize the latter. While brutalism left the building skinless, arguing that there was no need to camouflage the structure at all — quite the opposite — other idioms found more metaphysical ways to deal with the sensual experiences of architecture as a physical body.

In Western Europe and the U.S., roughness and opacity (flattering the tactile and being key qualities of an aesthetic based upon concrete) were increasingly and deliberately suppressed from the discourse, by focusing on smoothness and transparency (which in turn emphasized sight, and were centered around glass and metal). More and more, the choice of materials, surfaces and colors in modern architecture was intended to complement a unique sense, and thus to alienate the being from its built environment.

It was not a straightforward process, nor was it ubiquitously present in all national/regional architectures after the war. One can see it in France, from the late Le Corbusier (with his raw concrete masses which started a trend in the fifties and sixties in Western Europe and the U.S., only to flourish anew in the East in the late sixties and the seventies as "lyrical functionalism") to Jean Nouvel's "disappearing" glass tower in Défense and the recent Fondation Cartier, where there is no more resistance opposed to visually penetrating the architecture in its entirety.

One can obviously find it in the U.S., yet in a rather contorted manner; since Rudolph's mid-sixties, muscle-flexing at Yale was rather a reaction *against* the glass curtain of "Orthodox" (Venturi), corporate modernism, and post-modern opaque consistence brought back matter onto building façades.

However, one cannot find the same process in the East, where Khrushchev's *laudatio* for cement and concrete was absolute. One can make edifices out of concrete: rough, powerful, heavy, thus monumental. Concrete was "revolutionary", as it was an outcome of the heavy industry, and it was grey, which is, as pointed out by Schusev, the worker's color*.

---

* He used black, red, and grey stone for Lenin's tomb: mourning, communism, and workers.

Glass is cool, both transparent and reflective, fragile and easy, thus "feminine". It is present, corporeal as well as absent and virtual. Thus concrete is "masculine": rough, "as found" (Glendenning & Muthesius, 1994: 92), massive, immobile, the very embodiment of (heavy) industry, progress, and materiality.

There was discreet yet fundamental change in the nature of finishing. It became a quality of the surface itself, indeed of the structural system, rather than something applied eventually. Finishing could be a quality, something to enhance the surface's attributes, yet it could also stand for "accidental marks of shuttering" (ibidem), "out-of-form"ness (Stillman & Eastwick-Field), in order to obtain a "directness of expression" (ibidem). Obviously, a "revolutionary" discourse had to look for certain metaphors and be attentive to the metaphysics of matter.

Thus, following Khrushchev's emphasis on concrete, one can read the glass/concrete marriage as a key dichotomy in understanding Communist architecture. Sight was a key sense in experiencing Western architecture. But behind the Iron Curtain, due to a ubiquitous presence of concrete, the tactile was still present and relevant. Much like plastics, yet more impressive and heroic, concrete could be manipulated and could subvert the trilitic system as well. The so called "visual concrete" (Heinle & Bücher, 1971) stands not only for the immediate finishing of the structure, but also for expressive, unconventional forms like shell structures with complicated geometry, as well as for a whole range of "hard landscape[s] in concrete" (ibidem). Up to the 1970's in both West and East, concrete made it to playgrounds, interiors, schools, fountains and urban furniture.

One can hardly find towers with glass "curtain walls" in the East. First of all, because high-rises, as major features of Stalinist architecture from the Palace of the Soviets to the post-war seven towers in Moscow and Warsaw, were among the most important targets of Khrushchev's speech. Secondly, because one could not imagine unframed glass, i.e. uncontrolled building elements.

Thirdly, because architecture (i.e. the structure), although artificial, had to be present, visible, material, whereas glass offered but elusiveness, was slippery and metaphysical, could entail uncontrollable reflections under various light conditions: "a giant Hall of Mirrors, or Skyline of Mirrors (…) [which] implies, of course, total abdication" (Blake, 1977: 73). The concrete structure had to be emphasized, not camouflaged. It was exhibited, not allowed to be veiled by glass walls.

Why then reflect the reality, and not be real? The reflected city is not the real city any more, but an image, an interpretation of it, it's the other city from beyond the mirror. Mies van der Rohe could assert back in 1919 that "the important thing in a glass tower is *the play of reflections"* (quoted by Blake; ibidem; italics mine, A.I.); and perhaps in the West something needed now more than ever, a second cornea, a screen prosthesis to act as protective/interpretative intermediary between reality and being. Perhaps one could build with glass in the most ethereal ways, as in the glass skyscrapers in the desert outside Teheran (Iran), where only the chaos was reflected and multiplied, or as is SOM's Bank in Rhiad (Saudi Arabia), with its glass walls (facing the inner, empty, triangular court) looking into themselves.

Yet this was not the case in the East, where glass was heavily guarded and/or framed by opaque panels of concrete, occasionally stone, withdrawn behind heavy *brise-soleils* or colonnades. Enframing the glass panels was the norm in Romanian architecture during this period, recalling works like the Ministry of Education in Rio de Janeiro by Le Corbusier and Oscar Niemeyer, or, closer to home, Duiliu Marcu's CAM building on Victoria Avenue in Bucharest.

The outcomes were T. Ricci's "glass-within-stone/concrete-grids" Radio House and especially the Romanian Television building. The latter's façade is quite relevant in that context, as its boxes resemble TV sets, yet the emphasis is not on the glass screens, but on the green structure which holds the glass down toward the depth of the façade surface. Glass flanked between two opaque panels was also popular in the classicizing edifices before the war; D. Marcu's War School and especially Victoria Palace in Bucharest were sources for post-Stalinist edifices such as the Palace Hall in Bucharest, as well as for many city halls and "unions' culture houses" in the sixties and seventies.


## Original as Originary: Towards Archaic Modernism?

*"Andre Lurhat invokes the pile dwelling of the late Stone Age in justification of the pilotis so favored by architects in the thirties to liberate the congested city terrain."*

Alan Colquhoun (1986: 16-17)

*"Originality is the return to the origin"*

Antonio Gaudi

Alan Colquhoun raised the question of whether post-war modernism retrieved — deliberately or unconsciously — certain archaic structure, pattern and/or archetypes (i.e. "exemplary models") of architecture. After Collin Rowe, we know that modernists were not entirely estranged from compositional patterns used by architects beforehand. His comparison of Palladio and Le Corbusier was relevant in that respect. Steiner's Goetheanums, as well as Aalto's sacred spaces could indeed question in entirety the alleged gap between modernity and tradition. Yet an even deeper *raison d'être* of modern discourse has to be sought in connection with its *arche*-tecture (by analogy to Derrida's *arche*-writing). Such ontology might be proudly claimed, accepted as obvious, or rejected. Yet, regardless of the author's opinion, origins have to be accounted for when one looks into the nature and ingredients of their architecture.

A parallel with the official architecture of the 1930's might be illuminating in this respect. In *Celălalt Modernism (The Other*

*Modernism*, 1995: 125-37) I looked into the loudly celebrated, self-styled origins of "Nazi" and "Fascist" architectures. At stake there was the question of identity, differently tailored according to the respective regime's ideology. Identity in Nazi and Fascist architectural discourse was defined by nationalism *as* (aesthetic) ideology, whereas in socialist realism it was defined by ideology *and* (since the war) nationalism. Returning to (alleged) origins was then, once again after the French Revolution, the source for restoring the "revolutionary purity" of architecture. Racial origins would determine the architectural starting point: for Rosenberg, an architect who studied at Riga and Moscow, as well as for Speer later on, Dorians (i.e. the Aryan ancestors of German people) who had their own (Dorian) style. It follows that, when one wants to acknowledge and celebrate the origins of one's people, one can do it within the built environment by using that particular "originary" architecture seen by one's ancestors "as an expression of their racial awareness".

In *Revolution in der bildenden Kunst*, Rosenberg thus describes how the trilitic structure is genuinely Doric, thus aryan, thus "good", commendable, whereas the arch pertaining to a Southern, non-Aryan and (worse!) matriarchal population (Etruscans), was therefore "feminized", thus "weak", thus "bad"*. Conversely, for *stille littorio* (and, remotely, but with precisely similar racial arguments, for the Romanian Carol II style of the 1930's) by immediately or obliquely celebrating the Roman imperial tradition, it could revive and evince the values imbedded in the ancient built forms.

At least certain aspects of modern architecture before and especially after the war could send us to an alternative source. One recognizes the direct references to Mediterranean vernacular as a favorite source for cubist architecture: flat roofs/terraces, whiteness,

---

* "The trilitic system, eventually carried south by German tribes towards, did not flourish there with the same strength, because it met the resistance of a non-Aryan structure", the arch of a matriarchal society. (a.n.)

lack of decoration and rectangular shapes. One can also recall the opposition between the circular tent and *tholos* as the built expression of appropriating space by migrant populations of hunters, as opposed to the Cartesian *megaron*, made out of rectangular bricks of crude or burned clay, as in the homes of sedentary agricultural communities. Josef Strzygowski long ago stated in *Der Norden in der bildenden Kunst Westeuropas* just such a Semperian positivist idea that wood was originally the building material of his German/Indo-European ancestors, who were separated from the eastern Mediterranean and China "by a belt of brick and of tent builders respectively" (quoted by Rykwelt, 1993: 26).

Whereas it seems obvious that French and Italian modernism have favored the latter way of appropriating the built forms, one can hypothesize that — predominantly after the war — the architecture of troglodytes was, much like the projective "cosmic architecture", a (subconscious?) reference point for Anglo-Saxon, Scandinavian and German architects. After all, Semper believed, archaic forms are not affected by civilization: "even today Europe's overcivilized sons, when they wander in the primeval forests of America, build themselves log cabins" (vol. 2: 298, note 2). If Le Corbusier's primitive had rationally "designed the site" (a concept advanced by Vittorio Grregotti in his 1966 *Il territorio dell'architettura* and celebrated by Kenneth Frampton in Mario Botta's practice) of his walled home, the pedestrian walkways raised above street level at the second floor designed by the brutalist (and eventually built at Barbican and in downtown Cincinnati, for example), the metabolist pillars, Friedman's megastructure above existing cities as well as Archigram's Walking City and the 1960's and 1970's houses on pilotis could be seen as an effort to switch the "origins" of architecture toward "troglodytes" (Colquhoun, 1986: 121). This argument might eventually unfold as a means of investigating the alternative approaches to built forms/environment: the walled tradition returned in Romanesque, the Renaissance would eventually be found in its modern epiphanies in the rough concrete architecture of the late Le Corbusier and Paul Rudolph, in the Italian new-rationalism, in post-modernism as well as — dematerialized — in the glass/curtain walls of skyscrapers or in the transparent architectures of Philip Johnson and Jean Nouvel. The "structural", trilitic tradition of (Northern) Indo-Europeans and "troglodytes" could be found in Gothic (both vernacular and sacred), in constructivist experiments, and in the above-mentioned genealogy of megastructures leading towards the hi-tech. It is an uprooted architecture, without *Raum*, migratory, thus placeless and ephemeral.

Perhaps the most important event in the modern discourse after the war was the shift (in the fifties and sixties) from one origin to another. This shift did not happen in East European architecture.

## *Coda*

The scope of this text is not only to verify whether East European architecture after Stalin's death, while lacking a definitely critical, self-reflective edge, nevertheless echoed and employed major concepts of Western architectural discourses. It is, rather, a comparative study with rather optimistic conclusions.

While obviously trailing — at least temporarily — the Western discourse, it seems quite stunning that Communist architecture, regardless or, rather, in spite of ideological pressure, overwhelming state control, poor craftsmanship as well as obsessive industrialization of building techniques, materials and finishing, was in fact able to go roughly along with the same trends as its less controlled, more democratic counterpart outside the Iron Curtain.

This brings us to the question: how really important are ideologies and power manipulations when one observes the aesthetic discourse? Obviously, they could not turn the clock backward completely, as the Stalinist elite believed, nor could they completely control practice or stop inner processes from emerging

98

within the discourse. For most of the concepts enumerated before, one finds merely reflections, distorted copies or look-alikes. It was not, given the absent critical edge, a complete assimilation. Yet, it existed.

There were several directions in which East European architecture led, with little if any equivalent in the West. When Bolshevik ideology met modernism after Khrushchev's speech, it was love at first sight (or second sight for that matter, after the avant-garde). Certain aspects of modernity found, in the East, their most spectacular fulfilment: mass prefabrication of social housing, which was able to entirely reshape the existing urban structures; inventing new environments, as well as extending the megastructure concept to its "malignant variant" — the so-called "systematization of the national territory".

Perhaps the bottom line of this chapter would have to be the following sentence: Modernity is a totalitarian concept in the end, and the only places where its basic, most important goal, that of entirely reshaping reality according to its political/aesthetic plan, was abundantly achieved were the U.S.S.R. and (some) of its satellite countries between 1954 and 1989.

# III

# THE QUEST FOR IDENTITY
# IN ROMANIAN ARCHITECTURE

## III. 1. The Question

I intend to shape an overall view of Romanian architecture before and after WW II by using the criterion of the *particular (*as proposed by Georg Lukacs in aesthetic theory), in which the *general* would be illustrated by the manifestation of European styles; namely, in this case, modernism, but also the Neo-Romanian style as — roughly — an autochthonous version of Art Nouveau.

Romanian architecture eloquently illustrates the need to particularize as it constantly attempts to find its own identity, even when it adopts functionalism, a current which, by its very program, is little inclined to consent to give up its universalist temptations. In this context, the effort of Romanian architects has been almost heroic. To graft a national branch onto the trunk of a genetically universalist current, here is, grosso modo, how the creation of our modern architects can be characterized. Even those architects who obeyed the rigors of functionalism worked to adapt these not only to the architectural context, but also — in the larger sense — to the mentality of the society in which they were building. Thus the particular appears if not always by design, then at least as an intention, more or less consciously formulated.

The counter-argument to the statement above, especially where architecture after WW II is concerned, could be provided by the collective housing districts which do not and could not illustrate any national identity. However, the great names amongst our architects didn't build many such collective dwellings, but, rather, individual houses for the powerful. Nonetheless, when such architects did build them, they created *one-of-a-kind* collective dwellings instead of mass-produced ones (D. Marcu, H. Creangă, A. Culina, P. Smărăndescu, Gh. Nădrag, etc.). Romanian architecture seems destined not to experience a rupture. Not one of the styles having haunted our architecture in the last century has ever provoked a final divorce from a preceding style, to such an extent that the break should become obvious. The only moment when a stylistic fracture can be detected is in the second half of the nineteenth century, when the French-born eclecticism of academic descent massively entered the autochthonous picture, but the explanation of this can be found in politics rather than in aesthetics: the prevalence of the French model in architecture is only a reflex of the French patronage embracing vaster domains. Thus, the apparition of the Neo-Romanian style, usually classified as an autochthonic version of Art Nouveau or national romanticism, takes on a different, much more poignant hue when we view it within the entire movement of re-awakening of a national consciousness, a process intensified after state independence was won.

The Neo-Romanian style was not, therefore, a new stylistical connection (in Romania, the local version of the European National romanticism did not yield remarkable productions) but rather the impulse which Paris-schooled Romanian architects felt to find their own identity within their national architecture. The divergence from these international styles avant la lettre takes on a new meaning when it is parallelled with the current situation, when, once again, the national, local, contextual identity is favored over modernist architecture and against the zero entropy toward which it tended. But this attack against the lack of identity, circumscribed by the current of national affirmation, didn't interrupt the development of eclecticism and of the neoclassical style which had become the *styles of power*, of the vast administrative and representative buildings of the time. The establishment of the *type* and its "consecration" through this sort of building caused a widespread dissemination of these models in the vernacular architecture of the city outskirts and even of the village bourgeoisie.

In addition to this explanation, the persistence of the academic style has yet another: the paradoxical phenomenon of its alliance with a former "enemy", the Neo-Romanian style. At the very moment when the latter's vigor had almost collapsed into a heap of "ropes", cable mouldings, Brâncoveanu-style capitals, into the voluptuousness of a decoration which had forgotten the motivation of its very existence, the alliance with the stubbornness of eclecticism occured of its own accord but — surprisingly — still in the realm of kitsch, hence still in that of the consumer architecture of middle class urban dwellings.

The over-decorated juxtaposition of two defunct styles would be encountered again decades later when a marriage would be attempted between the ideas of the Neo-Romanian style and functionalism, in the name of national character (see Joja's attempts, but also Nicolae Porumbescu's, multiplied by an entire generation of their successors). This marriage, between the Neo-Romanian style (at least between the ideas that presided over its birth) and modernism was, however, in the beginning, tempting to those architects who had not been entirely won over by the functionalist virtues. The large apartment buildings most eloquently exemplified this type of stylistic cross (modern functionality/Neo-Romanian decoration, austere enough, however, to suit the modern morphology) as in the case of the Triumf Hotel on Kiseleff Highway (Petre Antonescu) or of the apartment buildings on Hristo Botev St. designed by Arghir Culina and Paul Smărăndescu — two architects who later on defected to the modernist camp.

This sort of "cross-pollination", timid at first, would later on become a preoccupation we could translate as a special interest to *particularize* Romanian modernism vis à vis the European functionalist modernism. There are three architects whose achievements are worth pointing out as successes in particularizing autochthonous modernism: Duiliu Marcu — in the area of representative architecture; Octav Doicescu — in programs of loisir and housing; and Henriette Delavrancea Gibory — exclusively in the domain of individual dwelling.

Also remarkable is the case of the cross between classicism and modern morphology. It may seem paradoxical, but here occurred the most interesting experience in representative architecture, i.e. *the architecture of power* as I call it. A certain decency of proportions prevented Romanian architects from begetting monstrosities — of decoration and of size — up until the House of the People. In fact, the encounter between these two styles — one long outdated, the other avant-garde — which at first sight may seem paradoxical, took place primarily in the realm of morphological *austerity*, of volumetric simplicity, and of monumentality. The examples of this type of cohabitation stand out positively at a time when European monumental architecture was moving from the Dorian giganticism of German architecture to the Italian rationalistic imperialism and to the pompous symbolism of Soviet architecture. In Romania, the architecture of power went from the purist classicism of the Royal Palace (1930-1937, N. Nenciulescu of the-column-in-the-axis fame) to the monumental Neo-Romanian style of the city halls in Bucharest (Petre Antonescu), Galați, Craiova, of the Opera House in Timișoara (D. Marcu), and to the modernism upon which classical principles of composition had been grafted (D. Marcu, P. Antonescu at the Bucharest Law School, G.M. Cantacuzino, Richard Bordenache with his "Palazzo Calcane", Octav Doicescu at the apartment building on Știrbey-Vodă Avenue, Florea Stănciulescu at the Institute of Agronomy etc.). This latest manner of designing the architecture of power was most convincing in terms of particularizing Romanian modernism and of bestowing national features upon the morphological images of the same modernism.

Yet some classic styles survived in unadulterated form, although they had become obviously outdated, well into the first few decades of the XXth century. This *old fashioned architecture* could also have another explanation beside the fact of its overt validity, a result of the evocative function of its language, which carried the overly-inflated prestige of classicism into the domain of the architecture of power (since it resorted to classical forms: colonnades, classical orders, frontons, friezes etc.). This other explanation could be the stylistic confusion of the first decades of the XXth century, when the National School was showing signs of fatigue precisely as it attempted to transcend its dimensional condition in order to have access to the architectural commands of power, while modernism still seemed too avant-garde and was practised only in the domain of individual houses. Thus classicism could still appear as the preferable alternative, since it produced verified images of the exact size which best fitted the desired representative character of the respective program. The case of the Royal Palace has already been mentioned. Works by G.M. Cantacuzino could be added, i.e. the Crisoveloni Bank and the building which screens the Kretzulescu Church in the Royal Palace Square.

Having its roots in the revolutionary movement of 1848, the wind of national emancipation still had to wait for a few decades before it could properly stress those of-a-kind elements which could particularize Romanian culture. Folklore, folk art generally, and the re-awakened interest in our national history (let us recall Kogălniceanu, who stated emphatically that for him the events of our national history, say the Battle of Călugăreni[*], were more important than any events in world history, no matter how famous) were the catalysts of this new spirit.

At first, the Neo-Romanian style couldn't help but be superseded by the imitation of historical styles (imported as a rule

---

[*] In 1595, where the Wallachian prince Michael the Brave defeated the Ottoman troops led by Sinan Pasha (t.n.)

via France) as a demand of political circumstance, as an image of power — in line with a model credited with the prestige of the ruling class — and as a credible proof of the modernization / europeanization of Romania. In fact, this wasn't so much a case of giving way as it was a necessary step which strengthened the national spirit by furnishing yet another argument: the resistence against alienation through forms of art. Proof of this is given by the merest glance in the direction of the place where the foremost names of the Neo-Romanian style went to school: Paris.

To be sure, the Neo-Romanian style came about as a reaction of satiety on the part of architects for whom eclecticism remained a lesson learned impeccably (interiors designed by Mincu prove it) but never *organically assimilated*. The departure from the model occurs through 1) a natural lack of adherence to it; 2) the aggressiveness with which this model spread its copies throughout its area of influence (we've said before that eclecticism was an international style avant la lettre; 3) the impossibility to ply this model onto the images inherited from their native country; 4) the national pride, in full bloom after the political success of 1877.

Without overestimating the influence of extra-artistic factors in the formation of this new style (although such factors were in fact decisive, in view of the strictly national aspect of the Neo-Romanian style), to explain it only within the bounds of art forms (as an artistic reaction to eclecticism, as a local version of sezzesion, or as a form of resistence against the capture of the construction market by a single morphology) would be too restrictive and quite impoverishing. On the contrary, the aberrations of the Neo-Romanian style begin to appear at the very moment when the current loses its extra-artistic motivations; thus, let us remark that the two most important stages in the affirmation of the style closely follow two crucial political events: Mincu appears after the 1877 War of Independence, and the forceful wave (in fact the last manifestation of substance) of such architects as Statie Ciortan, Iotzu, Smărăndescu, Arghir Culina, T.T. Socolescu, comes after the Unification of 1918. The intermediary stages are marked by a departure from the original conceptions of the movement and into an ever more pompous and more luxuriant decorativism, two moments of diminished entropy between two moments of maximum emergence and stylistical coherence. The asymptotical approach of the Neo-Romanian style to its own motivations thus has justifications mostly from without the territory of art.

In general, a style, even if it be inscribed within a vaster social tendency, does eventually achieve a sufficient degree of internal coherence (aesthetic principles, a morphology of its own, a particular attitude toward space — in the case of architecture) to cease to explicitly depend upon the tendencies which first circumscribed it. Yet the Neo-Romanian style, as mentioned, did exactly the opposite. Its "breath" was external. The explanation — or at any rate one of them — lies in the containment of the style within a single national area. The Neo-Romanian style did not really become a current (so that, while having its beginning in one art, it would spread to other countries and all arts) because it did not contain that germ of *generality* (I'd even say *impersonality*) which would have been necessary for its affirmation. Thus: it confined itself programmatically to the specific forms of artistic expression within a limited space, the Romanian one; it made use of artistic principles borrowed from vernacular architecture and folk art, principles which were radically different from those governing the urban art of the cultured classes; and, even within the bounds of this source of inspiration, it could only call upon the morphology and typology of *two programs*, namely the peasant dwelling of small dimensions and the Orthodox monastery. This was an enormous hindrance to its affirmation.

All styles which resorted to classical models either by adopting them (Renaissance, baroque, neoclassicism) or by critically evaluating and/or freely interpreting them (eclecticism, post-modernism) could easily take over specific solutions to a broad range of programs, and in particular to the programs of power examined here. Let us remark that the "victory" of a style, the establishment of a type inside this style are aspects related before everything to the solution of the program of power. The establishment of the *type* takes place in and through the architecture of power. It is an explicit form of recognition of the style's potency; reciprocally, this recognition of the style now invested with he corresponding prestige, causes the massive spreading of the given style into other architectural programs. In the case of the Neo-Romanian style, its starting point was a relatively small program, unable to develop through mere addition and amplification in size. When, in its wish to conquer, it tended toward the architecture or power, the Neo-Romanian style betrayed its own sources and severed the but frail ties which had kept it attached to those sources, through which it had received its oxygen, from which it derived credibility.

Now, as a limpid glance may be cast over an experience fully consummated in time, a few more observations could be added to those above:

a) the transfer of classical forms took place over an extremely long period, which allowed the shaping of adequate modes to utilize the vocabulary in question within new programs;

b) the transfer took place between vocabularies of the monumental and according to the principle of absolute measure (a detailed discussion of this problem appears in the chapter about C. Joja), hence between forms belonging to the architecture of power;

c) the transfer of monumental forms to modest programs still yielded kitsch productions as had the opposite transfer, in the case of the Neo-Romanian style;

d) the fact that certain details of decoration, ornamentation etc. came off their architectural context and slid over into other forms of art does not in essence prove anything, being a process often encountered in the art of all times. The problem is not why a certain decoration — the ogive, say — migrates from one art form to another, but when and how a decorative system takes this step.

The confinement of the representatives of the Neo-Romanian style strictly within the domain of morphological problems (since they brought no substantial modification to planimetries) is today more or less criticized. What ought to be remarked, however, is the absence of urbanistic questions from amongst their preoccupations — yet another weakness of the current in discussion. A handful of timid attempts at cheap housing districts (see also the cheap dwellings on Clucerului St. and on Architect Mincu St., designed by I. D Traianescu) in Dorobanți and Filantropiei, the diking and widening of what are now Bălcescu Blvd. and Grivița Ave. are not sufficient to offer us an image of these architects' intentions. In any case, the solutions would have been missing. The Neo-Romanian was a style of the individual object in architecture. It had neither the intention — nor would it have had the needed longue haleine — to systematize cities on a large scale.

In a possible repertory of successes in Neo-Romanian architecture, here are some that could be its fortes:

1) staying within the size limits of the model (i.e. the peasant dwelling, that of the small-town merchant, the dwelling of the small boyar, the manor) — Mincu / The Pub on Kiseleff Highway in Bucharest; Cristofi Cerchez / Villa Minovici; Traianescu / cheap houses on Clucerului St.; Socolescu / Villa Bebe in Cumpătu, (Sinaia); Duiliu Marcu / Villas of the Architect Delavrancea Gibory;

2) avoiding excess and redundancy in decoration — The Museum of the Romanian Peasant, formerly Museum of the Romanian Communist Party, by N. Ghica-Budești; P. Antonescu / apartment building on Kiseleff Hwy., The Marmorosch-Blank Bank; G. Simotta / The Patriarchal Palace; H. Delavrancea Gibory / individual houses;

3) using simple forms, close to those of modern morphology, in which the traditional element is present only under the

"disguise" of ratios, references and allusions — Octav Doicescu / Restaurant in the Botanical Gardens, houses in the old U.C.B. district; Duiliu Marcu / Villa Modrogan;

4) judiciously using the intermediary space characteristic of traditional architecture as a transition space and not (only) as a decorative element — Mincu / Villa Lahovary, The Pub on Kiseleff Hwy., The Girls' Central School; Henriette Delavrancea Gibory / dwellings; Octav Doicescu / restaurants, The Herăstrău Nautical Club etc.

As we can see, most of the names on this list of exceptional achievements belong to the two points of emergence mentioned above: the post-1877 moment (Mincu, Antonescu, Ghica Budești, Cerchez) and the post-WW I moment. Two superlative moments, joined in through decency, simplicity, modesty, and the science of proportions.

The importance of the Neo-Romanian style should not be evaluated only from a sentimental viewpoint. Raising the problem of identity in an architecture permanently submitted to exterior influences and pressures, in fact an immense receptacle capturing echoes from all directions, was the strong point of the Neo-Romanian style, even if we were to disregard its achievements — many of interest, some productive, a few masterpieces. From the Neo-Romanian moment on, the problem of the particularization of Romanian architecture will be a major touchstone theme in all attempts of our great architects: identifying images of the return.

### Tentative Conclusions

As we regard the stylistic panorama of a hundred years of national architecture (in 1886, the Lahovary House was its first product), we will remark the following phenomena:

a) The reflexes of international styles (and in the case of modernism, of the diverse tendencies within in) were promoted in their "pure" form in Romanian architecture by one or at most two representatives, while the remainder merely imitated the work of these personalities or practised variations on themes taken from it. The Neo-Romanian style counted among its front-line promoters Mincu, followed by Antonescu, the two Cerchez, Ghica-Budești; the second phase, flourishing after 1918, when access to the programs of power influenced the shift of the accent from the vernacular to the Brâncoveanu style and to the monasteries and churches of that period of national rebirth, had as protagonists I. D. Traianescu and C. Iotzu, and as challengers, G. Cristinel, A. Culina, T. T. Socolescu, Statie Ciortan, Duiliu Marcu etc.

b) The architects belonging to the second echellon of representativeness were those who as a rule "impurified" the style or tendency, by overdecorating and by amplifying scales and sizes; theirs was an exercise in the programs of power more successful, however, than that of the top architects. Mincu's monumental works, such as the Administrative Palace in Galați, the Bank in Craiova, the project for the Capital's Communal Palace prove his failure in monumental programs: the author did not achieve the same expressiveness, within the same style, as Ghica-Budești's works of equivalent scale or as those of Gr. Cerchez.

c) One and the same architect could go back and forth between different modes of stylistic expression. (A versatility without any pejorative connotations for me.) Here arises the problem of the rapport between style and an artist's own idiom. The important architects of this last hundred years in Romania have gone through two or three styles during their careers, and even through the hybrid styles — attempts at finding satisfactory compromises — already described in Chapter I. Thus, P. Antonescu went from academism to the monumental Neo-Romanian style, to stripped classicism; Mincu, the champion of the Neo-Romanian style, also employed the idiom of eclecticism in the interiors of the Vernescu House and the Monteoru House; G. M. Cantacuzino was in turn an academist, a modernist, and a theoretician of the particularization of Romanian modernism (showing a few peculiar nuances for which he could be considered a precursor of the post-modernists or of the regionalists). Duiliu Marcu was an example of sweeping through the entire range of stylistic options — academism, Neo-Romanian style, modernized Neo-Romanian style, modernism with principles of classical composition. N. Porumbescu went from Stalinism to "brutalist" modernism and to a modernism with tendencies toward national characterization, to the aberrations of a "national-communist" court style. Octav Doicescu illustrated neoclassicism, modernism of the national nuance, Stalinism, lyric functionalism. Finally, Cezar Lăzărescu moved from Stalinism to lyric functionalism and/or with some tendencies to autochthonize its vocabulary.

d) Another interesting phenomenon could be remarked, this time independently of the top architects and linked instead to the stylistic evolution itself. After a period of eclipse, each modernist orientation reappears, of course updated — for example, the constant theme of the national character. This theme was constantly present in the cultural preoccupations of the turn of century and of the inter-bellum period, but also had moments of powerful flux, sometimes created artificially, as was its latest comeback meant to justify a Communist dictatorship undergoing an identity crisis.

The functionalism of the Bauhaus made a powerful comeback immediately after the end of the Stalinist era (in the sixties): the stern refusal of adornment, with the ostentatious simplicity of decoration being (aside from a result of economic strictures) a form of refusal of a past which had been oppressed in an absolute fashion, the break with it marked not abruptly but conspicuously (for example, in the restaurant designed by C. Lăzărescu in Eforie Nord, in the Bucharest apartments built in Floreasca, in the Palace Hall Plaza, in Chibrit Square, in Băneasa etc.).

The architecture of power also observes, as can be seen, the same principle of the stylistic boomerang. Thus, architecture morphologically modern but classical in composition — as it had been practised by D. Marcu, P. Antonescu, Fl. Stănculescu before WW II — made a comeback in the same period of the sixties immediately following the Stalinist era, when these principles were adapted to suit a monumental architecture which would soon drift slowly but decidedly away from the thesis of the nationalist form with socialist content. Thus, creations such as the Radio Building (T. Ricci, M. Ricci, Leon Garcia), the Rail Station of Constanța (Teonic Săvulescu) but also the one in Brașov, some industrial buildings (such as the milk factory in Constanța designed by Ileana Iotzu) observe in all respects the "consecrated" monumental image of the pre-war model. The lyric functionalism of Le Corbusier as illustrated by La Tourette, Ronchamp and Chandigarh seems to have best suited our architects during those periods when the political pressure relented a bit (too few, alas, in this century). Nevertheless the years after the Culture House in Suceava was built (N. Porumbescu) mark the apogee of this orientation in Romanian architecture, as it unfolds in a multitude of tendencies — from volumetries somewhat freer of functional strictures to a decoration using the adapted vocabulary of traditional ornamentation.

A quick glance back at what has been stated previously unveils yet another truth about Romanian architecture: the initiators of a current (or in the case of modernism of a tendency) are paradoxically those who also represent excellence within that current. Mincu, the first Neo-Romanianist, was also its most representative exponent; H. Creangă — of functionalism; D. Marcu — of monumental architecture. An inexplicable fatigue overcomes the stylistic tendency at the very moment when it has sufficiently penetrated the space of our architecture so that a representative number of architects adopt it. An explanation would be the willingness, on the part of those architects who but carry on the given style, to distort its elements in order to make them fit architectural programs often inapt to illustrate the style. (The most significant case in point is the Neo-Romanian style).

On the other hand, we may remark a functional if not causal relationship between the stylistic derailment which characterizes Romanian architects (their ability to illustrate, decently, several styles) and the effacement of idioms of their own. We must needs make a related observation: even in the case of those personalities who illustrated several orientations, masterpieces did not appear in their creation until they securely adhered to a given orientation, which best suited their creative identity (and this even if these same architects produces works of different styles later on). The delicate rapport between idiolect and style is thus one of the keys to deciphering this paradox. Only by in-depth experimentation with a style may Romanian architecture, apparently, find its way to the masterpiece. Such is the case, for example, of Horia Creangă, the functionalist who was always equal to himself in calibrating his formal vocabulary so that the self-quotation was excluded from his work; or of Marcu, who achieved excellence in the domain of the architecture of power, which he helped develop through a few exceptional creations.

## III. 2. Official Architecture: Duiliu Marcu

The life-work of one of the best known Romanian architects of our century is a felicitous example of what can happen when a talented architect's idiolect successively embraces a series of different styles throughout a career which began in the last century and came to an end when elsewhere modernism was already showing signs of fatigue (1966). It would be more accurate to speak of a *dialogue* with his epoch, because, equal to himself in the classical rigor he had absorbed at the Ecole Nationale de Beaux Arts in Paris (at a time when neoclassicism and eclecticism were "international styles" avant la lettre), even when he would cross over into the camp of a vague modernism (though never in the functionalist camp), Duiliu Marcu remained nostalgic for monumentalism.

This perhaps is one of the reasons why his representative works are edifices of Power, at a time when Power was indeed spelled with a capital letter (in the third and fourth decades). It is therefore tempting to assert that Marcu's architecture represents the *Model* for the architecture of power in our country. Since the most interesting part of his work belongs to the sphere of modernism, we shall confine our discussion to it. The first phases of Marcu's activity, namely the neoclassic period (e.g. the house on Ana Ipătescu/L. Catargiu Blvd., the completion of the University built by A. Orăscu) or the period during which he flirted with the Neo-Romanian style (The National Theater in Timișoara, The Polytechnic School and its dormitories in the same city of Timișoara, the first version of the Villa Modrogan) show no special qualities beyond decent design and execution and do not count as remarkable creations within the styles they illustrated.

The "passage" through several styles was, however, to be of use to the architect when, in agreement with the spirit of his time, he adopted the modern expression; and this intuition of the present, which he saw fit to serve, proves once more the artistic intelligence of Duiliu Marcu and not the "chameleonism" with which his over-hasty critics labeled him.

Even when it changes its means of expression, Marcu's architecture preserves its classical vertebrae, the spirit of order, the formal purity and even some constants in the morphologic vocabulary. The "passage across styles" meant for Marcu an accumulation, afterwards synthetized into a modern architecture with obvious particularizing accents, in works of architecture of tradition. The departure from the paradigm is thus quite distinct.

The modern vocabulary marvelously suited the architect because it came in tangence with some of his own preoccupations. "His enduring preoccupation to always remain in contact with a classical equilibrium, with clarity and with a distinctive note, issued from his probably not always successful search for the correct proportions, from his habit of making himself check everything down to the last detail, without allowing anything to be improvised at the last moment, could be considered a constant" (Marcu on himself in his 1945 book of current works). Modernism offered Marcu clarity and rigor. The classical equilibrium brought him from his academic schooling, along with the taste for detail (an interesting parallel could be drawn between his and the purist oeuvre of Mies Van Der Rohe, another passionate pursuer of perfection en detail), the refusal of decoration, *the appetite for ample and simple forms*.

The sincerity of Duiliu Marcu's buildings is not akin to the sincerity of the functionalists, which meant the direct expression of the functions, structure and materials in the enveloping form. Marcu's form is not an immediate consequence since it serves the criterion of monumentality. On the other hand, the monumental — which, despite C-tin Joja's appreciation that peasant architecture though of reduced scale creates the impression of monumentality, cannot be achieved without dimensional ampleness — is rendered by more refined means than the mere exaggeration of size. The rigorous equilibrium of all the components of a building designed by Marcu (the internal scale is of an almost Greek coherence in his works), as well as of the whole to the human scale, makes all of his buildings plausible organisms. The organic quality of Marcu's monumental architecture manifests his assimilation of the autochthonous spirit. This architecture could have served as paragon of a tasteful autochthonous version of the architecture of power.

Here are some of the devices Marcu used to create monumentality.

a) *The colonnade*: classical reminiscence, seen in the version of the portico (The Utilities Building on Victoriei Ave., The Palace in the Victoriei Plaza, where it receives the aspect of an intermediary space provided with an arcade, one of the few successes in the interpretation of the traditional peasant-house porch in its proper spirit) or in that of the colonnade made up of engaged pilasters (The Palace of the Ministry of Transport) which runs the length of the entire façade, conferring it an ample, majestic rhythm which can be perceived from a great distance. The serialization of the vertical elements of structure is the major component of monumental expressiveness in Marcu's buildings. By marking the vertical dimension in his predominantly horizontal buildings, Marcu also creates the compositional equilibrium of his façades.

b) *The frontality*; the main façades of the administrative buildings designed by Marcu are always perceived frontally, are in fact *screens* sternly and suddenly raised in front of the view and thus arresting, dominating it.

c) *The symmetry*; the appeal to planimetric compositions disavowed by functionalism, but in constant use throughout the history of the architecture of power was yet another device from Marcu's classical arsenal. The Military Academy, The Palace of the Ministry of Transport, and The Victoriei Palace all employ the principle of symmetry, meant to signify equilibrium and stability, in a symbolic sense the firmity of power/symmetry as an organizing factor of life. Let us remark that at the Victoriei Palace the ample horizontal development of the colonnade was intended to dilute the composition of the façade so as to prevent the creation of a new axis of symmetry running east-west, which would have perturbed the main north-south axis which was to be the backbone of the urbanistic ensemble proposed by Marcu for this site. In any case, the device used to mark the symmetry is the following: flanking the glass-paneled portions of the building, rhythmed by colonnades, by two tympana set up at the extremities of the main façade and continued by a horizontal plinth above. This *frame* underscored and protecteed the fragility and dynamism of the middle portion of the building in the center of which was the axis of symmetry. Even when a compound was not conceived symmetrically, symmetrical details weren't lacking (the main building of the Băneasa Train Station, the staircase tower at C.A.M., the Athenée Palace-Hilton Hotel).

d) *The effects of perspective*; The Military Academy enjoys a long (cca. 0.65 mi) ascending perspective, so that, although it is no more than 30 ft. above street level and not at all ample in size (by comparison with the monster named The House of the People — now House of the Republic), the monumental effect is overwhelming. If the systematization plan (conceived in multiple variants both before and after the building of the palace itself) of the Victoriei Plaza had been followed, one other public building would have enjoyed an elongated frontal perspective from the direction of the Aviatorilor Blvd. and Kiseleff Hwy. This would have been a descendant perspective which Marcu intended to correct by amplifying the verticality and even by including a dominant high-rise of the (indirect) perspective at the intersection between Ana Ipătescu-Catargiu Blvd. and Ștefan cel Mare Hwy.

Marcu created his masterpieces by means of a vocabulary both classical and modern, characteristic of his time. His monumental works were strictly synchronous with those of Piacentini, Speer or Lutyens. We need hardly recall the profound utopian upsurge toward social justice motivating modernism, which, according to Marcu, "satisfies on the one hand the requirements of hygienists (...) and on the other the aspirations of mankind animated by the spirit of social equality, which translates as the right of every individual to the same standard of civilized living;" moreover, Marcu believed, "the modernist movement is even more justified after the war, as the international spirit energizes nations, which tend to suppress the frontiers between different countries and to form the United States of a better Europe, tempering thus the nationalistic currents." History, as we can see, repeats itself. "Anything un-useful must be purged from our lives" and "Architecture becomes purely constructivist."

Marcu was not a constructivist properly speaking, i.e. did not belong to the architectural current of this name, promoted by the Russian avant-garde*. Although in the above-quoted article he praised "the judicious use of reinforced concrete" and "the quality and aesthetic character of the new material which has revolutionized mankind," Marcu continued to use hard stone masonry (in *opus incertum*) for example at Villa Bebe (Sinaia) and, also there, wood, then ceramic and stone tiles, proving that nonetheless he didn't completely trust in the expressive qualities of concrete and preferred the classicism of stone — travertine and marble. Moreover, Marcu was not an internationalist but an architect preoccupied with particularizing his architecture even inside the modern vocabulary of his choice, by giving formulations of surprising clarity and originality to certain consecrated national elements, such as the aforementioned intermediary space.

---

* Before and after the October Revolution (a.n.)

One more remark in connection with Marcu's belonging to the modernist current and with his representative architecture: in an era when power swelled to dictatorial dimensions, the influence exerted upon him by the official Fascist architecture of Italy — the architecture of the E.U.R. and of the University of Rome, of Piacentini and Michelucci — can be easily detected. This is not an accusation, since this architecture offered in any case a better model than Germany's gigantic, Wagnerian architecture, through Speer and others. Certain striking similarities can be explained by the pre-existence of a modernist Italian model for the architecture of power, by the similarity between the Romanian and Italian programs, and by the recourse, on the part of both Marcu and the Italian architects of that same era, to classical molds for modern forms.

Duiliu Marcu's profile belongs in the foreground of our architecture in this century. He contributed overwhelmingly to the particularization of Romanian architecture in the context of world architecture through at least two fundamental gestures: the formulation of viable and convincing examples of representative architecture, and the first high-class solution given to an intermediary space in a modern construction, an interpretation of elements from the traditional repertory.

# III. 3. The Recourse to the Vernacular: Constantin Joja

To better understand why the contest for the Orthodox cathedral in Odessa was a failed start in Romanian architecture — on account of the fault created by WW II and deepened by five decades of communism — we must examine Joja's theoretical opinions as voiced in the studies published during the last part of his life. Practically all the principles enunciated in these studies can be detected in incipient stages in Joja's projects for the Church of the Nation and for Odessa, respectively. I deemed it necessary, in this context, to comment critically on these theoretical principles, after having introduced, on the one hand, Neo-Romanian and post-WW II architecture, and the aforementioned projects on the other. In the Romanian theory of architecture, C. Joja was and still is a point of reference. His opinion has in substance remained unmodified for decades, regarding the question of the national character which concern us here. Those who have followed the projects for cathedrals designed by Joja in 1940 and 1942 may find that practically all the theoretical hypotheses formulated afterwards are already in nuce in these two major projects.

The percussive ideas in the volume entitled *Actualitatea tradiției arhitecturale românești* (*Romanian Architectural Tradition Today*) were followed in 1989 by *Arhitectura româ-nească în context european* (*Romanian Architecture in the European Context*) which was thematically a prolongment of the former book. About this latter volume I wrote the only review at a time when Mr. Joja's opinions very clearly targeted the policy of demolishing villages, which he opposed by expressing the distinct value of Romanian traditional architecture.

Since a specialized criticism is quasi-absent, it could appear that C-tin Joja's opinions went unnoticed, or, conversely, that "silence is assent." This lack of critical responses could lend the author's opinions a false authority which would prejudice not in the last these very opinions.

Joja's intention to argue the profound dimensions of the national character can be related to Blaga, Athanasie Joja or Noica from among non-architects, to G. M. Cantacuzino, to the masters of the Neo-Romanian style, to Fl. Stănculescu, to Doicescu from among the inter-bellum architects or, more recently, to the isolated voices of Alexandru Sandu or Cezar Radu: only a few reference points, especially as they are tempered by the distance in time. Studies that could compare to Mr. Joja's practically do not exist in the last decades. The national character in architecture continues to be a rara avis in theoretical approaches. Practice reflects this theoretical gap, as I intend to show later on, in a manner I would qualify as tragical.

Compared to the former book, Joja's latest volume brings no new views; somewhat new is the extension of the area circumscribing Romanian architecture to the vaster European context. The author's intention is transparent and often explicit: to suggest the character of ancestral classicism of our traditional architecture versus the succession of styles in European art, a classicism dating since "before the arrival of the Greeks," as the author points out. Had this analysis been concretized in a strictly typological approach, things would have been much clearer, I believe. Unfortunately, Joja moves on to draw up hierarchies, after a fashion often blatantly reminiscent of protochronism. The danger couldn't be avoided as the author reached conclusions such as the striking resemblance of our peasant architecture — in its principles — to the modernism of the Bauhaus and even to functionalism.

C. Joja mistakes functional relationships for causal ones. Naturally there are inter-conditionings in the Thracian area extending into the Hellenic space, but it would be rudimentary to explain these by establishing filiations. In any case it is too easy to dispatch the problem of the apparition of the stone temples by the hypothesis of the transposition of wooden buildings into a different material. First of all, the *megaron* came from a region of the brick and of the stone (burnt or black, but for certain favored above wood) to reach a homeland where wood was scarce but stone plentiful: Greece. Next, even if the transposition hypothesis were granted, it would make sense to assume that were thus transposed buildings where a certain representative (hence monumental) configuration was already in place. Now that would have implied a more sophisticated treatment of coverings, however; and this in turn would lead — as can be assumed by making a handy comparison (with Chinese architecture) — to the superposing of elements themselves of a kind to lead to triangular sections, hence to frontons (pediments). These are questions of stress factors, where triangular sections better support the stresses of considerably greater openings between walls than those of the traditional wooden dwellings, covered by laying simple cross-beams.

The factors that could in fact explain this are actually far more numerous. For one, the planimetric origin of the Greek temple is found in the *megaron* (which we could consider the model of rectangular spaces, just as the *tholos* is the model of circular spaces) with its demonstrated source in the Syro-Palestinian area. In any case, the pre-Doric megaron is already well defined in the Aegean region, so that the origins of the frontispiece must be removed far back into the "dark pre-Homeric age." At the same time, a few other hypotheses could be considered, such as the profoundly symbolic character of the fronton of the Greek temple, related on one hand to the symbolism of the triangle and on the other to its function as a "stage" for the mythological representations of the frieze. The triangular frieze, simultaneously, is an image that underscores symmetry, that is the monumentality of the building, while giving relative positioning to the characters. The most important ones appear in the center and thus are bigger; the others, at the extremities, excentrically, are smaller. The device has been used and abused by the symbolism of power since the Egyptians at least: showing the importance of an element by making it relatively bigger than the other elements represented. The fronton (pediment) is much too complex an element to be given as its only explanation something about the protection against bad weather.

Let us return now to the alleged similarity between traditional Romanian architecture and modernist building. The author assigns a precise goal to this typological resemblance: to demonstrate the expressive potentialities of tradition for a modern architecture that would recall the Romanian space, that is for a contemporary architecture clearly possessing national features. Because in effect this is the very purpose of the author's undertaking, we shall have to examine it more closely. To simplify, Mr. Joja's idea is the following: Romanian architecture is classic (possessing all the implicit stylistic attributes), and has been for millennia equal to itself in terms of simplicity, dimensional rigor, asceticism of decoration, coherence of the intrinsic scale of its elements. Meanwhile — and, to preserve the tone of Mr. Joja's writing, we'd say: at last — modern architecture has rediscovered these qualities. Hence, after a few operations of elementary logic, it follows that now is the time to reevaluate folk architecture in an indigenous modern architecture whose intentions can all be served through the very spirit of our tradition.

First of all, the author errs in attributing an axiological tint to the *classicism* of our traditional folk architecture. By reverting the criteria, one could just as easily prove that our architecture is insensitive to the evolution of styles, that is, stagnant, autarchic, fettered by rigid forms, isolated, lagging behind and so on — value judgments that would turn the entire discussion into a sterile and irrelevant dispute. The formal structures of a folk culture cannot be compared with the structures of an urban architecture always fluctuating as it has to respond to evolving social commands. It cannot be always relevant to compare folk culture with the culture of the urban upper classes and to issue value judgments on the sole basis of this comparison.

The obvious explanation of its lack of development lies within itself: folk architecture has had but one program to solve, that of the individual dwelling. As soon as it tried to move on to another program, the religious cult one, it had to modify its expression, as in the case of the wooden churches built in Maramureş, or even to resort to borrowing formal structures from other areas, namely the Byzantine, to which Romanian architecture gave its own creative replies. The change of face could not occur if, the type having been built, the program were unchanged and its solutions found acceptable. Of course, certain similarities do exist at the level of the compositional principles of the form, but this cannot allow us to draw conclusions.

Here is the methodological error of Constantin Joja, otherwise a subtle critic of Neo-Romanianism. The Neo-Romanian style failed when, in order to solve ample programs, where a certain representative character was called for and monumentality required, it resorted to a couple of formulas which simply did not work:

1) the recourse to folk architecture, usually small and usually of wood; it led to the oversizing of the transplanted elements, which thus became misshapen and hideous;

2) the recourse to ecclesiastical architecture and to the palaces belonging to the Brâncoveanu period (by virtue of its being allegedly the first national style); because of the very nature of those programs (churches, palaces), it led to a departure from the specific features of our national peasant architecture, fundamentally linked to the dwelling.

Hence, they were both deviant formulas which were bound to fail, since we do know that:

— shapes may not be translated into other scales and materials without losing their expressiveness;

— shapes belonging to a certain architectural program should not be used to solve the problems of a different program;

— shapes of Byzantine descent, also tinted by Serbo-Armenian-Georgian influences, cannot be used to create a national ("Romanian") character;

— finally, the national character constantly defines and redefines itself in time, being profoundly related to history.

Instead, C-tin Joja believes that a national character could be obtained by applying the make-up of traditional shapes onto modern volumetric structures, by resorting to one or two features of the peasant house to cosmetize high-rises. The peasant-house veranda could thus be used, stripped of all decoration, in successive superposed registers: superposed images of the peasant house. In addition, instead of wood, other materials — metallic for example — could be used, which by diverse methods (such as veneering) could be brought to "resemble" wood. So, an invitation to falsity, profoundly harmful and contrary to the programmatical sincerity of modern architecture.

C. Joja even goes so far so as to propose diverse façades (in both *Actualitatea...* and *Architectura...*). After all, he believes, the formal elements of the porch and of the veranda, which impart rhythm, can be extended horizontally in rows of practically indefinite length, as well as vertically by superposition. Little matters the ungainly oversizing. Little matters the difference in function. Then what is left of all that led to the failure of the Neo-Romanian style?

In connection with the difference in scale, the author treats a few more topics open to debate: the note of monumentality of Romanian peasant houses, the principle of absolute measure, and the fact that "architecture doesn't consist in the roof but in what's under the roof," by virtue of which affirmation Joja postulates the *absolute horizontality* of our architecture and hence the possibility of its serial extension, horizontally, ad indefinitum. Let us review Joja's affirmations one by one.

First, monumentality. Clearly the author tries to identify this characteristic with a view toward postulating the feasibility of scale increases. The aesthetician Cezar Radu has very carefully analyzed all of Joja's concepts and has proved that montumentality is a characteristic of representative buildings and cannot be dissociated from a certain dimensional conspicuousness. The peasant house cannot be monumental because it is not large enough and has no reason to suggest monumentality. The Oltenian mansion is monumental because it was a building which already had to suggest power (as the residence of a member of the small local gentry), and thus monumentality had a reason to exist there. At most we can talk about a certain elegance of the traditional house, derived from the proportioning of the elements, from the ratio between the whole and the part (viz. the decoration), derived, finally, from the satisfaction of those criteria for which Joja appreciated it as classic.

Having reached this juncture in our discussion, it seems appropriate to further analyze an already-mentioned problem known in the aesthetics of architecture as the "principle of absolute measure" (or "size"). In short, this principle states the unlikeliness of successfully translating an architectural model from its own proper scale and materials into another, usually larger, scale and other materials. From this point of view, a peasant house built to the size of a cathedral is hideous.

It is well known that folk architecture provides, in comparatist terms, the source of all architectures "of the first generation" and acts as an internal source for all the other ulterior architectures. Thus the megaron is regarded as the source of all the types of rectangular planimetries with deep interiors, of the Greek temples, as mentioned above. In general, the imprint of folk architecture is more conspicuous in architectural programs that stay close to the traditional house of modest size, and this not only in Romania. The temple (church) — as "house of the gods" ("of the Lord"), the residences of the ruling class — as extensions of the program and size of the small dwelling, the palace — as a maximum of the residential program and already to some extent an administrative and/or representative program of power, all of these are adaptations of original themes having their source in the modest house.

Here is the example of the mansions in the Romanian region known as Oltenia; the dimensions increase, the material is masonry instead of wood, but the compositional principles — ground floor with outbuildings, habitable second floor — are those of the common Oltenian house, as are the elements of ornamentation. Apparently, we have a transgression here against the principle of absolute size. Another example is that of the wooden churches in the northern Romanian region of Maramureș, which belong typologically to the peasant house, are not much larger than it, and have very tall spires. Similarly, some churches built in Moldavia during Stephen the Great's reign (1457-1504) owe their structure to the same principles of folk architecture — the two-sided/four-sided roof, entrance on the south side or west-side porch; at Arbore, also on the west side of the church there is an intermediary space created by the prolongment of two antae of masonry and the hem of the roof, similar to the Straja type of house (cf. Gh. Curinschi-Vorona). Again we have an increase in size to correspond to the change in function.

In fact, grosso modo, architecture breaks the commandment of absolute size often enough, because after all shapes do generate one another, and any shape which at first appears strikingly new reveals, upon closer examination, an entire lineage. Not even modern architecture — despite that wishful originality pursued by its authors — can escape the conclusions of such genealogic investigation; the apartment building, for example, has had ancestors in both function — the tenement houses, beginning with those of Ancient Rome — and form — the terraced architecture, out of prisms stripped of decoration, of Mediterranean architecture.

Is the principle enunciated by Michelis therefore an error? No. The problem, however, needs to be qualified by introducing the temporal dimension. The development from small dimensions to large ones took place in time, across centuries and maybe more, in parallel with the evolution of the respective programs toward monumentality. Thus, the assimilation of the old shapes into their new sets of reciprocal proportions occurred slowly, naturally, by increments, without causing contrariety or shocking. The Oltenian mansion is indeed inspired by the peasant house, and in its turn it inspired the large, palatial manor where the boyar resided. It is a question of the model's prestige. Thus no sudden jumps (they are the examples that illustrate the validity of the principle of absolute size) but step-by-step accumulations, decantations, reformulations. Neither the sand-pile nor the grave mound of the mustaba type was the source of inspiration, the model of the Great Pyramid of Keops, but rather the smaller pyramids, akin to those at Saqqarah, in comparison with which the formal modifications, and not only the increase in size, are conspicuous. Programs that require monumentality borrow from pre-existing buildings which either contain this monumentality in a smaller dose, or contain the premises, the virtualities that allow the transformation into an architecture of power.

To sum up, the qualifying criteria for the principle of absolute size which in itself remains true are the following:

1) The transfer of shapes, with the corresponding re-sizing, occurs between constructions where the difference in scale is little (the case of Mincu's Pub on Kiseleff Hwy., where the adaptation of the themes of the country manor of the Wallachian hillside, though increased in size, is successful).

2) The transfer of shapes best occurs between similar programs: from the small peasant house to the country mansionette, from this to the palatial manor or to the religious building, and so on.

3) The adaptation of the ornamental themes causes them in time to become suited to the new spatial-functional requirement.

4) All of the above are tempered by the necessity to assimilate the new configurations, an assimilation which takes place in a sometimes very long time.

128

5) The same applies to material; Michelis would not have criticized the religious Gothic because it translated into stone the idea of the wooden frame of the urban dwelling.

Regarded from this angle, both the achievements of the Neo-Romanian style and Joja's proposals concerning modern architecture could be criticized not so much for having failed to observe the principle of absolute size as for having failed to observe its qualifiers as formulated above. A principle such as absolute measure, commanding (and commending) self-citation and self-reference in architecture, a principle that would be con-substantial with the development of architecture, cannot be in itself used either for or against an achievement; the multiple conditionings which qualify this principle must be considered, since only these can serve as axiological criteria.

C. Joja proposes some of the characteristics which could be the most typical and suggestive features of our folk art: the shadow as source of expressiveness, the importance of the intermediary space, the rhythms of the post/beam structures, the ratio of filled to unfilled space, the predominant use of wood. The danger consists in drawing up an abstract model of the national character, something akin to Blaga's, which could easily be trivialized or worse when its practical execution were attempted. The national character is a problem of aesthetic idiolect and of "a posteriori synthesis" (Cezar Radu op. cit.).

Finally, the problem of the rapport between the roof and the rest of the building; of course there is a certain conspicuousness of the horizontal vs. the other dimensions, especially in the architecture of the plains and of the hillside in Moldavia, Dobrogea and Wallachia. However, from the general volumetric aspect of any building we can hardly leave out the roof, be it only for the reason that in some parts of the country it is a compositional dominant (by reason of function). Does Joja take architecture to be only the interior space? It would be too restrictive; moreover, all considerations concern aspects of envelopment, hence of exterior design. Besides, not only the mountain houses but also the aforementioned churches of Maramureș, wooden buildings provided with extremely tall spires (shown by Joja himself in *Romanian Architecture in the European Context* on pages 212-216) are examples of traditional architecture where the verticality of the roof predominates. The fact that these churches appeared with a configuration that could suggest Gothic filiations, at a time when the Transylvanian Gothic had already expired, might indicate a folk filiation, vanished today. Are we excluding them from the discussion of the national character because they do not obey one work criterion, or do we dismiss the criteria? If in the religious Gothic we may perhaps escape the problem of the roof, in the lay — urban — Gothic the pinnacle powerfully expressed in the façades cannot be ignored. Seeing the lack of appetite of our architecture for stylistic alignment (Mr. Joja's viewpoint), the argument would not work in any case, in the sense of the comparison with the Gothic style. It has been demonstrated that for the urban civil architecture of Stephen the Great's Moldavia, the Gothic style was a source. If those buildings had been preserved, we would have had a Gothic mediaeval Moldavia, and then Mr. Joja, who justly deplores the destruction of the merchant architecture in our towns, probably would have had to rethink many of his opinions. If we leave the roof out of any discussion, almost all architecture begins to resemble the Mediterranean one and certain spontaneous confusions may appear. To sum up, horizontality is a characteristic but we may not absolutize it and, in any case, not at the expense of the roof.

130

## III. 4. Effects of Khrushchev's Speech on Romanian Post-Stalinist Modernism

By reason of the pressure exerted upon it by the political power, Romanian modernism in architecture had its fluxes and refluxes. Specifically, every stage of relative political relaxation was a return to the former models of the autochthonous functionalism; the sixties re-edit the austere architecture of the Bauhaus in programs of collective dwelling and public services, as well as the architecture of power pioneered by Duiliu Marcu before WW II. The same process occurred in literature, where the return, after the socialist realist phase, to the "hard-core" modernism of Tudor Arghezi, Lucian Blaga, Ion Barbu marked a rebel gesture of resuming "normality" and renewing the ties with its inter-bellum moment as if the Stalinist phase had to be actively forgotten.

This entire process, however, couldn't — and wouldn't — cover up an undeniable fact; Romanian modernism was "behind" the world, striving to recover its own arrested development while elsewhere functionalism, having proceeded without disturbing interruptions, was already entering those years of profound crisis from which it would never recover. In contrast, the years after 1957–58 and especially the following decade brought an ample eruption of functionalism in Romania (collective dwelling districts, civic centers, and the Black Sea coast resorts). On the one hand, architecture returned to the inter-bellum experience, on the other it experimented with "lyric functionalism" (i.e. Le Corbusier's late style of Ronchamp — La Tourette — Chandigarh), then with "brutalism" (in a local variant, which transposed it in a sort of volumetry more consistently inspired by the vocabulary of vernacular shapes, though highly magnified).

The comparison with the international style can be made only on the basis of similar forms. Few deviations from functionalist solutions occurred in Romanian urban drawing, and many of them lack any controversial substance, as they are merely decisions to thicken already existing districts or to build prefab high-rises as economically as possible. Most alternatives remained on the drawing board. What did get built were variants circumscribed, with all of their respective specific differences, by the modernist area. How much of it was the architect's decision and how much that of the politician is of no interest here. Suffice it to say that the modern phenomenon has not yet run its course in Romanian architecture.

One of the reasons of the stylistic immobility of Romanian architecture — riveted on functionalism — is without a doubt the sorry state of the industry of construction materials, of the technologies of construction, along with the ever lower level of expertise of the builders' force. In these conditions, a more spectacular attempt has had no chance of ever being built, shot down by counter-arguments ranging from estimated cost to building licenses and construction site. Hence an additional confusion which, as mentioned earlier, still reigns, between programmatic simplicity and the simple-ness, the poverty of expression effected by lack of means.

Thus surged that communist "hi-tech" style of the 1960's, which produced veritable sculptures in concrete sheets (Torroja, Nervi, Saarinen), special structures, free forms which were not derived from functional requirements. This wave arrived in Romanian architecture too, as there were architects who imitated the use of long cylindrical surfaces (Cezar Lăzărescu used them at his seaside restaurants and at Otopeni Airport), of the wavy-cupola type of roof (N. Porumbescu at the State Circus, an imitation of the same paradigm as the restaurant in Porto Rico designed by Tozo, Farrer & Mario Salvadori or the square in Royan by R. Sarger, L. Simon & Morisseau), of pleated surfaces (the sanatorium in Mangalia / Th. Săvulescu, Dinu Gheorghiu), of curved surfaces (the train stations in Constanța and Predeal, the restaurant in Mamaia as well as Bucharest International Airport, both by Cezar Lăzărescu).

These were among the most daring attempts to technologize Romanian architecture, and they did not escape the notice of contemporary research studying East-European architecture: "An additional center for shell construction in Eastern Europe was developed in Romania, due to the buildings of N. Porumbescu, C. Rulea, and M. Pruncu (State Circus in Bucharest, 1960) (*sic*)" (Kultermann, 1993, 152) or "Recent architecture in Romania has, as a priority, technological achievements relating to shell construction (*sic*)".

Outside of these few attempts, of all kinds of experiments with prefab elements (one of the pathological obsessions of the communist regime), and of the utilization of reinforced concrete with steel case structures in some of the edifices of power, much cannot be said about modern technologies in Romanian architecture. Of course under the circumstances it is almost moot to discuss stylistic "evolution", when it is known that without new programs, technologies, and materials, the development of styles in architecture is considerably slowed down if not altogether stopped. In the last fifty years of Romanian architecture, everything that has appeared as change was a form of *revival* of previous themes. While the architectural types crystallized and improved, aesthetic reasons alone could not change the face of an architecture where, in any case, the decision did not belong to the creators but to the power.

Clearly, the first tendency after Khrushchev's speech was then to "look backward" in order to bridge the gap created by socialist realism in the discourse of Eastern European architecture; the sources of this retrospectivism varied from country to country, and Romania oscillated for some time between the dual "stripped classicism/classicizing modernism." This was the celebrated

Carol II Style (see the article by the same name by I. D. Enescu in *Arhitectura* 2/1939, 4-5). Its promoters found inspiration in the Italian "Fascist" architecture (Piacentini, Michelucci, Libera, Terragni) for ideological as well as architectural reasons; the Romanian people was also Latin, and its original identity had to be signified through architecture, too. Architects like Duiliu Marcu and Tiberiu Ricci who had been active designing buildings for the pre-war political power were able to work after the Stalinist intermezzo, too. Duiliu Marcu was even President of the new Architects' Union, created by decree on Nov. 13, 1952. Let us recall the similar effects of the April 23, 1932 decree in the Soviet Union. Tiberiu Ricci, who may have been the author of some of the projects that had come from Marcu's studio before the war, designed after the war the Radio Building and Radio Hall (General Berthelot St.) in almost the same manner in which Duiliu Marcu's Studio had built the State Monopoly Building of Victoria Avenue in the thirties. Palace Hall (an add-on to the Royal Palace) recalled Marcu's "classical" palaces, i.e. Victoriei Palace[14], but owed more to the functionalist idiom than its inter-bellum models, while the apartment buildings on the perimeter of the new Palace Square employed the stern aesthetics of Bauhaus[15].

An edifying example of this "classicizing modernism" (or "stripped classicism") is Romarta Copiilor, a commercial-residential building located opposite C.C.A. (Casa Centrală a Armatei — Army Central House). In 1954 a contest was held for the square in front of the C.C.A. building and the buildings on the perimeter. Project 18 won the 2nd place (Al. Zamfiropol, Al. Hempel et al.). All the projects that received prizes or mentions were clearly indebted to the Soviet realist-socialist architecture. Nonetheless, the building which in the end was actually built[16] — with a symmetrical composition and pilasters running all around the ground floor of the building — belongs to the vocabulary of the 1930's rather than to the Stalinist one[17].

In "Notes Regarding the Contest for the Systematization of the Army's Central House Square in Bucharest" (*Arhitectura R.P.R.* 4/1955, 9-22), G. Pătrașcu explains in detail the results of the contest but extracts no conclusion whatsoever about the future of the program. The very fact that the first prize was not awarded suggested dissatisfaction on the part of the organizers, who probably sought some other image for this busy downtown intersection in the Capital. The architects of that period, however, seemed to have more trouble than expected ridding themselves of the realist-socialist cliché, as suggested by another contest — the 1956-57 contest for the systematization of N. Bălcescu Plaza, today the Intercontinental Hotel-National Theater Plaza. Here, the alternative to socialist realism was at most the classicizing modernism of, say, Hensellman at the Stalin-Alee in Berlin. The two projects which won ex aequo prove by this the lack of enthusiasm as far as building either one in its "pure" state; the two are practically identical in urban conception, reminiscences of San Marco: a campanile as dominant of height in a plaza displaying a continuous front of identical façades.

The differences do not suggest two different ages of design. Project 37 (Titu Elian, C. Hurmuzache, Aron Brimberg, Pompiliu Macovei, A.S. Teodorescu) is an example of realist socialism, displaying the obligatory frontal symmetries on all the façades of the central building, which is neoclassical in a Joltovskian style (provided with a terrace, though), located on the site of today's National Theater, as well as on the façades of the left side building, located "under" today's Intercontinental Hotel. The campanile was exiled across the street in an extension of Colțea, as an articulation of the street corner. The entire context, in these architects' vision, had to be modified in the same spirit, as had happened with Warsaw's downtown. The authors of Project 37, amusingly enough, won the third prize with another neoclassical pile, which was merely a permutation of the pieces of the first project, minus the campanile.

135

Project 49 (Victor Adrian, Carol Hacker, Dan Ioanovici), in its turn, cleared the entire portion between Batiște and Sf. Gheorghe, over-widening the boulevard and leaving only one intervening accident: Colțea Church. The centerpiece of this ensemble was an asymmetrical building, its heavier wing towards the Ministry of Agriculture; attached to it through a short portico was the campanile. By their shapes, the buildings in this proposal rather recall Fomin.

The "modern projects" (though in the hensellmanian manner) began from the mentions on. All of them are cut out according to the principle of the screen-façades, without articulations of volumes, without "accidents" to trouble their Olympian serenity. However, nothing can prevent us from seeing in the administrative buildings of Project 10 (Gh. and N. Negoescu, Aurelian and Ianola Trișcu) the prototypes of the political-administrative headquarters built in county-seat cities ten years later, nor the kinship between the "tower" building in this project and the towers designed by Doicescu on Știrbei Vodă and in the Senate Plaza. There is only one project — 31 (Traian Chițulescu, Niculae Ioniță, M. Gh. Enescu, I. Bălănescu, Sanda Almosnino, Paul Focșa, M. Enescu, Arman Cristea) — in which the plaza is trapezoidal instead of rectangular, relying on the in-depth effect and utilizing the real directions of the two boulevards, which cross one another at an angle greater than ninety degrees. Finally, the most "modern" project — Project 5 (Anton and Margareta Dîmboianu) — from a formal aspect, which received a mention ex aequo, was in fact the most classicizing one in terms of urbanistic solution.

De-Stalinization was not in Romania a sudden process, as it was in Hungary. The transition from socialist realism to the strict modernism of the seventh decade took place by increments, during a period of cross-pollinations. In those years, inter-bellum precedents were revived — neoclassicism, stripped classicism, classicizing modernism — and vernacular architecture was courted; also, the limits of the discourse were forced to make it

136

accept the stern bareness of Bauhaus. In a different manner, the same idea was underlined by Grigore Ionescu; during the 1955-1960 five-year plan, the historian noted, radical mutations occurred from "those methods of design which relied upon narrow, antiquated concepts of the rapport between form and content in architecture and in urbanism" (1969, 59). Also, the period immediately after Khrushchev's speech meant "a phase of preparation for the ample activity, on an increased scale, which was going to make itself felt after 1960" (ibid.).

The late fifties, marked by the 1956 rebellion in Hungary and by an increased social preoccupation on the part of the Romanian Proletarian Party (R.P.P.), bring us the official recognition of major architectural and urbanistic problems. The R.P.P. Plenary Session of Nov. 26-28, 1958, criticized the slow response of the construction industry to the economical problems of the country. ("Let us build good, inexpensive housing.") Also criticized was the backwardness that plagued urbanism. Gheorghe Gheorghiu-Dej's speech at this plenary session recycled the favorite themes of this Khrushchevian period in constructions and architecture. The building of vast numbers of social dwellings overwhelmed the production of construction materials and — for that same reason — cost estimates were constantly overrun. "THE MAIN CRITERION IN THE CONSTRUCTION OF HOUSING IS COST" (ibid. boldfaced capitals in the original) — was Gheorghiu-Dej's emphatic announcement echoing with some delay the explicit requests of the Soviet leader in December 1956. Nothing new, in other words, no autochthonous local initiative, Dej's message being already behind the Soviet directive.

As suggested by Professor Nicolae Lascu's recent research, "the backwardness" consisted (also) in the continuity, in Bucharest, of the same legislative and urbanistic arrangements which had been set up before WW II. Thus, Professor Lascu underlines "the absence of any systematization plans till the early 1960's, for most cities "...)" and "The beginning of the destruction / modernization

137

of our cities consisted in isolated interventions, unrelated to one another" (Lascu, 1995, 174). The few attempts to conceive a new urbanistic plan for Bucharest failed en route, it seems, although this did not prevent the constant reference, on the part of every published project, to these piously observed plans in spite of their... non-existence. Two explicit mentions do exist, however. One is the sketch for a general plan to systematize the city of Bucharest, presented in 1958 at the Moscow Congress of the International Architects' Union, with the theme "The Reconstruction of Cities 1945-1957." The other concerns the plan of a "square" whose perimeter coincided with that of historic downtown Bucharest; but the plan is attested only indirectly through circumstantial evidence. Thus, the Lufthansa Building on Magheru Blvd and the twin buildings Eva-O.N.T. across the boulevard were supposedly devised so as to allow this hypothetical perimetral boulevard to run by, respectively between them. Similarly, a part of the same plan would have been represented by the systematization of Știrbei-Vodă Avenue in the vicinity of the Military Academy (although the obvious objection is that here we are dealing with a revival of Duiliu Marcu's own pre-war plan). In fact, oral testimonies heard during my research confirmed that the plan conceived in the thirties was still in use; and this ought to cast a new light on the hypothesis of the continuity between the two moments — the pre-WW II and the immediately post-Stalinist one.

In the February 8-10, 1959 plenary session of the R.P.P., the "aesthetic exaggerations" which contravened to the "economic factor" in the building of social housing were again criticized in due Khrushchevian spirit. Simultaneously, in the same document the party officials of the C.S.C.A.S. (State Council for Building, Architecture and Urban Planning) criticized the lack of coherence of the urbanistic approaches, especially in the large districts of social dwellings: the groups of apartment buildings were either too scattered or too small, the density was too little, and services were lacking. The same 1959 brings to the fore the so-called

138

"systematization of the national territory." This will become the predominant tendency in reformulating the autochthonous environment, a tendency that gained more and more momentum and became ever more radical until 1989.


## *The Seaside*

Among the first projects to "improve" an "aleatory" and "irrational" reality was the systematization of the Black Sea coast. Various projects for Mamaia, Năvodari, Vasile Roaită had existed since before 1954. They had been coordinated by the same Cezar Lăzărescu — ubiquitous male lead of Romanian modernism in architecture after WW II, an architecture he piloted as chief of design teams and of its institutions, as well as officer of the liaison with power.

The second half of the sixth decade revived[18] these seaside projects and broadened them, but only the sixties and seventies would vigorously execute them, as the entire seaside was terraformed. To follow the projects for Năvodari, Eforie, V. Roaită, Mangalia, and, later, for Mamaia is to accurately describe all the stages of Romanian architecture after Stalinism. From the strictly socialist-realist perspectives for a Năvodari built by the forced labor of political convicts and the Bucureşti Hotel in Mamaia (I. & C. Ghiţulescu, A. Corvătescu; but any pre-war architect could have designed it) on the one hand — to Perla Restaurant (1959), the restaurant-club in Eforie ('57-58) or the Niemeyerian restaurant on the cliff in Mangalia ('59), synchronized with the spirit of their time, on the other, a radical change had occurred along the way. It was a change of attitude and perspective in the way Cezar Lăzărescu and his staff, along with other architects involved with the seaside, understood architecture. It was the deliverance from the official expression, from rigid symmetries, from misplaced classicism unsuited to the leisure function in order to move on to an occasionally radical modernism which was also somewhat inadequate to the small scale, picturesque, integrated image the site would have required.

The 1958 contest for Mamaia on the Black Sea is in this context an enlightening testimony of the Zeitgeist. It called for "economical buildings made of durable materials capable of withstanding the marine climate (...) conceived in a realistic fashion as parts of a socialist architecture to harmonize with the environment (the sea, the beach, the lake, the plantations) and with the function of the buildings" (*Arhitectura RSR* 5-1958, 3). Twenty-three projects were submitted, surprisingly few in view of the importance the development of the seaside was then given. The jury, headed by Octav Doicescu, awarded only a third prize and three mentions. Perhaps worth noting is that all the projects were more rigid than what Cezar Lăzărescu and his team had already done in Eforie. Aberration were also present — i.e. Project 17, Motto "45381," which filled the area between the sea and Tăbăcăriei Lake with pentagonal, cloistered hotels, entered through monumental portals cut out to the same classicizing pattern which up to then had belonged to socialist-realist architecture and which was painfully unsuitable to either the scale or the scope of such a project.

The architecture of the seaside (which continued beyond the period examined here, through the development of the resorts of Olimp, Neptun, Saturn and Cap Aurora) is probably, aside from Bucharest and the civic centers scattered throughout the country, the most consistent and important phenomenon in understanding Romanian post-war architecture; moreover, it boasts some of the more applauded buildings of the period.

In order to achieve the enormous program aiming to modify the natural environment, the prefabrication celebrated by Khrushchev was indeed the key. In Brussels (1957) the U.S.S.R. presented numerous type-projects and prefab buildings. There was even an international exhibition of type-projects in Berlin[19] (Oct. 23-Nov. 10, 1957), while at home many contests were launched

for the design of type-buildings with definite social functions —
and even the call for typified administrative edifices came.

In addition, once again vernacular architecture began to attract
architects as a possible source of inspiration heretofore "forgotten"
or, more accurately, over-ideologized. The information furnished
by architects of the period in the interviews conducted during this
research — and indirectly confirmed by the published documents
of that period — proves that Romanian folk architecture was indeed
regarded as "leftist" architecture. In a dispute on how would
representative buildings look after Stalinism, peasant vernacular
architecture outdid the Byzantine architecture (of the kind
promoted by Simotta at the Patriarchal Palace) and carried the day
on mostly ideological grounds. While the latter was regarded
suspiciously as the architecture of the allogenous "exploiting
classes" (politics after Stalin would possess, let us recall, a
distinct nationalist chauvinist flavor), folk architecture (i.e. of the
"exploited" classes) was instead made positive by its very "social
origin" or heredity.

The vernacular became a possible source of "rationality" (i.e.
of modernity from the standpoint of Khrushchev's speech; efficient
use of materials, restrained decoration) which thus could once again
irrigate the "urban" architectural discourse having temporarily
forgotten its natural roots[20]. The vernacular would also assist
architects by allowing them to justify the propensity for rationality
without having to appeal to the theoretical "cosmopolitan"
approach. The sentence, "Vernacular architecture is leftist
architecture and at the same time authentically national
architecture" could serve as motto both to Nicolae Porumbescu and
his autochthonic school in Iași and to Joja's architectural
nationalism (as he had been absolved of the guilt of having
belonged to the extreme right before the war and recovered for the
new nationalist spirit / current which swept over Romanian
cultural policy). The logic of the text devoted by Radu Crăniceanu
to the new "folk" architecture along Valea Jaleșului was "to mend"

the perception of both vernacular and "rational" architecture, i.e. modern architecture.

The vernacular also contained implicit moral attributes; aside from its ancestral "large aperceptive dowry" — a new name for Blaga's "matrix" — as. N. Porumbescu called it, folk architecture had the ability to absorb and make rational sense out of the influences "of urban/cultured" architecture, to improve and temper them. Peasants do not boldly rush to embrace alien perishable models (that is, have more sense of discernment than city dwellers.) Of course, influences and renewal do exist, but "peasants assimilate these improvements over the span of generations, as they mistrust certain novelties and technical adventures" (ibid.). In a comparable spirit — simultaneously modern and wishful-archaic, since the archaic was being rediscovered as a possible source of the modern language — were built for example minimal apartments (Mihai Bravu Hwy, T. Niga et al.). Their justification was two-fold; on one hand, modern housing arrangements (i.e. one-room apartments) supposedly had their origin in the peasant "traditional house," on the other they would replay common themes from those architectures with vaster experience in this area — the text didn't say which architectures but in any case the context clearly suggested they were not those of the socialist camp.

Was this autochthonist orientation a consequence of the above-mentioned speech? Partially, yes. The apparent celebration of the "national", emptied however of all content of its own so that it might decorate at will a "socialist" one, also informed the Stalinist political/aesthetical discourse on architecture, explaining for example certain decorative details in the style of Brâncoveanu's period on Casa Scânteii — today the Free Press House — or the presence of some local, Dobrogean details on the social houses aligned at Năvodari. Of course there were not and never had been row houses in traditional Dobrogea, so the "national character" was reduced to the decoration. In Romania, as it were, it was difficult to invoke some classic national tradition as in the German Democratic Republic, for instance, where Schinkel quickly became the paternal figurehead of the new "socialist" style — a local version of the Soviet socialist realism — in which Stalin / Karl Marx Alee was executed in Berlin. The architecture of the Brâncoveanu period — reduced to a handful of details — and a smattering of vernacular architecture were the only two sources which could be called upon from the "national" hope chests, and they were inevitably and every time lost without hope of recognition in the imported "socialist" content.

During the Stalinist period, marginal programs were also built where the "national character" supposedly came out, namely train stations. These could have been built anywhere else, since they owed nothing to the spirit of place or to the architectural dialect spoken in the region where they were placed. They show no regard for the geography of the site or the local / regional cultural spirit. Rather, they are "picturesque" buildings, with the pointed roofs of mountain houses and with stone girdles; meager chalets built on a shoestring budget. They could have been typified and exported anywhere in Europe. "The traditional house" has little or nothing to do with these buildings, for which no Romanian precedent existed, in either function or form. Only in 1956 did the construction of a hotel in Poiana Stalin (today Poiana Brașov, a resort only a few miles above the city of Brașov) begin (Dinu Hariton, N. Porumbescu, C. Rulea) which was to he endowed with a "traditional line" as well as "an air inspired by the architecture of the peasant house, with it well-known proportionality, grace and sensitivity (sic)[21]." Unlike the train stations of the previous period, eulogized in *Arhitectura R.P.R.* 6/1957, the hotel recognizably and above all explicitly alluded to the mediaeval peasant fortresses of the area.

A less investigated area of manifestation of the binome vernacular / national is the architecture of apartment buildings, of social housing. Until the seventies when the concept of "national features" would once again come to the fore, the architecture of collective dwellings was at most a promoter of Bauhaus (in the happy cases) or of the minimal, pre-fab lodgings of post-Khrushchevian inspiration (in all other cases). Nevertheless even in the late fifties we do find a few references and explicit texts on the subject. Tiberiu Niga's apartment buildings in Cățelu District (1959) perhaps need not surprise us, in their attempt to somehow recall some recognizable features of the traditional house, in view of the author's similar works before WW II. The reference to an identitary mark is more surprising in the case of certain relatively obscure works. An example would be the ensemble of apartment buildings in Cotroceni on Ana Davila St. (M. Slomnescu, collab. V. Iliescu), executed in 1957-58, where the author has an a) contextual approach; "The characteristic of the site is the rich plantation and the beauty of the old trees... especially as the buildings are situated in a neighborhood of villas *with which they must harmonize...* This way the ensemble is an integral part of Cotroceni, a city district where parks and planted gardens abound" (*Arhitectura R.S.R.* 10-11/1958, 44; italics mine A.I.), and a b) referential approach; "The loggias dominating the façade allow an interpenetration between architecture and nature which is a *characteristic* of Romanian architecture especially in the country-side" (ibid., italics mine A.I.). Still in Bucharest, on Ion Scorțaru St., the same architect will commit another building with the same m.o., a two-storeyed residential building riming with Niga's already-mentioned type of approach: arches of masonry on the ground floor surmounted by pillars with the sections of traditional wood posts, tiled roof, entrance through a loggia / porch open to the exterior.

It was once again, then, permitted to talk about and quote from the vernacular architecture (i.e. "national" architecture). A few of the panels exhibited by Romania at the Vth Congress of the International Architects' Union were dedicated to the celebration of the sacred architecture of wood in Maramureș / Transylvania

144

and that of masonry at Curtea de Argeș; Mogoșoaia Palace and the traditional houses are once again invoked as prestigious precursors and therefore as possible models of inspiration. Even more — when a new building was envisaged on 1848 Blvd. in 1957, the theme of the project required the valuation of the Russian Church as "a church which has been decreed a historical monument and at the same time is a remarkable work of architecture" (idem 40).

## III. 5. Romanian Post-Modernism?

The critique of modernism in architecture is neither the exclusive property of the eighties — of (im)pure, brawny post-modernism — nor is it, for that matter, limited to architecture. A basis of comparison with socialist realism, for instance (and by further analogy, with the official styles popular between the wars) is in the first place the anti-avant-garde and anti-modern reaction. The reaction against modernism, however, is only skin-deep, and as a rule directed against personalities or groups, rather than against manifestoes; in the substratum, subtle and substantial (modern-post-modern) continuities occurred.

Boris Groys offers an even more radical view on this phenomenon: he sees socialist realism as a continuation beyond all expectation, beyond all imagination even, of the aesthetic and political program of the avant-garde. In other words, when Stalin was appreciating that reality no longer needed any aesthetic retouch because it had become in itself beautiful as a result of the political intervention, he was also implicitely announcing that one of the main objectives of the avant-garde had been reached: direct action — not just through the medium of representation — upon reality. Avant-garde architecture was created by an elite and, being radically different from the traditional meanings of architecture, it could seem "illegible" and elitist to the masses. Their opinion became important — if only to be manipulated — between the two World Wars. Founded on populist notions, i.e. promoting identitary-nationalistic[22] views along with a "public image," centered on the exaltation of the archaic, mythical origins, the architecture of official buildings between the wars both in Europe and North America eclipsed incipient modernism and exiled it to

146

the marginal position of industrial and residential architecture (villas, housing districts).

During the same period an eclectic architecture emerged, based on compositional patterns and a formal vocabulary of classical origin (colonnades, architrave, basso and alto rilievo, statues) and stripped ("modernized") through lack of decoration as well as use of new materials (steel, glass, reinforced concrete) and technologies. It is the architecture of international fairs and universal exhibitions between the wars (especially Paris 1937 and New York 1939), the architecture of power, designated by its affiliation with a certain ideology — "Fascist," "Nazi," "Stalinist" architecture; or, generically, "totalitarian" architecture — and the architecture of the American New Deal, with its post offices and federal buildings and the works of the then-famous Tennessee Valley Authority. In all of these political contexts, architecture was at the same time "conservative-nostalgic" (based on ideal urban patterns, traditionalist, monumental, classicizing) and "reforming-projective" (centered on rewriting physical reality, utopian, sternly functionalist).

Only after the Second World War did "orthodox" modernism (Venturi) or corporate modernism (especially in its most austere form, the *international style*, the extreme-functionalist architecture) become images synonymous to capitalism. As they were winning ground especially in the United States of America, "modern movements" (Jencks) rewrote history and in their turn banished all alternative discourses from schoolbooks and, often, from the very texture of the city itself, considerably weakened by the war.

This is not to say that modernism was an unanimous image or that it was unanimously accepted. The international style was often criticized even as it peaked. British brutalism, for example, radicalized the modern discourse by pushing it to its ultimate consequences. Buildings became not only austere but downright poor; not merely functional, but unfleshed, exploded expressions of the functional system itself; they were not only mechanisms but

147

machine organs whose functions were outwardly displayed: pipes that ran on the outside, every function expressed by its form, clearly delineated from that next to it. We confront here the disfigurement of architecture; its corporeal envelope is blown to bits.

Houses became écorchés, where the integument having formerly isolated them from the exterior was peeled off. The "skinning" of architecture and the destruction of its "corporeal" integrity, however, were not the exclusive properties of brutalism, but also, systematically, of all high-tech, metabolist architecture, as well as of the building of social housing, at the other end of the scale of values. In this latter case, underscoring the lines of demarcation between living cells destroyed the intimacy or at least the privacy previously afforded by constructions. Now we knew precisely where the bedroom, the parlor, the kitchen begin and end. Bare, dis-spelled, this architecture of the functional "verity" will be re-draped by post-modernism in pasteboard décors.

The critique of the genetic chain brutalism–Archigram-metabolism–high-tech would come from inside it, just as the "megastructural" utopianism of the sixties had caused the disappearance of the building's outer skin — Yona Friedman, Nicholas Schoffer, the pop architecture of the Archigram[23], (sub)aquatic cities or those gliding through interstellar space. Paul Rudolph (whose 1963 Yale School of Architecture building flexed muscles of reinforced concrete[24]), Philip Johnson or Minoru Yamasaki also grew inside the modern paradigm — they who believed that, to cease to be dull, modernism had only to drape its "apparent" concrete sheets in the sweet style of the classics.

Modernism experienced other gentle schisms, too. The regional, "peripheral" versions of modernism (Scandinavian architecture, Czech cubism, Catalonian-Portuguese[25] architecture and, more recently, "ethnic" architectures such as Hasan Fathi's in Egypt, Jon Utzon, England in Malta, or Balkrishna Doshi in India) are considered by Kenneth Frampton progenitors of his critic regionalism, and, more recently, by Colin St. John Wilson as

148

worth while directions outside of the modernist mainstream. Finally, our review of the critique of modernism ends with the New York Group of Five which began its activity in 1964 at the Institute for Architecture and Urban Studies (coordinated by Philip Johnson) and published the magazine entitled *Oppositions*, devoted to extended theoretical studies. This was the group behind late modernism (Meier, Gwathmey, Hejduk); it also produced a historicizing post-modern (Graves) and a deconstructionist (Einsenman). Both Venturi and Einsenman "danced" against the backdrop of the semiotic and linguistic studies of the sixties and were preoccupied by architecture as language. Einsenman wished for an architecture that would be pure syntax, as neurotic and unsettling as the times.

We are more interested here, though, in the 1966 moment when two landmark books were published, fundamental texts for de-structuring modern architecture. One was Robert Venturi's *Complexity and Contradiction in Architecture*, prefaced prophetically by Vincent Scully as "... probably the most important writing on the making of architecture since Le Corbusier's *Vers une Architecture* of 1923." The other is Aldo Rossi's book *Architettura della Citta*. Both dealt fatal blows to modernism. The new architecture and the city had to be tolerant, more permissive, duets and choruses instead of solos no matter how brilliant. Less is not more, but more boring. The American city ("Main Street is almost all right" for Venturi) with its disconcerting diversity of images, symbols and signs, is richer, more meaningful to the life of the community than are sky scrapers poking the landscape at random. The same is true of the mediaeval town with its organically intertwined streets and lanes. In it, Rossi sees how the types (exemplary, Platonic models: archetypes) develop and persist, above styles and more meaningful than they because more profound. Diversity and even adversity must be admitted in architecture. Ambiguity is productive, contradictions amplify the meanings (where they are left to stand instead of being cut down,

149

like Gordian knots, by modernism) decoration (the ornamentation) and décor (the apology of the urban façade) recover their right to dwell in the city. Venturi will dissociate the significance from the making of architecture and will set it up as a poster / sign in front of the building (the "decorated shed").

Nothing was the same after these two books and derived works. The seventies crush the modernist discourse in many prestigious universities — Charles Moore is Dean at Yale instead of Paul Rudolph, Vincent Scully eulogizes Venturi, architects attuned to the change begin to appear, such as Robert A. M. Stern and Michael Graves, as well as conspicuously non-modern buildings, though still confined to the woods of Connecticut and the glossy covers of magazines.

Even if Charles Jencks gives an exact "hour" when modernism "died," it is safer to observe that two are the post-modern edifices widely regarded as the "first" — Portland Public Building (Michael Graves) and the AT&T Building (Philip Johnson). The rest — the association with the conservative revolution, the implosion into supermarket and Disneyland architecture, the exhaustion in less than ten years — is now well-known history. One may not be and in any case one may not stay in the avant-garde if adopted by mass culture. Without a critical edge, said Kenneth Frampton, the discourse becomes degraded and collapses. Post-modernism died like Patrick Suskind's character: of too much love.

However, post-modernist theories outlived post-modernist practice, yielding many fertile concepts; fragmentation, collage[26], pastiche (quotation for aesthetic purposes); simulation (the eulogy of the façade, of the artificial and the superficial); the theory of simulacra and the critique of interiors where furniture is seen as a set of bourgeois monuments (Baudrillard). All these concepts are useful today not only to the study of the American megalopolis but also to the interpretation of the "New Civic Center" in Bucharest. These concepts are also essential to the interpretation

150

of socialist-realist architecture, showing us, of course, not that Soviets were making post-modernist architecture in the 1930's, but that, between the lines, both of these populist-conservatory, eclectic, nostalgic, schizoid discourses are informed by similar grounds.

## *The Theory of Catastrophes Applied to Romanian Architecture*

A brief excursion in our past will set on firm ground what must be said afterwards about Romanian post-modernism. For Romanian architecture designed after Ion Mincu's Lahovary House of 1884 (the first neo-Romanian building), Stalinism was a sort of axis of symmetry (although of course more of a gap or black hole than an axis). What is on the left of the axis (i.e. before Stalinism) must be repeated on the right (i.e. after Stalinism), with certain necessary nuances. By superimposing upon this scheme[27] the concept of "two-gear architecture"[28] as characteristic to countries with totalitarian regimes where alternative discourses may, however, exist (Fascist Italy, U.S.A. during the New Deal), we shall in fact obtain two levels of interpretation.

1) In Romania's pre-World War II "official" architecture, no significant detours occurred; there were neither priorities nor delays. The eclecticism of the XIXth century — which had meant the monumentalization of the city of Bucharest but also the destruction of its mediaeval architecture — makes a comeback in the 1980's, considerably abased, however, as a language, when the architecture of the new civic center replaces significant portions of the historic center and blows up much of its urban silhouette. The Neo-Romanian rhetoric returns in the 1970's in the architecture of administrative and cultural buildings, under the guise of the "national character"; many "civic centers" in county seats are variations on folk themes at monumental scales. Finally, "stripped

classicism" returns, too, as a plausible source of post-Stalinist architecture, not only because many of the authors of those pre-war edifices (or members on their design staffs) make a comeback and/or continue to work (the cases of Duiliu Marcu and Tiberiu Ricci), but also because the anti-Stalinist reaction after 1960 allowed the new generation of architects to resume the modern experiments of the former generation at the point where they had been interrupted. (Many of those inter-bellum experimenters — Marcu and Creangă, Duiliu Marcu, P. Em. Miclescu, G. M. Cantacuzino — were also the teachers of this new generation.[29]). Urban legislation and building by and large followed the defining characteristics of the city's downtown in its between-the-wars aspect. New buildings after 1945 and especially between 1954-1970 were either fillings or continuations of the fronts of large boulevards and squares (Kogălniceanu Square, Roman Square). Duiliu Marcu's research concerning the systematization of Victoriei Plaza was continued (still under his tutelage) into the 1950's, as attested by the two volumes of projects and articles of 1946 and 1960, respectively. A statue of Lenin and probably the aesthetics of the façades would have told the difference between the two eras.

2) The top level, that of the architecture of power, "trickles" into the "marginal" level(s) below, a diffusion, however, which makes things less obvious. Nevertheless, the pseudo-architecture of the city *outskirts* is promoted in scale by the buildings of the new civic center" — a sort of larger and grander market district signifying — among other things — the triumph of the peripheral space, of the city outskirts, and implicitly of their low-brow subculture over the center and its high-brow culture. The older high-rises decorated with traditional motifs — cable mouldings, girdles, biforial and triforial windows — are redesigned after 1977 in the much degraded version of the cheap apartment building made of prefab panels, though with shingled attics and traditional motifs transposed from towels and wooden spoons into concrete. The stern

modernism with a hint of classicism — Horia Creangă at the ARO/Patria Building or D. Marcu's Magistrate Bldg. on Magheru Blvd. are examples built between the wars — also returns to post-Stalinist architecture (Roman Square, Romarta Building, Nations' Plaza). Industrial architecture, on the other hand, having remained even during Stalinism a haven for our talented modern architects, is an atypical example from the standpoint of our hypothesis.

.Perhaps a qualifying nuance is worth adding to this unavoidably schematic grid used to interpret a hundred years of "national" architecture — from the Lahovary House to 1990 (the latter year picked for methodological reasons). Between the wars, architecture consistently eluded the "official" discourse — whatever it may have been at any given moment — and also catered to a free market which developed many marginal programs. Although unmentioned by history textbooks, their presence in the organism of the city makes it more complex, more ambiguous (thence, Venturi would add) more expressive. "Florentine" and "Moorish" architecture was all the rage in Bucharest between the wars. For some — kitsch, for others — picturesque, such villas of the upper class are today the delight of the (few) islands of architecture unconquered by the multitude of prefab apartment buildings. Even Neo-Romanianism produced credible images on the level of the individual dwelling, of the urban villa, where it could conjugate — almost playfully — the most exotic glosses. Romantic / exotic images, such as the crenellated building on Ștefan cel Mare Hwy. or the "Zodiac" Building (Radu Dudescu) on Dorobanților Ave., and Oriental "impurities" having reached us through the architecture of fairs, such as bow windows, can be found scattered here and there throughout the Capital.

Cross-pollinations between styles must be added to these "aberrations." Thus we shall encounter eclecticism and/or modernism with Neo-Romanian details, buildings between modernism and Art Deco; allusions, reciprocal contaminations, prestigious quotes. "I seek the 'signatures' and traces of precisely

153

these 'exemplary marginalia' because such fragments (also) constitute Romanian post-modernism, the one without post-modernity" (Mircea Martin).

## Nationalism as Cure for the Identity Crisis

Until the early 1980's, when the relentless campaign of building entire prefab neighborhoods of apartment buildings in order to "solve the housing problem" slowed down and slackened a bit, no changes occurred in the poverty-stricken physiognomy of mass architecture other than plastering it with "national motifs".

The attempt to give an "ethnic" profile to architecture was (more or less from behind the scenes) motivated (and flattered) by the movement toward nationalism amongst Romanian communists. A theoretician like Constantin Joja, whose genuinely autochthonistic views were warranted by his Legionnaire past[30], became the flag bearer of certain "protochronistic" opinions, according to which the much-praised features of modernism could be found in Romanian vernacular architecture (so-called "traditional" architecture) for some two thousand years, as well as in the "true" urban tradition, that of the mediaeval inns. In folk architecture, Joja believed, the roof didn't matter, being strictly functional. The "essential" was under the roof: horizontal series of pillars, rhythmically shaded. Hence, nothing else to do but to transform the rhythm of archaic porches in serial structures extending horizontally or piling up vertically in however many floors, as needed.[31] Contemporary materials should imitate the traditional ones; "wood" could be thus obtained out of veneered metal, "brick" or "adobe" out of concrete and so on.

Lifting folk decorations and applying them to monumental structures was/is the specialty of the architect from Iași Nicolae Porumbescu. Joja the theoretician and Porumbescu the practitioner are the cornerstones of an entire rhetoric, immediately embraced by officials and transformed into a dogma which was, alas, soon to be degraded into the minor architecture of the prefab neighborhoods. Another stumbling block was the translation into monumental scales, the same misstep which had been taken by the Neo-Romanian stylists decades ago. In the last pre-1989 creation inspired by Mr. Porumbescu's autochthonic vocabulary, namely the Civic Center in Satu Mare, the local Habsburgic tradition was neglected in favor of folkloric hysterias transposed into concrete. The "wooden" details are falsely made of concrete. The decorative details seem to have been torn out of their context (towels, spoons, porch beams) and magnified to gigantic scale. An elementary principle of architectural aesthetics was thus disregarded, that of "absolute measure".[32]

In order to achieve "specifically national" connotations and a ubiquitous (because eclectic) "identity" modern architecture had to suppress otherness. Regional and local identities, which accounted for the remarkable differences among the architectures of our historical regions would be at first concealed, and later on violently annihilated.

Ion Mincu had favored the rural middle class architecture of the Wallachian hillside (of Muscel), which from a regional style became exemplary on the national scale. Mincu's followers used the style of Brâncoveanu's period (early XVIII[th] century) and (therefore) the architecture of monasteries as a source of inspiration. As in the case of the merchant architecture of the XVIIth-XVIIIth centuries celebrated by Joja, we have serious reason to question the epithet "national" attached to these architectures. We are in the midst of essentialism. Sometimes the intermediary space (porch, veranda, covered entryway) with its symphony of (pen)umbra, sometimes the "style" of one prince or another, sometimes an architecture regionally and socially circumscribed (the peasant house) is considered Romanian. All of these "obviously Romanian" attributes mutually exclude each other from their own monologue about power.

## Atypic Modernists, Non-Modernists and Post-Modernists

When we study Romanian architecture, we must divide our attention between those who escape the modernist net and those who could be called properly post-modernists. Post-modernism in Romania is so scattered and fragmentary that the detective-hermeneutic work involved in finding and explaining it has to sample the entire context having made it possible. We are interested here especially by those modern architects who did not respect the "right half" of the time line suggested earlier (i.e. the post-1953 period), namely the officially orchestrated succession of aesthetics in the order given above. In addition, we will investigate the "relaxation" of the 1980's, when details and elements of late modernism and post-modernism had arrived in marginal architectures while at the top the design and execution of the "New Civic Center" were in progress.

What has been said so far suggests a preliminary unified answer: in post-Stalinist Romanian architecture there are deviations from modernism (i.e. from the international style, from lyric functionalism or from Bauhaus functionalism). They take on the guise of "alterations" of the official East European post-Khrushchevian aesthetics by the officials themselves — the architecture of "national identity" and that of the "New Civic Center" — or that of minute divergences, neither overt rebellion nor alternative discourse (as was Hungarian organic architecture). Rather, they were "accidents" without great significance to the official discourse. Built with the indispensable complicity of provincial party leaders or under the wing of the heir apparent Nicu Ceaușescu and/or of his "court" (the Young Communist Union and the Communist Student Union, the two powerful youth leagues in which people were groomed for later Communist Party member-ship, and of which the dictator's eldest son was the boss), these edifices acted as safety valves, in the same way in which little off-color remarks (called "lizards" in the jargon of those times) were allowed to slip by in the very well-tempered literary works of "court" writers.

Beyond the "politically correct" architecture, there was a parallel, fragmentary, peripheral architecture, obsessed by the beauty of architectural shapes more than by any kind of explicit or implicit rebellion. The youth hostels designed by teams led by Professor Emil Barbu ("Mac") Popescu (Dorin Ştefan, Viorel Simion, Petre Ciută, Alexandru Andrieş and the other authors of the memorable exhibition at Căminul Artei in 1988) are examples of atypical vocabularies for the time and place of their construction. They were the products of an eclectic cosmopolitanism, more or less synchronous with Western experiments, if inevitably second to these. Louis Kahn[33], Japanese metabolism (Kisho Kurokawa's 1986 visit to Bucharest was a triumph), Stirling and Meier, contextualism and Mario Botta, the neo-rationalists and high-tech architecture — all this bouillon of formal references was in its day the charm of certain architects in the School of Architecture in Bucharest, such as Zoltan Takacs, the most imitated professor from the School in the past twenty years. Late-modern "eclecticism" lacked, however, a revolutionary or, even critical, or self-reflective agenda of its own, other that the implicit refusal of the official uniformity.

The Hariton brothers, Alexandru Beldiman, Radu Radoslav, Florin Biciuşcă, Viorel Hurduc, Cristian Severin, Andrei Vlad, Şerban Sturdza, Vlad Gaivoronski and Ioan Andreescu are only a few of the authors and/or chiefs of projects and works where volumetry became relatively complex. The (more) consistently decorated façades began to display timid arches, columns and gables of "post-modern" inspiration. The modification was confined, however, to the level of decoration (the very fact of its re-appearance was a sign of change), of the shape of balconies. The group never questioned the official policies regarding urbanism or the monolithic, single-block character of edifices and screen-façades in residential ensembles (Ştirbei-Vodă, Tei, 1 Mai). A late issue of *Arhitectura R.S.R.* celebrated a lateral façade (by Hurduc) of a residential compound on 13 Septembrie Avenue (today the first floor is occupied by Sexy Club). The presence of two semicircular windows and of an also curvilinear balcony on an otherwise blind front, or that of face brick for the entire compound seemed such triumphs, such heroic achievements... In fact, the main façade was rigidly symmetrical and quite simple, resulting from the interplay of long balconies.

"Post-modernism" was satisfied with its own marginal condition: isolated details on a lateral façade. Under the circumstances, the very fact of getting any money at all for façades and finishings from the incredibly thin building budgets seemed extraordinary. The surfaces (allowed by the government per resident) had been increased somewhat, after the Communist leader's announcement of a new ideal: each Romanian should have a room of one's own by the year 2000. Consequently, more elaborate partial projects could be designed in comparison with the standard-sections heretofore allowed, while at the same time the living space could be increased. The results were seen in buildings where the volumetry eluded the standards of prefabrication and which, oddly, were in consonance with the socialist-realist comeback in the new civic center despite their conspicuous participation in a completely different stylistic epoch. What do I mean to say? Some testimonies indicate that some of the better architects involved with the design of the civic center intended to produce, in fact, historicist post-modernism. It seemed possible to manipulate the regime in that direction; was it asking for historic references and prestigious quotations from the past? Very well, it would get them. Bofill had already done likewise in the same epoch. Some brought Bofill albums to the studio as documentation.

A parade of Bofill-isms, Krier-isms and other idioms of the post-modern decade joined hands in this contest for the "New Civic Center". I don't know if or where the sketches submitted to the many successive internal contests for every building variant and even for every hall might still be around. In 1984 or '85, Mr. Patriciu showed us the slides of the contest, underscoring, naturally, the proposals of his team. They had designed the entire boulevard of the Victory of Socialism as an homage to "hard & heavy" post-modernism. Ancient Egypt, Palladio and Caracalla's Baths all congregated on one and the same façade. I don't even want to imagine whose would have been the — tens of — statues atop the attics of this boulevard, had this proposal been accepted. Examples taken from Marne-la-Vallée bloomed overnight on the drawing boards of Romanian architects who competed for the honor of building on the ruins of historic Bucharest, in a demiurgical, Faustian (as Anca Petrescu labelled it) frenzy to immortalize their names, by replacing history with their own masterpieces. It was an opportunity unmatched by any since Carol II, that of rebuilding Bucharest from the ground up. It was the chance to edify a post-modern Bucharest, the amplest such intervention in Europe. Many foreign architects who saw the pile actually gave this verdict. The guilt for the demolitions would forever belong to Ceaușescu: dictatorship often provides such immeasurable joys to architects. Was Mitterand not doing the same sort of thing (in Paris)? Yet the renown of the new buildings would forever belong to their creators.

It appeared that, by an utterly weird turn of events, architecture would (could) fare better than all other arts and the rest of society, too. Moreover, architecture seemed to become a flagship art, as it had been before under other dictatorships. The Institute of Architecture "Ion Mincu" already regarded itself as bulwark of "liberalism," although it had little grounds to justify this renown. The Institute, in fact, lived out the lingering memory of the ex-Rector Ascanio Damian and organized, through Mac Popescu's personal ties, "research" trips in the West from which some even returned — otherwise the "eighties-ist" atmosphere was as frozen here as anywhere in the country. The architecture school was in effect the outpost in a bitter confrontation between generations, turned into a "stylistic" conflict. The entire authority of the institution was brought in to prevent the infiltration of post-modern discourse. A few Stalinist dinosaurs were left — toothless, but still kicking — in our school. The remainder of the professors were "sixties-ists", hard-core modernists, owing their style less to an intimate conviction than to the practical impossibility of any other type of design at that time in Romania. Their assistants betrayed them, flirting with the latest styles, gleaned from the few magazines that still made it across the border. They were not all-too-young assistants, because hiring in all universities had simply ceased. This created an important generation gap camouflaging (also) aesthetic tensions.

As a graduate student between 1984 and 1990, I was in the midst of the post-modern breach and witnessed its extinction into deconstructionism after 1988. Back then, at the architectural conferences organized by Club A (the architectural students club), Dorin Ștefan and Viorel Hurduc showed us slides from Paris; the contest for Tête Défense (where the Romanian entries outnumbered the American and Japanese ones), the La Villette Park, Bofill's projects. Those who (still) returned from the trips to the West organized by Mac Popescu also brought slides to the club, as did then-assistant Sorin Vasilescu, a child of his own good fortune. We watched them with a sort of wishful religiosity.

To flirt with the "latest fad" of the West was to earn an infamous label which I wore with concealed pride, as a Jew would wear the yellow star. Some of our professors were vigilant in sniffing out red columns, historicist quotes, and ironies, although their assistants were post-modernists. Dinu Patriciu presented his works for the United Arab Emirates and his proposals for the Victoria Socialismului Blvd., copies of Ricardo Bofill or Leon Krier. Being post-modernist was a sweet subversion, in which we luxuriated ecstatically, gambling with our grades and, implicitely, with our future job assignments. There were still sparks of life in the famous Club A where all kinds of tiny sidesteps were still permitted, mostly in song lyrics (Alexandru Andrieș, Timpuri Noi) or in the little jokes of stand-up comedy (Divertis-Distractis).

The projects commissioned by the U.A.E. and executed by the team of architects headed by Cornel Dumitrescu (then Rector of the Institute of Architecture) in the mid-eighties were examples of "historicist" synchronicity. Hotels that reminded one of the Falcon of the Sheiks, palaces for emirs, phantasmagorical apartment buildings — all were Freudian releases of late-modern and post-modern unfulfilled desires on the part of our young architects. Among these the most visible ballet-dancers were Dinu Patriciu and Romeo Simiraș, Viorel Simion, Petre Ciută, Francisc Echeriu.

On the theoretical level, echoes of the current events in world architecture still rang in the pages of the trade publication *Arhitectura* (for example in the series on contextualism produced by Dorin Ștefan or the presentation of recent achievements). The magazines available at the American Library — if one dared to go there, and not many did — filled our informational "black holes" with bits and pieces about Jencks, Collin Rowe, Blake, and other post-modernist topics.

Perhaps not by chance, therefore, did the first signs of a timid, skin-deep, meager "change of face" — nevertheless a change — arrive in the mid-to late eighties from outside Bucharest. Soon it became obvious, however, that Romanian "post-modernism" had no connection, other than "façade-ism", with the Western discourse, and that the vast destruction of the center of Bucharest was not going to be followed by vast architectural experiments.

### Communist Disneyland

"The amplest post-modern intervention in Europe?" The Victory of Socialism Boulevard and the House of the Republic are products of the same type of urban intervention aiming to "rationalize" and monumentalize the organically-developed cities[34] of Europe. These artificial implants into the mediaeval tissues of cities are to be found everywhere, after the utopian projects of the French Revolution and those of the Enlightenment, especially in inter-bellum Europe. Important Italian cities, including Rome, then Berlin, Moscow (1935) and Bucharest itself (1932-35) are "monumentalized" on paper and — partially — in fact. The urbanistic plan for Bucharest provided for the configuration of a new civic center. Where? Surprise: on Arsenal Hill, that is, precisely where Ceaușescu's regime would build it in the eighties[35].

The methods of composition — collages of classical / eclectic elements, quotations[36] with an evocative/aesthetic function[37], simulacra, eulogy of the urban façade[38] — are without a doubt analogous to those celebrated by post-modern architecture. Essential ingredients are, however, missing: the irony, the double coding, the aside or clin d'oeuil to warn us, jokingly, about the concessions to kitsch meant to flatter mass culture. The ensemble, on the contrary, is starched and dead-serious, taking itself and expecting to be taken seriously, like a group of party officials and Security members (the Romanian Securitate was the equivalent of the Soviet Cheka/OGPU/NKVD/KGB) in black suits with dandruff on their shoulders, white cotton socks and loafers. The humor here is involuntary, the irony belongs to the critics, not to the authors, to the interpretation and not to the creation. Robert Venturi carefully took apart the failures of modern monumental buildings and concluded that they wanted to "speak" with the "wrong" words. He called them "dead ducks". The new Civic Center in Bucharest is one such dead duck; unfortunately, following the example of the Soviet dwarf, it is the largest in the world.

The palace which, along with the devastated area around it, made the object of the architectural contest "Bucharest 2000", changed its name after the Revolution and became the beloved child of Parliament members. The results of the contest have most likely left them unimpressed. And why would they be? (Not only) the members of our Parliament believe that, above political differences, their building is an expression of the constructive genius of the Daco-Roman people. The House of the Republic is also an international "smash hit". This kind of architecture pleases not only scores of upstarts (for weddings, baptisms) but also entire schools of diplomatic small fry (for symposia, conferences).

After a detour, the ex-center of absolute power in Romania has become just what it should not have, that is the absolute edifice of the new power. The retouches are skin-deep; the hall formerly called "Romania" is today an official concert hall; the ground floor houses an art gallery, whose entrance is flanked by thick rows of anti-terrorist troops as colonnade of atlantes. The official character of the building lives on and continues to be nurtured through the manipulation of the interior space and of the symbolistic of the national collective identity. If the Presidency moved there, Ceaușescu's urban testament would be fulfilled to the letter. The fact that changing the destination of the House of the Republic (now Palace of the Parliament) was not allowed during the competition for the "rewriting" of the zone is in itself an eloquent piece of evidence supporting what has been said above.

The international urban planning competition "Bucharest 2000", the largest ever organized in Romania, already has its own history. Hundreds of hectars on the south side of downtown, the area where the most brutal intervention took place in the 1980's, await the financing schemes that would make possible the execution of the buildings conceived by Meinhard von Gerkhan. The same as Défense (the district of architectural/urbanistic experiments in Paris), this mangled area of the urban tissue could be regenerated, on the basis of and following a master plan obtained thorough the contest, within a few decades. Safeguarding the function of the House itself, a stricture imposed by the officialities of the day, did, however, alter essentially the final results, only to confirm once again Speer's opinion that architecture can be manipulated through the requirements of the given theme[39].

Restructuring the area around the House / Palace of Parliament was on the Architects' Union agenda as early as 1990. In 1991, a national contest of ideas was even organized, concerning the House of the People, its adjacent zone, and what to do with both. The ideas submitted then are still quite interesting, even those whose execution remains in perpetuity pure utopia. Above all, they are worth quoting here because they are chiefly post-structuralist ideas.

Having the children take over the House and paint it every which way — the deflation of a pompous architecture, as in the United States of America, by covering it with graffiti — was one of the solutions proposed. The pseudo-paper entitled *Mîine (Tomorrow)* edited by architects Florin Biciuşcă and Dan Adrian for the contest, announced the results of a "national referendum" according to which 85% of the population of Romania had declared that the edifice was "beautiful". As a result, a decree was issued that pronounced it so. The symbolic re-building of Arsenal Hill by turning the place into a grave mound would have left only the top floor of the House exposed. Of course, Parliament would have continued to function in it in an underground bunker. The immense space is nearly impossible to manage even as it is, so it's hard to imagine the cost of burying over 18,000 square meters. Another project suggested that the façade be covered with a huge glass triangle. The result, beside the concealment of the hideousness behind it, was clear: the Great Pyramid in Little Paris. The reference to I. M. Pei's pyramid at the Louvre Museum was transparent. The grand prize, however, was awarded to a project deconstructing the zone, whose architecture was to be once again criss-crossed by the streets and lanes of recent memory.

Unfortunately, all of these are limited and essentially utopian interventions which do not resolve any of the functional problems of the area: the traffic, the rending of the street tissue, the gap between the extant and the proposed to exist. In addition, no solution has yet been given to the apparent impossibility of ever finishing the building other than superficially. The leaders of

Parliament, in love with their edifice, continue to pump important sums into finishing it. Opening the huge art gallery toward Izvor is part of this program. Inaccessible to any but the elite of power and money, the gallery is deprived of its reason to be. Similarly, there is the Parliamentary restaurant, which can be rented for weddings and baptism feasts. Thus the House becomes a privileged landmark for staging rites of passage — something that ought to be food for the thoughts of anthropologists.

The well-tempered optimism displayed by its organizers with regard to the results of the "Bucharest 2000" contest was justified. The winning project is intelligent and flexible enough to be able to accommodate future pulsations of the city center. Although it preserves the House in its present stage — a requirement of the theme which was probably a gaffe and above all a blunder of the jury — von Gerkhan's project does offer solutions for dissipating its character of condenser of the visual vectors, shown as it is in flattering perspectives from every available angle. However, the vivacious changes occurring even as we speak in the physiognomy of the boulevard could suggest another way out of the situation. For better or worse, private property inevitably has cut its own slice out of the totalitarian pie. A general phenomenon of pseudo-vernacular virility[40] has already wiped the traces of the "victory of socialism" from the façades and replaced them with marble, granite (or imitations thereof), air conditioners and screens of billboards.

The post-modern solution could be provided still by Disneyland and the American Main Street, but in the version Venturi introduced in *Learning from Las Vegas*. For him, urban theatrical props — architecture as symbolically decorated shelter, with façades functioning as signals — are proof of the vitality or urban civilization. After all, the architecture of the boulevard at stake is a market-district architecture, like the one of "Voaleta" (Gabroveni and Lipscani Streets, for instance), except on a gigantic scale. Accepting its condition of a commercial-residential

165

neighborhood for the low middle class ("mahala") located in the very historic heart of the city could have been its salvation. Everything that today is kitsch, once it were pushed beyond the limits of its aggressiveness, could be tamed and could become picturesque through simple operations we can learn from the aforementioned models. We would have had today a possible communist Disneyland in Bucharest. The profile of the House as Absolute Edifice should have been played down to the minimum, while the centers of interest in the area would have proliferated. The political attractiveness of the House should have been annihilated, the totalitarian symbol in the national collective imaginary, undermined. It could truly have become — when it would have acquired enough substantiality — a post-modern success: commerce, entertainment and, it goes without saying, mass culture. Which would have been the best function for Casa Republicii? A huge casino: Caesar's Palace, its atomic-bomb shelter turned into a monumental safe.

The two plazas, one in front of the House, the other in front of the department store Unirea, could be the sites of a couple of engaging amusement parks in which, coming out of McDonald's (indispensable from such cityscapes)[41], children could ride the roller-coaster, octopuses — orgies of lights and advertisements. Red columns, green and blue capitals, Coca Cola and towers. Does it seem too "apocalyptic"? No, not for a market district. No, for Bucharest. And here's why: Romania's capital city undergoes at intervals "plastic surgery" which almost always radically transforms it. In the XIXth century, earthquakes and fires caused the replacement of almost all important buildings they'd destroyed, with the exception of churches. In her study, "Bucharest — City between East and West", the late Dana Harhoiu talks about the martyrdom of our own urban memory. Thus, although the first documentary mention of Bucharest occurred in 1459, the oldest still-standing edifices were built in the second half of the XVIth century. The urban works undertaken during the Kingdom, which

166

filled downtown Bucharest with eclecticism, were built on the ruins of the old mediaeval inns and lanes. Magheru Boulevard, which was the first consistently modern axis of the city (being considered at the time an European priority and increasing the scale of the patriarchal city), in its turn replaced pre-existing buildings. Simu Museum, the delicate Ionic temple/art gallery, was crushed in order to make room for the twin apartment buildings Eva-ONT. Carol II and his architects planned a Bucharest of the kind hoped for by Călinescu: heroic, marmoreal, neoclassical. Only the course of history prevented the transmogrification of the capital into another Fascist EUR '41.

This perpetual state of palimpsest of the city, of geological stratification of its ages manifests itself, however, through the lack of continuity of street fronts. Victoriei Avenue is the most eloquent case in point. The alternating styles, heights of corniches, squares and plazas confer its distinctive character to Podul Mogoșoaiei (the old name of this old city way). Perhaps this is why, in Budapest's dense street front, the office building recently raised by Buick respects the alignment, the height and the registers of its neoclassical neighbors, although it is a high-tech edifice. At the same time, American high-rises can be proposed in Bucharest, without having anything to do with the site or with its history; where? Near the Athenaeum, or the Savings Bank CEC.

Discontinuous, fragmentary, eclectic — downtown Bucharest is all these. This is why a master plan must guide the future urban development of the area which is still in ruins today. If such outrages can occur in an established area of the historic center, it is difficult to imagine what would happen, without a structuring urban vision, in an area where today only wastelands remain. The adventure of building a city center for the years after 2000 is, therefore, a risky endeavour on the thin blade that could separate an unmanageable city of headless high-rises, like Hong-Kong and Singapore, from an articulate and fluid European capital, intelligent from a urbanistic standpoint. The ball is quickly moving into the

167

court of real estate and financial policies, which urbanism can steer only discreetly, from underneath the surface.

## The Post-Modern Gypsy

At the international seminar *Beyond the Wall — Architecture and Ideology in Central and Eastern Europe*, which took place in 1995 in Bucharest, Ioan Andreescu, professor at the School of Architecture in Timișoara, presented the situation of those Gypsy "palaces" in his native city. The best among these super-houses are replicas of the French eclecticism of the last century, executed in genuine materials, carrying million-dollars price tags. There are even architects who have specialized in this classic(izing) architecture, honestly, therefore estimably, executed.

My colleague's argument was that residences of this type are in fact manifestoes of a heretofore marginalized world which refuses to continue to accept its social status of a pariah. However, like all manifestoes, they are excessive. And if their intention was to come out of and dispel the isolation outside, the result now is an isolation at the top of the money hierarchy. I believe, therefore, that these houses send no "integrationist" signals, but rather defy the city/community, by violating the norm and the prevailing, accepted common sense. I am not in a hurry to condemn the phenomenon, but I cannot be too "post-modern" either, and see in it who knows what frenzied (ethnic?) energy, worthy of our applause. Quite often, the apparition of such houses in non-Gypsy neighborhoods leads to a negative contamination of those areas, which are abandoned little by little by the non-Gypsies; it leads to the sharp fall in real estate value and to their transformation into slums.

An interesting aspect, though, is that the Romanian upstart does not refuse the pompous architecture of doubtful taste so dear to the Gypsy billionaire. On the contrary, Ioan Andreescu showed, wealthy Romanians build gypsum and plastic copies of the aforementioned palaces, which are, in turn, marble copies of a style — eclecticism — itself assembled exclusively through cut-and-paste devices, loans and collages. The indefinite mirror-reflection, amnesiac and recessive, of the original motif disfigures and impoverishes semantically an architecture designed to proclaim the social prestige or at least the opulence of the proprietor. This new/pseudo-vernacular, in no way inferior to the one celebrated by Charles Jencks among possible ramifications of post-modernism, plays today the role of anti-modern rhetoric, visually the most violent of urban relationships, quantitatively the most explosive.

A case in a league of its own (vernacular architecture, pop culture and Disneyland all in one) is the "post-modern" *Southfork Ranch in Hermes Land*. Unique in Romanian architecture, Mr. Ilie Alexandru, owner of the group of firms "Hermes", sponsored the TV game show "Robingo" and the local Orthodox cathedral (whose feast-day had to be, therefore, St. Elijah/Ilie), threw oranges out of his carriage as Christmas gifts for children, bought computers for the school attended by one of his own children and renovated the maternity ward where another child of his was being delivered. But the most spectacular product of his magnanimous spirit of a benefactor, for which he deserves the attention of any serious study of contemporary Romanian architecture to be undertaken from now on, is Hermes Land, the post-apocalyptic compound just outside of Slobozia. Here a replica of Southfork Ranch[42] of "Dallas" memory where the Ewing family saga unfolded (itself a product of post-modernism) co-exists with an artificial landscape dotted with mediaeval castles, artesian wells, pagoda-like Gypsy houses and a replica of the Eiffel tower. For a small fee, anybody can visit this Hollywoodian ensemble. Hermes Land is deservedly a public success, allegedly attended by two million visitors every year; however, since these are figures given by the proprietor, they very well may be like him — that is, exaggerated.

If we wish to find what Ceaușescu did not succeed to build — a major post-modern intervention (where post-modernism, however, utterly lacks irony and is in fact more in the eye of the beholder, i.e. the post-factum interpretation) singling Romania out as the site of a pasteboard Jerusalem — we should look for it not in downtown Bucharest, but near Slobozia.

## *Instead of Conclusions*

The question whether or not there is a Romanian architectural post-modernism does not have an easy, straightforward answer, but an answer which is polimorphous, ambiguous and complex-contradictory, like post-modernism itself. We cannot give this answer without and in the same breath qualifying (effeminating) the affirmation.

Here are some possible answers.

a) An atypical modern architecture and an un-modern architecture, as we've tried to show above, may be identified. The atypical character of this modernism is determined by comparison either with the international phenomenon (the architecture of the "national identity") or with mainstream architecture inside the borders (one-of-a-kind buildings with late-modern and post-modern nuances).

b) We have not had an explicit, manifest discourse directed against modernism or the manner in which it was used in the ex-communist space.

c) There was a post-modern decade in the Romanian school of architecture, practically coinciding with the worldwide pheno-menon itself, a decade in which were prominent a handful of then young architects; Dorin Ștefan, Alexandru Beldiman, Dinu Patriciu, Viorel Hurduc, Florin Biciușcă.

d) What has a post-modern appearance, or is constituted by the same methods as post-modern architecture does not in fact belong to post-modernism: the new civic center. Since the potential does exist, this can be recovered, however, for post-modernism, through the very devices suggested by the fragmentary interventions of the new vernacular upon the "Victoria Socialismului" Boulevard.

e) We are the spectators of a virtual communist Disneyland taking concrete shape in the Southern Plain (i.e. near Slobozia).

f) On the contrary, what does not seem post-modern — the pseudo/neo vernacular architecture, from the Gypsy palaces in Hermes Land and the residences of the rich upstarts, to new churches and certain weirdly flamboyant holes-in-the-wall — has common genes with the American post-modernism: perennial ephemerality (poster-façades, pasteboard décor), simulacra (ceramic granite, linoleum tile, stucco marble), nostalgic eclecticism, pastiche and allusive reference, celebration of popular culture. The inexhaustible vitality of this architecture is also "American" and, at the same time, a beneficial "breaking" of the monopoly that state and administrative power heretofore have had on the expression through monumental edifices.

## III. 6. On Poisoning Places

In what follows, I will confront the instruments of one of the most coherent ways of understanding architecture — founded on Heidegger's philosophy — with the empirical data of a traumatized space — Bucharest. In the process, we shall rely on *The Origin of the Work of Art* (tr. rom. Gabriel Liiceanu and Thomas Kleininger, Bucharest; Humanitas, 1995) and on the collected works of Christian Norberg-Schulz (whose name is abbreviated in the following text as CNS), but most of all on his *Genius Loci — Towards a Phenomenology of Architecture* (New York: Rizzoli, 1979).

In a related essay, published in the special issue of *Secolul 20* featuring Bucharest, and reprinted later in *Khora*, I was using a more recent book by CNS, *Habiter* (1982), which structures the themes of his work. His former studies, however, the first to be devoted to concepts he introduced, have a freshness which later on was lost; meanings or directions the author had not completely developed as yet seem more useful to us today in the interpretation of an, alas, too well-known segment in the history of our architecture. The post-modern decade, post-structuralism and most of all, in Romania, an operation of dismantling almost an entire city unmatched in contemporary history have all washed in the meantime over CNS's work. All could cause a crisis of a view which must be founded on calm, on an organic development, on being at peace with the world and with the space of one's own living. Can it then still be useful? To answer this question, even tentatively and by introducing the notion of *poisoning*, we shall have first of all to circumscribe and to define, inside the "existential space", the notions of *place* and *genius loci*.

172

After commenting on the poisoning of places, we will also suggest possible ways out of the doldrums, in accordance with principles afforded us by modern philosophy. We will be able thus to offer answers and to suggest, to those who believe that philosophy and theory of architecture are two intellectual activities removed from the "real" problems of architecture, that, quite the contrary, it is no logger possible to examine and understand this domain or at least a part of its problems without the theoretical metadiscourse.

## *"Existential Space"*

The space in which we dwell (but "Dwelling is the manner in which mortals are on the earth" said Heidegger in *Building Dwelling Thinking,* tr. rom. p. 179) is two-fold: what it is and how it is perceived as phenomenon. 1) On the one hand we talk about *space* itself (but, Heidegger reminds us, at stake is not that *spatium* whose attribute is *extensio*; it is *Raum*, room in the sense of place, of the place of one's own, the native place where one builds one's dwelling, the earth-place which pro-poses[43] itself in the work of art[44]); for CNS, space is the "tri-dimensional organization of the elements that make up a place".

2) On the other hand, we talk about the *character* or the spirit of that space of existence. CNS uses this Latin term — *genius loci* — to warn us that every place has its spirit, its guardian angel. The character of a place is defined by CNS as "the general atmosphere", which is the most comprehensive property of any lived-in space (1979, 11). Character is "the basic way the world is given" (14); it is a function where time and by extension season are variables changing the phenomenal aspect of the place. But, for the same reasons, CNS believes that light is what determines character and, in rapport with the materials and shape of the place (or of its buildings), the vertical dimension (the qualitative axis of space) answers the following questions: 1) how is the building set on the

173

ground and 2) how is it raised toward the sky. Character is an attribute of what is built by man, as it depends on the manner in which things are made and, therefore, "it is determined by the technical achievement ('the building')" (15). At this point we must observe that natural places cannot have character, which once again ties up CNS's demonstration with Heidegger's observations in *The Origin of the Work of Art,* concerning the latter's being an artifact, hence in opposition to natural beauty.

Space has as distinctive property *orientation*, by which is meant a *permanent rapport with the centers* and a *vectorial displacement* toward those centers — a perceptual field, a "concrete" space, far from the abstract distance of Euclidian geometry (11). Instead, character has as distinctive property *identification*. Architecture gives density and concreteness to the properties of existential space; it amplifies (it should and can do it) the potential attributes of this Heideggerian "always already" which is[45] the earth on which it stands[46]. In this manner, architecture renders visible the *genius loci*. Moreover, architecture can quantify that character and, afterwards, transmit it somewhere else. It does this through *motifs* and *patterns*; they are to some extent the algorithm for the character of a "family" of buildings which constitute a place (15) and, more than that, they "serve to transpose a character from place to place" (ibidem). Artifacts such as works of architecture "explain the environment and make its character obvious" (15). In other words, character may be i) given — it is found already constituted in a site where we are to build — or it can be ii) proposed by us where it does not yet exist.

A given character, in its turn, can be 1a) simply *visualized as such* in its stability (the architect builds what he "sees" as datum of the place) or it can be, as a corollary to 1a, 1b) *amplified* through the new building, but it can also be 2) *complemented*, if it is still in a state of ambiguity, or if it misses certain data to become decidedly manifest. Character is somewhat of a "Nude Descending A Staircase": the sum of phenomenal aspects related to change as

174

much as to stability, of which I will treat directly. Nonetheless, character must not be regarded as an "ideatic reduction", as an essence of all successive aspects the place might put on. We do not study in a place only the shape it presents itself in (and even not primarily this shape) but the sum of the evanescent attributes it earns, or it affirms, in the confrontation with time.

An immediate observation is that an essential dimension of this change is light, which so radically distinguishes between a building in Crete and one in Iceland, especially as it is not just the given light but also the reaction of the place, of the earth and of the other added materials, to this light; the play of light on things is as important in defining place as, in prosaic terms, the amount of photons reaching it from the outside. The place, as is immediately apparent, has an alchemy of its own which the architect will "hear" — and by saying this I am also implicitly reminding us of the necessity to take possession of a place through all of our senses; having become more and more centered, after the invention of perspective, hence after the rationalization of the view, on the sense of sight to the detriment of the other senses, especially that of touch[47], the architect as well as the user became alienated from the materiality of houses, from the concreteness and the plenitude of the experience of space.

A place, therefore, must be experienced through all five senses, as well as — most importantly — remembered especially through childhood memories, probably the most powerful. In the exercises I assign my second-year architectural students who take the Theory of Architecture/Phenomenology course, and in which they are asked to describe a significant place in their lives, the theme of the childhood place returns time and again, along with, naturally, the grandparents' house. The affective memory, as it were, shows the data supplied by empirical experience in a favorable light. In these conditions, it becomes obvious why notions such as "utopian architecture" or "typified/standardized buildings" are aberrations that depart from a vision of architecture derived from Heidegger's philosophy.

In addition, character derives from a tectonic relationship; on the vertical axis of space (i.e. its qualitative axis), character accounts for the manner in which buildings a) rise to the sky and b) sit on the earth. An intelligent architect, like the one celebrated in Kenneth Frampton's *Studies in the Tectonic Culture* (Cambridge-London; Graham Foundation /MIT Press, 1995) will build at the interface of the three vectors (2) of which one is the tectonic, while the other two are *topos* and *typos*. Tectonic, Frampton underlines, is the "art of articulations" which accompanies the gesture of *techné*, that of producing a built-in space; a gentle modification of the earth which pro-poses itself in the work of architecture, so that the final result should be reminiscent of that *Gelassenheit* Heidegger recommends or the "Let it be" of Beatles fame. Architecture, in this view, amounts to a "placing in the Open", to use Rilke's subtle phrase in Heidegger's interpretation, of the dynamics of forces "un-loading" into the ground, of the resistance against gravity (27).

All these preliminary co-ordinates configurating the concept of genius loci had to be given because one of its essential attributes is *stabilitas loci*, CNS believes; if the spirit of place is present it is thereby stable despite its imponderable character, that is, it is capable to absorb change within certain limits. The changes absorbed by the spirit of place are, of course, those that continue, amplify or complement it; a "change" that disposes of it out of hand cannot be absorbed by definition. What are these "certain limits" (18), however, CNS omits to clarify, but we do know that one of them is mono-functionality; "a place which is suitable only for a certain single function will soon become useless" (ibidem). The "functional" diversity of a place is thus an essential condition of its survival *as* place. Otherwise it will disappear at the same time as its spirit. A certain *degree of invariance* of the properties of a place is to be presupposed so that it may preserve its spirit, once it has established itself as such. Sedimentation (a function of time)

176

is the process by which a place receives the consistency of its attributes and even, I shall venture to say it here, the consciousness of those attributes.

## *Poisoning a Place*

What happens then to a place whose "character" does not lie in invariance but, rather, in the — radical — change of its constituting projects? Clearly we cannot talk about the capacity to absorb change inside certain limits anymore, hence about any *stabilitas loci*. In the terms in which it has been so far defined, this character would be more of a cruel destiny. The "djinn" of a place such as Bucharest (I don't quite dare to call it evil genie although so it seems to me), weird as that may sound, constitutes itself out of the inter-killing of the barely sketched, successively born and quickly dying "genies".

I call this process *poisoning a place*; in a poisoned place, unrelated stages of the different epochs having come and gone coexist uncomfortably; these stages have continuously replaced one another in part or in toto, most often by violence (fire, earthquake, bombardment, razing). If, as CNS thinks, "every place ought to have the capacity to receive different contents", in the case of a poisoned place, it pays dearly for its past — the reality of having undergone the violent reciprocal replacements of so many divergent projects — by becoming unable to "say" anything to the architect who would come to "hear" it, in order to inaugurate, at last, a stable character.

The poisoned place becomes mute and this, more often than not, is a permanent affliction. Its muteness is no less violent than the former battles. The place becomes wasteland. It is no longer a space of order, but a topos of chaos. The palimpsest-like quality (layers upon layers, blind walls, fragments) of Bucharest, so eulogized by some architects as the city's defining trait, is in fact the sign of its incapacity to sustain the continuity and the internal coherence of a place. Such a poisoned place becomes quite easily a favorite object of interpretation for deconstruction — so wallowing in traces, negations, divergent layers, scars inflicted by temporal power — but ceases to be of any interest to phenomenology.

From this point of view, Bucharest is of more interest to a theoretician of deconstruction such as Peter Eisenman than to, say, Kenneth Frampton. The former rediscovers and places in a favorable light as many different traces and previous layers of the site as can be in his new buildings (see for example the coexistence of the Armory with the Center of Visual Arts in Wexner Center, Columbus, Ohio, or the old house translated on the ground to draw a new one at the extension of the College of Architecture of the University of Cincinnati, Ohio). In contrast, the latter wrote that it is a lack of professionalism to level out an undulating terrain in order to build new houses, instead of using the potential of that site and terracing it; after which, coming to Bucharest as head of the jury of the International Urban Planning Competition "Bucharest 2000", he saw what was left of Arsenal Hill, which had been leveled out in order to accommodate, after the previous site had been razed and burned, the House of the Republic.

And so inevitably divergent views compete in the research of the character or of the manner in which to build in a poisoned place. Thus, some seek to valuate one or another of the "successive layers" — Constantin Joja regards the inns with windowed balconies as a characteristic not just of Bucharest, but the very sign of a protochronist priority in rapport with modern architecture; for others, Bucharest is a "little Paris"; Dana Harhoiu likens it in her 1997 study (which I will comment upon a little later) to Istanbul because of its wastelands; finally, others, myself included[48], saw it begin to turn into another Phenian into the hands of the Ceaușescu regime. Other architects support the violent overturning of such layers or their continued coexistence — seeing Bucharest as a "palimpsest" as Alexandru Beldiman does or as a place of dramatic urban diversity, such as Victoriei Avenue typifies, according to Professor Dr. Alexandru Sandu. Naturally, if there is no agreement on what is the character of a poisoned place, there is even less hope of an agreement on any plan to develop it in the future.

As proof of this we can also adduce the following occurrence. On one hand, the winning project of the "Bucharest 2000" competition (Meinhard von Gerkhan, Joachim Zeiss) abandons all pretense of trying to understand the/any "spirit of place" and proposes a new urban structure, utterly different from any of the previous, historic stages undergone by the poisoned city. The only link to its past is the old street pattern, reduced, however, to a series of passageways criss-crossing the rigorous system of urban blocks in a manner which, contrasting with this rigor, appears haphazard and, therefore, introduces a welcome tension within the project, a tension that dynamizes the now merely virtual urban space.

On the other hand, the study concerning protected urban zones, winner of several prizes at the 1998 Biennial of Architecture held in Bucharest and made by a team of which I had the honor to be a member, co-ordinated by my colleagues Dan Marin, Radu Florinel and Hana Derer, proposes a vision of two-geared urban development at multiple speeds; "excising" those city areas which possess an identifiable character and, within them, amplifying that character, even at the risk of losing a coherence of the whole which though desirable would be achieved too slowly.

We must remark that phenomenologists from the school of CNS or Frampton prove to be lost when they have to pass judgment on poisoned places and especially when they must offer healing solutions for such places. The notion of character of place obliterates their perception. We know, having painfully learned it first-hand, that there are also tainted characters, such as the character of the new civic center in Bucharest or of many cities

179

in Romania. How should we build now and from now on in Țăndărei, Fetești or Slobozia, where all that is left are prefab apartment buildings of unparalleled ugliness? Should we perhaps "flatter" the character or such places as it is given now? This is what the jury of Bucharest 2000, headed by Frampton, seemed to believe; the House of the Republic is a datum of the site and must be included as such in any solution for healing the area. Therefore none of the projects submitted to the jury took into consideration the idea of an intervention upon the House itself, either to hide it or to enter into a dialogue with it through a variety of compositional devices, thereby interrupting its single-minded, unending monologue.

A poisoned place needs to be looked at as being the resultant of all the strata which cohabit in it at a given moment and by no means should it be frozen in the latest phase in which it is offered to us. Probably more attention should be given to the projects for Sarajevo belonging to such teams of deconstructionist architects as those of Coop Himmelblau or of Lebbeus Woods. The latter belongs to a direction which entitles itself "radical deconstruction"[49], and proposes to mark the scars left by bombardments and other dramas on the respective buildings and to transform these into a sort of cancer cells which pervade in a later phase the entire building. The key image is that of ruin, of an active ruin that acts like a virus, instantaneously infesting the organism and transmogrifying it even as it is devoured.

In what follows, we shall be able to critique, in light of what has been shown above, a recent book about Bucharest, and, afterwards, we may be able to take on the risk of suggesting a few possible practical solutions regarding the configuration or the amplification of the character of one or another of the pieces and bits of the city which have not yet been permanently overpowered by the cancer of self-destruction — which eats us up not only as a society but also, even, at the level of our urban environment.

## *Bucharest — Ideal City? Critique of a False Character*

Questioned under this heading is the main thesis of a book published by the regretted Dana Harhoiu, *Bucureşti între Orient şi Occident* (*Bucharest Between East and West*), Bucureşti; Simetria, 1997), a thesis which at the same time constitutes the novelty of the book. Namely, the author proposes the hypothesis of a Bucharest — ideal city, organized by and according to sanctifying geometrical principles.

The hypothesis has three "heads": 1) Bucharest churches are supposedly arranged along the radii of concentric circles having as *omphalos* Church Sf. Gheorghe Vechi; 2) this "navel of the city" is the head of the corner in a square matrix constituted by Sf. Gheorghe Vechi/Mihai Vodă Monastery/Patriarchal Cathedral/Radu Vodă Church. The axis running through Sf. Gheorghe Vechi — the Patriarchal Cathedral would be the bisectrix of the angle Mihai Vodă-omphalos-Radu Vodă and is continued by the most important commercial road arriving in Bucharest from Moldavia, toward Wallachia's northern border — Calea Moşilor; 3) in general, Bucharest would have been founded in accordance with an ideal diagram akin to Philarete's — a circle "mandala" in which two squares are apposed at 45 degrees.

I am surprised by the lack of press echoes to this revolutionary theory by comparison with the accepted version of urbanistic history: Bucharest, "spontaneous" city, developed "organically" if not downright chaotically, without fortifications because of the Turks, organized around trade and guild churches, with wastelands, with successive layers, competing openly and violently replacing one another and so on. If it were true, a verification the author does not provide convincingly, this theory of the ideal geometry of Bucharest would immediately elicit the interest of researchers wishing to continue and to systematize it, to say nothing of the adherence of at least two kinds of undesirable "defenders" — those single-mindedly obsessed by synchronisms at all cost, all too eager

181

to jump at the opportunity of establishing yet another European "connection" as ideologic-nationalist outlet for the pent-up frustrations of the inferiority complex of the "small culture"; and those all-too-easily mesmerized by anything that feeds their pseudo-esoteric, pseudo-mystical velleities, or that is construed as feeding them, and who see Bucharest as the latest Jerusalem-upon-Dâmbovița and the House of the Republic as an expression of the Temple. Of course, such interpretations would considerably distort the good intention of the book, which cannot be held responsible for its misreading. However, I cannot help but notice in the author's fervor to deny the empirical data, not all of which complement the object of research, an affection for it which impairs her objectivity. Dana Harhoiu "discovers" a hypothesis and then manipulates the data of the city to prove it.

Despite the temptation of its novelty and charm, Dana Harhoiu's theory is methodologically unsound. It combines aspects of the sacred space as interpreted by the phenomenology of architecture (Eliade, Heidegger, Norberg-Schulz) — *axis mundi*, for example, would pass through St. Gheorghe Vechi in the case of Bucharest — with morphological analyses of the urban structure. The tracing of the concentric circles leaves quite a few churches outside of the diagram, which proves that it might not be such a rigorous diagram after all. The identification of the corners of the two apposed squares, derived from Philarete, is difficult to maintain on the map of Bucharest. Batiștei Church is not exactly in the northern corner, nor are Radu Vodă and Sf. Apostoli where they "should" be, while in the north-western and north-eastern corners there are no churches at all.

Very likely, among Bucharest's many old churches, enough can be found to draw among them any geometric diagram one may wish, more or less ideal, on the city map; it does not follow that such diagrams would necessarily have any meaning other than that of playful amusements. Therefore the interpretation of the author of *Bucureşti*... appears to have been made up a posteriori: first the diagrams, then the explanation. The only argument to support the similarity with Philarete would be, I am paraphrasing, that there was a Latin translation of his treatise at the court of Matei Corvin and that another copy of it was found in Russia. From these two examples, D. Harhoiu extracts the risky, to say the least, conclusion that "these ideas had a wide circulation throughout Europe, hence in Eastern Europe as well." Is this not a bit too simplistic, especially when we are talking about an epoch in which books were not as widely available and read as they are today? And what about the missing link between the presence of a book in the library of a prince and the "situation in the field", inside the masonry guilds?

There is no doubt that in the act of founding any city on a pre-established plan there is an incipient geometry, more or less ideal (i.e. Platonic), more or less sacred. Such geometric diagrams can be discovered in the case of cities founded as castra, in the midst of which *cardo* and *decumanus* — the rectangular system of axes of the Roman Empire — still survive today. Even in the case of cities having developed "spontaneously" or "organically" — terms which are actually quite far-fetched when applied by history to the description of a city's becoming — rudiments of a structuring geometry do in the beginning exist. The intentions to pinpoint such rigorous schemes organizing the urban space should not be, therefore, rejected de plano, even in a case as hopelessly tangled as Bucharest. I do not at all exclude the possibility, therefore, that rigorous future studies, based on documents as yet undiscovered, should confirm one or another of the aspects of Dana Harhoiu's theory, or that new work hypotheses should be formulated. For the time being, the beautiful book published by Simetria offers us an enchanting, daring, intellectually stimulating tale — but a tale from whose spell we are awakened as soon as we close the book and go out for a stroll in the empirical city. I am afraid that Bucharest is but *unreal* (meaning chaotic and confusing) or surreal, and hardly *ideal* — no matter how much I wish this were not so.

183

## Is It Possible to Heal Bucharest?

Are we complaining that Bucharest does not have a pronounced profile, a character that can be defined as such, quantified and, hence, continued in new architecture? The clearest thing that may be said about this city's character is that, in the course of its becoming, many different competing projects have shoved each other aside through violence.

A diffuse, uncertain or partially virtual character, to some degree as yet unconstituted, may be emancipated, however, and promoted through a building which valuates its natural gift. We can recall here the example offered by Kenneth Frampton in his text about "critic regionalism" of 1982; designing architecture on a hill can be done two ways — in an inane sort of way, when the hill is leveled (see Arsenal Hill) and on it are built houses totally indifferent to the relationship with their site; or in a thoughtful way, when the undulating site is, on the contrary, valuated and its natural gift is put into a favorable light by terracing. If a tower is to be built, then it is advisable for the tower and for its urban context that it be set up on a height and not in a valley, so that it should be perceived looking up and not the other way. This is why, looked at from Victoriei Avenue, the Bancorex Tower is ill situated, a great deal of the building effort being spent just to raise the tower to street level; in contrast, looked at from Dâmbovița, the tower does not seem tall enough, precisely because the site would have allowed for such a height, but is not used.

Of course, there are a great many places in Bucharest which meet all the requirements outlined above, all of which must be, however, reunited under the umbrella of *coherence*, the attribute that gives them all substance. We will recall, though, that most commentators speak about the discontinuity, fragmentariness, eclecticism of the urban organism. Bucharest is a palimpsest. Its defining traits do not necessarily coincide with desirable attributes of the city that ought to be configured from now on. In other words, examples of city places where the character must be preserved and amplified (Magheru Blvd., coherent and consistent in its pre- and post-war modern structure, practically continuous in height and, a rare thing in Bucharest, even in its modern style) are fewer than examples of places whose character must be completed, outfitted with what is missing from it or even completely replaced. Magheru is a typical example of an area whose character has constituted itself by the violent elimination of the previous one, as is the Lipscani-Victoria Ave. area where the eclectic city displaced the mediaeval market town without leaving a trace.

If this is indeed the character of the city right now, we must cease to pronounce sophisms such as "Bucharest's character consists in the periodic aggression of the different layers succeeding one another through violence." We cannot seriously affirm that the city is a battle-ground and that this is also a desirable attribute of the future city. From materials to style and from its tectonic aspect to the relationship with light, Magheru is a PLACE showing coherence and consistency, which must be preserved as such and where localized interventions must necessarily observe the already aggregated features of this place: level of height, continuous street front, restrained expression, appreciable material consistency (predominance of wall over glass, of the opaque over the transparent).

These features must be quantified in a building code for this area, which would establish the defining traits of the place so that they be reproducible by any subsequent intervention. Also, any such building code would have to provide some leeway, because, its character being very consistent, the place can absorb a certain dose of variation or even divergence from the general rule. Under no circumstances, however, should the building of high-rises be permitted along this perimeter.

Magheru, like the entire downtown, should probably be closed to any but pedestrian traffic and public transportation. Streetcars, trolley-buses, taxis, scooters and bicycles excepted, all vehicular traffic should be shunted to the outer city, with all the subsequent modifications concerning the introduction of a *park-and-ride* system (parking on the perimeter of the inner ring, with the parking fee also covering the cost of public transportation anywhere inside the ring). In addition to safeguarding the center of the city and all those who inhabit and/or use it daily, as many European cities already do to protect their historic centers, the measure would also have preventive value as it would deflect the enormous influx of vehicles bringing upper and middle class suburbanites into the city, a problem compounding the already suffocating city traffic across downtown.

The commonplace of Bucharest-city-of-blind-walls must also be disabled. Those blind walls we cannot help but see everywhere are the sign of a failed urban policy; in the name of the desideratum of a future continuous street front, buildings which are being raised today are deprived of one and sometimes two façades which become at best walls to hang billboards on but which are for certain one source of uglification in the city. More often than not, the nearby building is never torn down and replaced with another equal to the first, thereby absorbing the "reverence" paid it by the city code and, willy-nilly, by the architect and the client. The result is that the blind wall remains in place, testifying to an inadequate manner of understanding the city and its true capacity for continued building. The solution? A realistic city code and licensing policy, which would allow the building being raised today to attain the plenitude of its urban relationship, and leave it to the future building, if it should ever be built, to solve its own set of problems concerning the adequation to the future urban context.

Discontinuity, fragmentariness, eclecticism, thus urban incoherence represent for certain the "character" of a causeway such as Calea Victoriei. The next question though is whether it is to be wished that this "character" be favored and continued (with buildings of different heights, eclectic/equivocal in style), or that it be compensated for and supplanted in what it is lacking, i.e.

continuity, homogeneity, coherence. Placing vertical accents destabilizes such a context even more; it brings to the fore precisely that character of place (i.e. incoherence) it is not desirable to underscore. We may refer to that kind of positive diversity which characterizes neighborhoods such as Parcul Ioanid or Parcul Filipescu, a diversity which, paradoxically to some extent, constitutes the character of those districts. But even so, coherence (both are upper class residential areas, in which prevail the same height and individual lot treatment, relationship with the street and vicinities, as well as lawns, gardens, and parks) is essential, and the differences appear only in the stylistic treatment of the façades.

In other words, this is a different type of diversity than on Calea Victoriei. Victoriei Avenue is the battlefield where different city strata confront one another. These seem to detest each other, with the result that every once in a while one of them is victimized so that another can replace it. The carnage that ensues as the new displaces the old adds nothing relevant to the urban context, but, rather, fractures it even more, making it even more illegible, harder yet to suture. If diversity is not subordinated to a common integrating theme, the character cannot "seat itself" in a place. It has no time to do it. Incoherence is never and nowhere a quality of the urban organism. The violence of grafts and implants allows no respite and no foundation for the configuration of an identity of this renowned Bucharest neighborhood. Its renown, however, is undeserved, and must be quickly emended. If both aforementioned types of differentiating among buildings in one and the same neighborhood are characteristic to Bucharest, it seems obvious, from a phenomenological perspective, but also from common sense, that the restrained diversity of the residential neighborhoods is preferable and to keep, while the major discontinuity of Victoriei Avenue is dysfunctional and to discard.

In the end, all of it is a question of manipulating values. In a self-respecting culture, attributes that derive from a classic understanding of symmetry (order, equilibrium, hierarchy) are promoted as positive. The conclusion of this text seems to be that, in an urban tissue such as Bucharest, diversity is necessary, but incoherence is to be avoided. We can no longer afford to continue this process of poisoning the places of our own existence. This, of course, provided that we care at all about them — something which, alas, is not at all, but at all, evinced neither by the authorities nor by the "consumers", and not even by the members of the architectural profession. In these conditions, we gleefully await — in the midst of the "natural" destruction owed to poverty and lack of sensitivity — the next devastating earthquake, which will once again level the terrain clearing the way for a new stratum of poisoning...

# IV

# ARCHITECTURAL CRITICISM AFTER 1989

## IV. 1. BUCHAREST: UNMITIGATED HISTORY

### The Collapse of the Modern Project

Everything that happens around us in architecture nowadays is the collapse of the autochthonous modern project. Imposed from above — first by King Carol I and the aristocracy, next in its vulgarized form by communists — modernity succumbs without being replaced by an alternative project as temerarious and complete as it has been. Instead, "here comes the grass" (Radu Drăgan); the anomaly is already generalized. Perhaps nothing bears testimony to this state of irrepressible dissolution as does architecture. Although the other arts also have enough to tell, architecture (as remarked by Manfredo Tafuri and Frederic Jameson, the post-modern critic) borders directly upon the societal and ideological projects, to which it is related in a manner more complex than merely as an effect to its causes. In the absence of accurate (or credible) information about functioning of the first system, we can get a general idea by examining the state of architecture and urbanism.

What will we remark? The deplorable state of our historic monuments, which only in the last couple of years has shown some signs of being perhaps reverted (for the moment, the money for the necessary work of maintenance and restoration comes only through state channels, as for many years the state has refused to authorize concession of pilot-projects to private companies; now, even if the state changed its mind, the private enterprises have vanished). Ten years have elapsed and the historic center (the market district around Lipscani) is still a slum right in the middle of the city; nor have the major churches or the modern buildings along the large boulevards been restored. Under these circumstances, to request the discussion of the "statute of post-war historic monument" becomes almost hilarious. (And yet Germany is redoing Stalin/Karl Marx Alee in Meissen porcelain; Tafuri, like all architects I met in Berlin, praised it with restraint.) But why should we deplore only the fate of the historic monuments, when so many shaken buildings in Bucharest await their anti-seismic consolidation? That a "UNESCO expert" was found to propose the demolition of all pre-war architecture, too costly and too complicated for construction engineers to consolidate, is perhaps not such a great feat, after decades of demolitions. However, it is surprising and too much even for Romania that a part of the press has found room to print the aberrations of said expert and that no one has entered into a professional dialogue with this deluded character.

All of this calls to mind yet other "old, yet always new" problems: the lack of communication inside the profession; between the profession and the authorities; amongst authorities... A sad example is the project of the law of architectural practice, which, although submitted more than three years ago, still lingers somewhere in an office in the Ministry of Public Works (MLPAT), a gamepiece on a board where entrepreneurs, construction engineers and small barons of architecture itself call all the shots. No consistent architectural press has been able to quite coalesce; the trade magazine *Arhitectura* is published too infrequently, *Arhitext Design* has strayed from the fresh beginnings of Radu Drăgan and Mihai Pienescu, *Axa* has just come out and lacks writers, and *Virtualia (www.virtualia.org.w)* has been launched just now, with hyper-enthusiasm for hyper-texts, and, I trust, with greater success than the others. Very likely the absence of a professional architectural critique signifies that architecture has not yet reached that "critical mass" which would necessitate its apparition (too few architects, too few remarkable architects, too few worthwhile buildings, and, instead, too many blunders ready for either the psychoanalyst or the fraud-embezzlement-corruption squad or both). However, this absence also denotes the lack of an appetite for theory, of a longing for meta-text and for introspection on the part of architects; it also shows that the lack of a proper artistic education at all levels and in all schools avenges itself by producing mutants who could not care less about our monuments and about our own space as a community; people who, when they find the money, build houses that resemble them: illogical, gaudy, adorned with superposed towers of zinc plate.

And then the banks, oh, the banks! The only bullish investors in their own public image, raising palaces in the midst of a ruined cityscape, defiant provocations thrown in the face of the country's high entropy! Utterly uninterested in the context of their building sites (see Lipscani but also the rest of the country), bank headquarters (and branch offices) are the only edifices where money, quality materials, new technologies (at least in Romania; even if, like the curtain-walls so beloved by our bankers, they have been visually passé for decades elsewhere, cf. Peter Blake's *Form Follows Fiasco*), and even imagination have been in plentiful supply. The bank designed by *Avangarda* on Vasile Conta St. was one of the first clean examples, minus perhaps the cheap allusion to the Statue of Liberty, owed to the fact that the lot on which the bank was built had been the U.S. Embassy parking lot... The main office building of BCR (Romanian Commerce Bank) located in Ghencea, designed by Ştefan Dorin by converting an old factory building, also proves that corporate headquarters continue to be a potential ground for quality architecture, especially since the School of Chicago on. Mammon plays a serious role in the history of architecture, as did its "traditional" clients, Caesar and God himself.

Meanwhile, we continue to finish up the Palace of Parliament cum House of the Republic for our many, tiny caesars who so enjoy

191

cogitating inside. Instead, for no logical reason, City Hall postpones the execution of the project Bucharest 2000, perhaps reluctant to part with the perimeter of the Civic Center, out of which so much sweet honey can be extracted in the form of bribes and other tax-free income from potential investors. These investors, however, are about to become extinct, ousted by the horde of aggressive, lazy and unprofessional rednecks, yet full of airs, who have their seats on the City Council only to oppose any vision that might heal the city.

For the Supreme Creator, too, we are eager and impatient to build gigantesque abodes. The Cathedral of the Nation is already designed, despite the legitimate outcry of responsible intellectuals — duly admonished, with almost proletarian wrath, in the trade journals published by the Patriarchy. What caused and causes indignation is not, of course, the building of a church, but, rather, how and what will be built. The legal means to decide upon and commission a serious project have been ignored; the professionals, snubbed; and a fact which ought to have been spiritually and morally uplifting has been turned into a jugglery trick, where the swiftness of hand of the prestidigitator and the unmindfulness of our society have co-operated. Thus yet another gigantic edifice will pop out of this magic hat — gigantic and therefore stupid, inadequate, like all *hybris*. This syndrome of giga-building on a cosmic scale appears to have infected all of us overnight — architect and client alike, yesterday collaborating as a matter of political course, today, of economical course, yesterday for the victory of socialism, today for the defeat of *minima moralia* and *spiritualia*. Next to the disdain for the space of our dwelling-together, this is the most serious disease — and so gleefully contracted — affecting the health of the national being.

Here we are now at the grand finale of the Romanian modern project; the city is destroyed, and we sing in praise of some doubtful auroral states belonging to its between-the-wars past, because that's pretty much all that's been left untainted. The houses, now abandoned, return to the elements from which they had been called into service. A general urbanistic plan is missing. There is no project to develop the city — the most recent round of local elections proved it. The center is in ruins, a wasteland and a site for tank parades. We do not restore the historic monuments, because we are too busy making high-rises. Scandalous villas dot the contour of the city, and the entrances into it are the most eloquent true-picture of Romania today. As our architecture is, so are we.

## Who Scrapes the Skies of Bucharest?

In a recent issue of the political-cultural weekly "22", the building code and licensing policies of the Capital's historic center are questioned. It would appear that the excessive caution exerted for the protection of the historic center is in fact a resistance to "the apparition of new buildings with a modern look." The overly-cautions Board of Monuments would have become an impediment to progress. Examples are provided, too. An architectural contest was held for the site of the former National Theater. The winning team proposed a tower of comparable size to the Art Deco "Sky scraper", designed by the Americans in the late 1920's, of the Telephone Company. To my knowledge, the requirement to somehow recall, at least on the façades toward Victoriei Avenue, the former presence, on that site, of the National Theater, was met. Today, the project has been taken over by BIP, the same company that designed the tower on Victoriei Avenue, and I hope they will not build yet another opaque bunker, without public spaces, indifferent to its context, praised only by the newspaper *Curentul*. In a different contest, this one for the Palace Hill Plaza, the team who won the second place also proposed a tower in this plaza. "I for one am at a loss," declares the interviewee in "22"'s article, wondering why the first project did not make it past the "conservative" Board of Monuments while the second was to some extent given praise.

Sky-scrapers used to be, it's true, the emblems of modernization, but forty year ago. Nowadays, they continue to be built with fervor only in Asia and in China's special zones; the Petronas twins are probably the most edifying example of the late identification of the illusion of progress with the phallic architecture of high-rises. Hi-tech architecture in China, in turn, is a sad example of what lurks behind a forced and unassimilated development. We know now that even in economy the Asian tigers are not, perhaps, a praiseworthy model.

The architecture of high-rises has become outdated in the rest of the world. Business districts have moved to parks located outside the historic centers of cities (Edinburgh Business Park, designed by Richard Meier, is one example). In American cities, tall buildings have overcrowded downtown areas to the point of saturation. As a result, these areas became depopulated, and then died. Surrounded by rundown districts inhabited by minorities and left to the mercy of delinquents, these downtown areas are strangled by crime and destruction. Coming to work from the suburbs, city and bank clerks need to cross dangerous stretches. I've known the fear of crossing these inner cities in Cincinnati, Seattle, but most of all in Detroit, where the inner city is several miles deep and looks as if it's been bombed. Such are the former historic centers of cities and they look like our Lipscani. The price of land and the isolation — oddly — at the very heart of the city have forced corporations to break through the encirclement and move their headquarters to the perimetral rings, where the malls and large shopping centers were already located. American cities are imploding. There will be no reason to go downtown after five o'clock and, pretty soon, at all, if the destruction continues in the same rhythm. The few measures taken by local administrations or foundations are still timid and isolated. For example, the conversion of warehouses and silos into art galleries and studios is an interesting approach, but it does not solve the high crime rates of the inner cities.

In Western Europe a similar phenomenon is unfolding. Businesses need to be kept in clusters rather than scattered here and there, wherever there's the possibility of a "filling" in the too-dense historic centers, which have extremely strict building codes. For this reason, a division has started to appear a few years ago, by which corporations cut themselves in two; public service, interfacing with the customer, and everything that entails dialogue keep residence in the center, in pavilion-like buildings, often low-profile, inscribed in the street fronts. What is not contact with the public, computers and bank personnel, production studios for television companies and so on, take to the suburbs. Even Meier's center has no high-rises and, paradoxically, no white buildings.

The question we must ask in all seriousness is this; do we need to go through the same stages and at the same speed as did those more advanced than us, or do we try to plug into contemporaneity directly, as long as our arrested development has offered us this strange opportunity? The adepts of modernization give it stylistic meaning by celebrating modernist architecture; however, this can no longer be promoted today under the same guise that brought it post-war glory.

Finally, it's a question of strategy. We must accept our investors as they are, and concede that, being neither urbanists not afficionados of the latest architectural theories, they do wish to build phallic sky-scrapers, in order to celebrate visually, on a urban scale, their new power. Let's be cynical and admit, like von Gerkhan, that such a desideratum cannot be wholly repressed, and, as is already happening, building licenses for high-rises will be requested. At the same time, we have the ruined, frail, shattered historic center, begging to be protected against the aggression of high-rises and to be secured through our commitment to re-set it on viable economic foundations. Thus we seem to be in a dilemma: we must safeguard the historic center, already too crowded; but we must also allow for its economic development, which appears to mean, for reasons that have less to do with market economy and more with the power of symbols and the symbols of power, that we must put up with towers, high-rises and so on.

At the very heart of this apparently insoluble dilemma, however, we are in a privileged position. Why must we choke the historic center, when the one hundred and fifty hectars razed by Ceaușescu are available? They have been the object of an international competition which has produced a winning project which provides for the building of high-rises along the entire north-western side of the Palace of Parliament. We have to make the choice of filling an already-extant vacuum, which awaits us, and which, in becoming filled, will also in the process solve the problem of camouflaging the national shame called House of the Republic. Few cities have this boon, granted them by a previous destruction. The time has come to take advantage of it.

## Upstairs, in One's Apartment in One Building in One Dormitor City on the Outskirts

After long decades of uniformization of the architectural expression through type-projects, through standardization and prefabrication, the tables are turned and the promotion of individual differences is, at last, in tune with the times. Dwellings are the prime domain of difference; every family expresses itself through its interior, even in the apartment building, although perhaps the pool of "identities" is not large. Mass-produced furniture and the few archaic schemes for furnishing a room further reduce the range of individual options.

My parents' generation caught the wave of change at its peak. Enthused by "progress", they abandoned their houses in order to move into an apartment building in the sixties and seventies. Why? In retrospect the reasons seem amusing; so that they would no longer have to put fires in their wood- or coal-burning stoves, since central heating exempted them from purchasing wood or coal, from the chore of cleaning out the ashes and so on. And, so that they would become true city-dwellers. To live in "civilized" conditions. Thus a massive migration occurred toward and into the apartment building, as families traded some of their liberties (as earth-dwellers) for certain comforts (as city-dwellers): sewers, central heating, electricity.

My parents bought the kind of furniture everybody else bought in the sixties, paid for in installments. They bought a radio. Then a TV set; first one made in the USSR, then a Romanian-built one. Paid in installments. Then they bought a refrigerator. They still have all these appliances today. Most people, when they moved into apartments, transported their way of dwelling into a different space, which had not been designed for it. Apartments had certain "optimum" furniture schemes and, in fact, less flexibility than the peasant house, on account of the countless perimetral doors (hallway and room-crossing doors, balcony doors etc.). But the "optimum" schemes dreamed up by modern designers were not observed. Nobody set up "functional zones" in the living room. Romanians turned the living room into the "good" room of the peasant house; a room with somewhat better furniture, "parlor" furniture (table and chairs in the middle, cupboards on the contour, glass cabinet), out of use in the absence of guests. Furniture was vigorously polished, doilies were placed on it and, on the walls, kitsch landscapes hung, in gilded frames. All along the walls, also framed, were black and white family pictures: baptism, wedding, service in the army, loved ones. Then came the knick-knacks. Many knick-knacks. Perhaps some stuffed birds, too. In a visible spot, the electronic display would proudly boast a wooden-case radio, or, later, one in a case made of white plastic, a TV set with rounded screen corners. In the hallway, enthroned on lacy frills, sat the telephone.

This is the becoming-into-being of the Romanian apartment building: a peasant house on the tenth floor. This perching, however, provided it in time with an alternative identity, containing also a new and disturbing chromosome — the slum.

## Derision, Slum, Post-Modernism

The notion of *gentleman-architect* refers, in the history of architecture, to a character belonging to the upper class, educated in an aesthetic taste suited to his rank, and wealthy enough to be a patron, likely to commission the building of major works of architecture. He is the one that hires a team of master masons and commissions a work drawn up along the lines of those models — types — which are in use at the time, and which he, together with the master, adapts to the site, to his social status and to his personal taste. This *architecture without architect* (in the sense in which we use the word today) belongs to the high sphere of vernacular architecture and is associated with the great architecture of all times. The interest shown by this architecture to the architecture of power (palaces, but also churches) is not an accident. The City, center of power and prestige, broadcasts its models toward the outskirts. The stately, bookish, prestigious culture of the social elite is often echoed into the folk culture, even if in disguise. At the inter-face between the two, the vernacular borrows, assimilates, invents models and patterns.

In other words, there is a kind of direct contamination, at the points of contact between the two cultures, but there is also a contamination occurring through a link, a "moderator". An example is the displacement of the traditional folk culture of the village — mentalities, aesthetic taste, clothing — by and via the "suburban culture", by the slum. This is the topic we shall mostly deal with here. The agents of this intermediary culture are usually representatives of the "imitating" culture, invested by their native villages with a prestige at least equal if not superior to that of the legitimate representants of the authentic "high" culture. But the kitsch inter-face, the de-structuring agent becomes in time autonomous. The Gypsies' houses already do not resemble the House of the People anymore, but Chinese pagodas, or, as Ioan Andreescu argues, in the best cases, local adaptations of French neoclassic architecture, made from catalogues of that epoch, using quality materials and — to top it all — with an almost humble and painstaking respect for the accuracy of the copy. Mr. Ilie Alexandru copies in Slobozia, in his surrealist Hermes Land, Southfork Ranch, a mediaeval castle and the Eifell Tower. The music of the slum is already no longer (just) the corrupt version of authentic and autochthonous folk lore, but a variation on Oriental and mostly pseudo-Oriental folk music — from Yemen, for example, or Bengal.

In fact, the entire architecture of the Civic Center is an intrusion of the slum, a maneuver to occupy the very center of the city. By destroying historic centers (urban culture) as well as villages (folk culture), the slum sets forth a single alternative, which is not inspired by either of the cultures it has subverted, and sets itself up as the only reality. The incredible, unreal character of a gigantic scale model which singles out the House of the Republic in rapport with the perimetral urban tissue is perfectly comparable in all respects minus scale with the discrepancy between the "commuters' apartment buildings" built in the center of many villages and agro-industrial towns in the 1980's and those sites. From the very first "agronomists' houses" to the first attempts at rural systematization, which — as only a few still know today — belong to the seventies, the signs were already plain. In fact, the very notion of "civic center" was first of all tested in the "county-seat cities" after 1968.

The peri-urban vernacular parasitizes prestigious models, amplifying what it deems "essential" in this architecture, be it secular or religious. For instance, eclecticism is reduced to its details and accidents, to what appears, upon superficial inspection, haphazard and playful. The Neo-Gothic, to give another example, which thrived in the last century, picked from the Gothic its "mystery" and created somber houses in acute angles, cottages that only ivy and the geraniums in the ogival windows saved from hopeless ridicule. Like all upstarts, the Neo-Gothic proved "more Catholic than the Pope", with the result that many cathedrals, for example, received their bell tower only in the XIXth century, because, as Viollet Le Duc, author of an "ideal" cathedral, pronounced, this tower *had to* exist. The houses on the outskirts of Bucharest at the end of the last century, whose tenants — Caragiale tells us — moved out every St. Dumitru, are more "eclectic" than their "originals". In stucco and cheap plaster, the outskirts of Bucharest a hundred years ago were carnavalesque mirror images of the French-isms en vogue in the center of the city.

The vernacular architecture of the slum underscores dimensional "excellence", taking its own architecture out of scale and disfiguring its proportions: the towers become too tall or too many. Also, it imitates "expensive" materials — stucco or, anymore, self-adhesive linoleum instead of marble, Ersatz granite and tile. If it uses originals — materials or models — it does it all wrong. This wrong-ness or inadequation is in fact the essential characteristic of this type of architectural discourse. Always careful to overstate its belonging to a social group which, in effect, refuses to grant it membership, eager to impress, this type of vernacular wants more than anything to be recognized, to be admired, while at the same time it denies itself, knowingly, this chance. The solution to the inferiority complex is, in this case, an acute complex of superiority.

In the modern era, the circulation of the sources is no longer one-way only: from power to the masses. Leaders belonging to the middle or lower classes, raised to power through the convincing argument of military force (Napoleon was the inventor of kitsch, says aesthetician H. Istvan) or through the vote of the "people" often impose the imitation not of the originals but of the copies and of the interpretations of the originals by the low-brow vernacular described above. Thus are promoted in the architecture of power inferior models, belonging to the periphery of culture and of authentic arts. The House of the People is an expression of the eclecticism of the periphery, a gigantic slum. Hitler was fascinated less by Imperial Rome than by the buildings on Ringstrasse in XIX[th] century Vienna. Stalinist architecture often copies "rustic" versions of consecrated styles, disregarding the high-classical ideas of a Joltovski or Fomin.

However, this kinship between vernacular and kitsch, between the official architecture of the Ceaușescu regime and the nearby market district, would have been the chance for urban recovery of the ensemble of the new civic center. Except in scale, Lipscani and Victoria Socialismului Blvd. are blood relations. Today, the balconies which many owners have windowed in, the parabolic TV dishes, the dynamic billboards and the luminous ads, all sketch — as yet timidly — my project. It is at bottom a cynical project — but the cynicism is directed against an architecture of hybris, edified on the ruins of the true center. The vernacular resurrection already humanizes this cardboard architecture — an unreal architecture, as Peter Eisenman wished it — which has "frozen" as a design and has ever remained a scale model, as yet unformed. Even the official attempts to use the place in a solemn manner end up appearing ridiculous, because the place is simply stupid. Had it not been built on the cadaver of its victim, but on some neutral and suburban lot, it would have been a changeling and nothing more. The solution therefore is to push the kitsch beyond the limit of its intrinsic aggressiveness, into a realm where it becomes innocuous Disneyland, architecture afflicted by the Down syndrome.

By comparison, the recent project, proposed by the group of firms America's Partners, to build a Transylvania/Dracula Theme Park into the side of the House (with Michael Jackson's money), casinos and commercial gallerias (with the money of some

American tribes), is less radical than the idea to turn the House into a huge casino, insofar as it preserves the edifice of our national derision intact as well as its supposedly solemn function. Few of those who have heard out the representative of America's Partners (strongly supported by the Embassies of both the United States of America and Israel) appear to sense that it is impossible, despite any seeming evidence, to make and pass laws, after all, in a circus arena. I appreciate the post-modernist taste of our nation's elected representatives. In a way, when I see my proposal of 1990 one step away from being approved and launched, even if in a sensibly different shape, I am rather inclined to opine that urban life can perhaps be resuscitated in this place of death. But even post-modernism, and even its inherent derision, because imprinted in its genetic makeup, may not cross the boundaries of common sense. At least the appearances of a state life must be preserved — or mustn't they?

## *The Architecture of Snobility*

Snobbery was, is and will be a privileged agent in propagating prestigious architecture. This tells us nothing about the quality of the model, but we must observe from the very beginning that, in principle, the "pollinating" role of snobbery has been beneficial to architecture and its becoming. Often, for reasons that are better explained by semiotics, this assimilation of prestigious values (in oneself or in the groups of persons promoting these values) results in kitsch. Nevertheless, we owe the propagation of a style or current from one art and one place into arts and across several countries precisely to this circulation of prestigious models. Snobbery — as an attitude embraced by those who wish to be accepted by (or perceived as) members of a superior social group — encourages the circulation of new techniques, rare/special materials, new ways to inhabit or utilize a space; snobbery is what changes the face of architecture.

With the understanding that I will, in the process, somewhat stretch the meaning of snobbery, I will advance a few examples (not all of which, I realize, show the positive character of snobism). To the circulation of models from urban to rural architecture, we owe certain "forms without meaning" such as the four small towers around the steeple of some wooden churches; in the walled cities it was copied from, this was a distinctive mark signifying that the respective town possessed jurisdiction, while in the countryside, it signified nothing but a decorative element. French eclecticism in Bucharest is an example (also) of snobbishness, by means of which the Romanian elite wished to signify its belonging to a certain cultural model (which had arrived here via Russia and only later on through direct import by the Paris-schooled youth). More recently, the gigantesque architecture of the nouveaux riches, of the extravagant residents of Oaş, of the House of the People, of the Romanian banks built after 1989 — all of these are expressions — some bearable, others awful — of the snobbery of those who commissioned them. The wish to have a Versailles of our own, as rumor has it, was the driving force behind the "New Civic Center". In an interview, Anca Petrescu, architect-in-chief of the project, even went so far as to say that, *like Speer*, she, too, had made the pact with the devil; this, I'm afraid, is the only resemblance between her deluded self and "the most famous architect of the XXth century," as Krier called Speer. What in fact did happen was that the city limits, the faubourg about to become slum, which in the past had used the models located in the city center as source of inspiration, now took possession of this center and displaced it.

While between the wars the Romanian school of architecture lingered in a more and more baroque zone of Neo-Romanianism, the "market" was becoming modern, although it may be of interest to remark that the modern infusion took place almost exclusively among certain minorities, at first ethnic, then social. In fact, modernity was never assimilated on a social scale, even after its association with the communist projects; as soon as it was possible, the houses built after 1989 imploded into an eclectic language — both "etymologically" through the bric-à-brac of the sources assembled, and "historically" through the vast age differences among these sources. In Timișoara, the exorbitant Gitano villas are — the more successful ones — built after catalogues of French eclecticism, the very same ones that Gottereau probably used. Nothing modern was kept — other than the retarded (here) reinforced concrete, mis en oeuvre exactly the same way it would have been a hundred years ago. On the contrary, architecture runs away from modernism and either into vulgarity or into post-modernism and deconstructionism. However, these two, unassimilated in our country, always appear reduced to an outer shell which lacks profound critical substance. In Suceava, I saw a bank whose façades were explicit quotes, one from Richard Meier, another from Ricardo Bofill. Such schizophrenic architecture cannot go, as it were, unpunished. Executed in cheap or poorly used materials, unsuited to the intended architecture, the new façades age quickly and hopelessly; no doubt you will have noticed that Romanian modern architecture is in a pitiful state, and, on the inside, the apartment buildings of the eighties are infinitely older than those of the sixties.

Snobbism implies exactly this kind of superficial intake, often without assimilating the respective models. Today we can boast with our own set of losers, although, measured against the respective styles/fads — eclecticism, modernism with all its "wings" — our (counter) achievements are but marginal. We have imported practically everything and contributed only the transfer from city to town to village, the re-sizing, and the play/permutation of sources. At the Monastery of Horezu, the "temple" of the Brâncoveanu period and style, the sources can be quickly reviewed, along with the dynamic indication of the sustaining pedal — a blur, transformed by the passage of time into a picturesque impression. Dionysius' Tower, cited as such in the architecture of the Cotroceni Palace, also carries the successive echoes of "other rooms, other voices" — for instance the twisted columns — here with less drama because with less skill — of the Berninian wing of the San Pietro Cathedral. A play on imported words, a "mutual ordering" of lingering sound waves which "strike each in each" with the last vibration before extinction.

I've encountered only one other architecture in which models having come to breathe their last on distant, foreign beaches reach such a dramatic peak: Russian sacred architecture. There, too, we look as if into a kaleidoscope at fluid patterns which must have been originally distinct. There's the baroque, resorbed into brick and strong colors; there's the Gothic, surviving in awkward window frames, as it does in Moldavia; there's neoclassicism itself, tamed, right next to the Ottoman arch or the Indian cupola — reverted sky, with the stars on the outside. We are reminded that Peter the Great, in his zeal to modernize Russia, imported (through Trezzini) for the benefit of pravoslavnik architecture the most monumental thing the Occident had to offer, even if it was by no means French: the dome of the Amsterdam Stock Exchange.

And why not? The snob often forgets the interior rule by which is constituted the model or the style he takes over, its "escorting discourse" as I have elsewhere called the story of the house — from the political speeches about it to the short anecdotes that explain it. This is how, suffering from multiple amnesias — changing social class, function, scale, materials and geography — Palladian architecture made its most successful career in the United States; how a certain German palace became the emblem of Disneylands everywhere; how the Great Pyramid of Keops, made of glass, got to host baseball games in Memphis, Tennessee; finally, how the Parthenon will survive — intact but done in stucco — in Nashville. Some of Le Corbusier's late works (the city of Chandigarh in India, a typical example of snobbery, set by Nehru, or the Church at

Ronchamp) had a great influence, twenty years later, on the architecture of many Romanian civic centers. Thus models travel, carried by the guilds of masons or imported by the new snobbery. Of course, as they travel, they also change, increasing or, conversely, diminishing their scale, corporified in marble or in stucco. Nothing prevents us hence from "seeing" with equal reason for the analogy now pagodas, now tent camps silhouetted in the puzzling roofs topping the residences of wealthy Gypsies.

This weak or non-assimilation of the borrowed model is also the reason for its rapid disappearance, here today and gone tomorrow. A lived-in and lived-with environment, having assumed its shape and character over a relatively long time, is more difficult to give up than a cardboard décor. The density of being of the former does not allow it to disappear without a trace. The pedigree, the fanciful genealogy is a snobbish invention which becomes somehow necessary precisely as the genuine ancestor, the true being, the spirit of a place has been put out. Case in point: when the misguided girl-guides who enlighten foreign tourists visiting the House of the People tell them that the House is built in the style of Prince Constantin Brâncoveanu (†1714) they only repeat what their Parliamentary bosses have told them. Do not laugh at the girls; rather, cry at the House bosses, who stated only recently, on live television, that, far from being an accident, their and the people's House was the compensatory achievement of Ipsilanti's burnt palace, as well as the realization of the 1935 master plan for Bucharest. It represents, therefore, an "objective" apparition in our town, in the same way presumably in which Ceaușescu too was objectively present in the official paintings between the princes of old days.

There are also ways to fight back against "bad" snobbery. One — the original and most radical — is to remove the ladder, as Prince Negru did, in the legend of Master Manole, leaving the ten masons stranded on the roof of the Argeș Monastery, which they had just finished building. The modern and less painful measure, similar in its effects, is the exclusive-right contract.

Another way is education, with the drawback that the fascination of the power behind a model will supersede it every time. The "californization" of mass culture is not just an import of burgers, caramelized drinks and cowboy jeans, but, above all, the communication of the American model of a successful life, supported by the visual aid of so many movies ardently glorifying it. Education helps, but it will never be able to check the impetus to climb, by any means, to the top, or to imitate those who have climbed, which is the snob's not-so-secret energy. An artistic education, sustained at least through grade school and high school, could reduce, of course, the distance between model and snob, could direct attention to the authentic models and, by way of consequence, could hem in the possibilities of the apparition of kitsch. In other words, snobbery could be channeled from the Turkish rags and trinkets to the renowned clothiers and indigenous fashion designers. Instead of buying heavy, carved furniture of an undefinable but oppressive style, the snob could be taught to like Ikea furniture, which, far from being a masterpiece, looks decent enough to create an acceptable interior. Instead of sky scrapers, which continue to thrive only in battered Asia, we could expect from our snob, now a strategic investor, conversions of historic buildings, or buildings that say something, of course, about their patron — buildings always will — but something flattering.

## *Town Hall or Disneyland?*

At the time of its building, Drumul Taberei was a civilized example of putting into practice the urbanism of the Chart of Athens. Apartment buildings were placed at wide intervals from each other in a greening landscape. Commercial centers were grouped here and there amongst them; alleys wound their ways freely in between different groups of buildings: some tower-like, some P + 4 bars. In addition, the district was built outside the city, so that not many old walls fell victim to progress. Later, however, the communist regime began to thicken the high-rises, destroying lawns, small parks etc., suppressing the residents' privacy, straining the public utilities systems, i.e. electricity, sewage, central heating, and congesting traffic. Public transportation to and from the city continues to be inadequate. Where they were missing, improvised open market places have sprung, thumbing their noses at the architects and urbanists of thirty years ago.

The center of this satellite town is across the street from Moghioroş Marketplace. A hilarious penance for a Communist hero (Alexandru Moghioroş), to have become the eponym of an open marketplace, the very kind of thing he and his had "fought" against... Opposite the marketplace, in any case, is the Post Office. Next to it is a large, vacant lot, which was to have been the site of township offices — a town/district center gathering together administration, commerce, and facilities. Surprisingly, the site is still unoccupied, having emerged from Ceauşescu's final years without a "Hunger Circus", that is, without one of those buildings which had appeared in other outskirts of the capital, and under whose immense, circus-like cupolas, the wilted carrots and turnips of the First Architect of the Nation were bought and sold. A few projects for this site were undertaken as graduation projects by students of the Institute of Architecture "Ion Mincu", and not much else.

After the Revolution, we have been threatened every now and then that some sort of second-rate amusement park is just about to be built here. Vain threat. The vacant lot is still here and still very much the same vacant lot where iron sheet shanties elbow each other selling counterfeit rum and hot sausage, and SC Tradiţia s.r.l. (Tradition Commercial Society, Ltd.) sells cheap furniture from a corrugated iron lean-to the size of a baseball field. The amusement park consists in maybe ten bumper-cars bumping into each other in a half-crazed sort of way, like the nation itself.

208

Corrugated iron, corrugated plastic, wrought iron fences, Gypsy music, vomit and mud forever.

A sizable bidonville has sprouted, bearing witness to the stupidity and callousness of local administrations in the past and of the urbanism offices both at City Hall and at the local Town Hall. The prevailing air is that of a cheap itinerant circus. Building licenses for these hucksters' dens, if they exist, can only be temporary and/or obtained through bribery; there is not the slightest sign of any intention to put some order into this chaos, even a bad one.

Meanwhile, the marketplace across the street, which has grown and grown in extremities like a patient with acromegalia, has no parking space to speak of. Town Hall is hidden somewhere near the train station. And why would it be where it should be, in the very geometric center of the city slice it purports to pilot? Well-hidden in their offices, warming themselves around improvised electric heaters, the "brains" of the local administration sit and cogitate, no doubt, about the future of the nation, counting the days to retirement or unemployment pay, whichever comes first. Meanwhile Drumul Taberei also counts its days to a true center and true aediles, willing and capable to lead it.

## *"Mythological" Tidbits*

As early as 1992, I have signaled the danger we run of treating the question of communism in architecture too lightly, in pamphlets or verbal volleys alone, without any serious research into the topic. We run the risk of leaving this copious theme exclusively to the foreign academics (one estimable example is Brazilian Maria Cavalcanti's doctorate at Oxford) and failing to interpret our own past with all due rigor. The studies of oral history concerning the House of the Republic are missing. So are the sociological studies. And also missing from the roll call of the duty to understand are the historians, urbanists and architects who could inscribe and explain, through comparative methods, a phenomenon which continues to appear to some an accident, to others the highest expression of the Romanian genius (notwithstanding the presence of such persons of doubtful taste in Parliament, where they are evenly distributed in all political parties).

Serious studies are however, beginning, to appear. Professor Lucian Boia of the Faculty of History from the University of Bucharest organized last year a session of scientific communications on the theme of "Communist Mythologies". One of the two books in which the materials presented have been collected, released recently by the University of Bucharest Press, contains three contributions on architecture, which I will discuss in turn.

Ms. Mariana Celac (Director of *Arhitectura* journal) writes "a comparative analysis of totalitarian languages in architecture," which would require at least a tome, should she intend to develop the theme. This excellent essay examines and compares the architectural interventions in Berlin, Espozitione Universale di Roma, Moscow, the Civic Center in Bucharest, the ceremonial axis of Persepolis, of 1977. The strongest hypotheses of the paper are: 1) that the author of the new civic center in Bucharest must be Ceaușescu himself, and 2) that the architecture of the Civic Center was and is an image of the country, reflecting a new social class which is "numerous, unprejudiced, endowed with vitality and social ambition (...) which has no history and no roots. It does not bear the guilt of its own apparition; communism does. It is the class of the ill-made and ill-bred 'new people'*. The first hypothesis uses as minor premise the obvious fact that despite the presence of an army of architects, many of them competent and respectable professionals, the Civic Center is laid out without any rhyme or reason; so many good architects could not have designed such

---

* Creating the "new man of the multilaterally developed socialist system" was the highest and most sinister goal of communism in general and of Ceaușescu in particular (t.n.)

chaos, reasons Ms. Celac. And why not? The major premise in this syllogism is more difficult to grant, i.e. A group of good architects will always design good buildings and urbanistic ensembles regardless of tyrants. Then why didn't any of these good architects dare to oppose the destruction of a single church or historical monument?

Alexandru Beldiman, President of the Architects' Union, published a short description of the becoming of Bucharest, also using to this end Dana Harhoiu's ideas. (The text was published by the University of Bucharest). In it, the author underscores the seismic-fault character of the totalitarian intervention in Bucharest. Mr. Beldiman has often characterized Bucharest as a palimpsest, a text which is erased, rewritten, annotated, glossed over and over and over again, without ending, ever. It is also, I'd extrapolate, an unfinished project and a perpetually open wound.

Last but not least comes the contribution of Professor Alexandru M. Sandu, Rector of the Institute of Architecture "Ion Mincu", a text remarkable not only for its theoretical acuity but also for the profound analysis of the serious problems of our architecture, to which I enthusiastically adhere. What would these problems be? On one hand, "the endemic incapacity of Romanian architects to go into battle for an architectural solution," that is, if pushed to its last consequences, the absence of a critical, self-reflecting dimension in our architecture. This interrogational collapse took place, I believe, before communism, probably at the same time that French eclecticism crossed the border into Romania at the turn of the century. The Neo-Romanian style and the modernism that followed did not manage to raise the level of the theoretical discourse much. The result? "In Bucharest it is hard to find today an architectural-urbanistic achievement of the last twenty-five years which would be at the same time an act of cultural merit." The text discusses the need for a participatory urbanism, for an understanding of sites and places, ideas which are still (and,

211

after 1989, again) almost insurrectional in the autochthonous context. ˙

On the other hand, Professor Sandu argues, with restraint and force, the necessity of an architectural critique. Former editor of the architectural journal *Arhitectura* and Rector of the Bucharest School of Architecture, Prof. Sandu's is clearly one of the most authorized opinions in this area. I was the beneficiary of his understanding in 1989 when I proposed the first theoretical graduation project in the history of "Ion Mincu" and Prof. Rector Sandu accepted it. In addition, Professor Cezar Radu and I owe him the moral and institutional support for the first critical course held within the Institute's Master program.

When, in 1992, Mayor Crin Halaicu announced the intention of an American investor to turn the House of the Republic into a casino, he either ignored or forgot to mention the paternity of this proposal, which I had advanced and supported already in 1991 at the Competition of Ideas for the House of the Republic, organized by the Architects' Union. The magazine *Contrapunct* (Counterpoint) published my text immediately after the contest. The idea was to turn the entire area into a zone for entertainment, an amusement park of the Disneyland sort. It was the only way to annul the totalitarian symbol and, at the same time, recover that gigantic slum for urban use.

In that as-yet utopian phase after the Revolution (or, rather, a post-distopic phase) we did not know that the edifice would prove to suit the taste of our democratically-elected representatives, without distinction of political color. To my knowledge, only Dinu Patriciu, being an architect, showed some skepticism and proposed that the hill be planted thickly with trees, to cover the hideous House, which, he also thought, should be dressed in ivy. We did not know that the budget for finishing up the House would become almost as consistent as the budget of education and culture put together. We did not know that at the head of the project would be Anca Petrescu, without a single hind thought, or batted

212

eyelash, or trace of shame having darkened her face in all these years. Also we did not know that not only the man-in-the-street liked this building. In his case, lacking a minimum of an urban and artistic education, lacking landmarks of certain architectural value, it was somewhat understandable why the "giga-house" seemed "beautiful" — different anyway from his own environment of prefab buildings, grey, cold, damp and mouldy. The affectionate nickname "House of the People" bears witness to its "adoption" by the masses. But the House is more recently a great international success. Here are held conferences and symposia that make all the diplomatic small fry throughout lands near and far look busy and important. Hafez Al Assad is not the only one to have found "impressing" this "Romanian Versailles" as Anca Petrescu and Paul Everac* called it (only infinitely worse put together).

To top it all, para-psycho-pathological theories have been circulated that the House of the Republic is no less than the epiphany of the Temple of Jerusalem on the bank of Dâmbovița. If we accept that the Victory of Socialism was the New Jerusalem of the communist ideal, so be it! The proportions of the House, leaflets tell us, would be the very same ones the Bible indicates. As far as the water of life goes, it might find its equivalent only in the underground infiltrations. Speaking of basements: they have always been, Bachelard tells us, magnets for the subconscious. For the always hyper-functional collective imagination of the Romanian people, the House basement has been the fuse detonating loads of explosible fancy; here were found terrorists, rockets were stored, and high-speed monorails stopped by to fetch Ceaușescu to safety and impunity.

Willy-nilly, we have to dialogue with this reality. A contest for the "camouflaging" of the Warsaw Palace of Culture, a "gift" to the Polish people from Stalin, yielded no conclusive results in 1992. Since then, "imperialist" sky-scrapers have begun to sprout

---

* Writer playwright of the Ceaușescu era; 1989–1994 Director of the national television company, TVR (t.n.)

around the building, defying the Stalinist palace built with the trowel by their last-cry technologies, for the terror of the regime in question of new technologies and sciences, such as genetics or cybernetics, is notorious. The question we must ask our officials and potential investors is whether a commercial architecture, without an ounce of understanding for the urban tissue, similar to the architecture of an American downtown, represents a solution for today's dismantled Bucharest.

## "Court" Architects

The apparition of so-called "official" styles in architecture is often the expression not only of the potentates' taste, but also of the architects' slavishness. Familiar with the basic ideological commandments guiding the theme, these architects often flatter what they discern to be the expectations of those political leaders who will approve the building, and present more and more flamboyant versions of what they know is "liked" and approved, then versions of the version. Architects come out to greet the political power. To a regime that is unsure of its aesthetic options, they offer their services with fawning frenzy. If van der Rohe had won the contest for Reichsbank in 1933 and if his supporter, Goebbels, had prevailed over Hitler's personal opinion, we would have had today an entirely different history of architecture. Mies and Gropius both took part in the exhibition *Deutsche Volk, Deutsche Arbeit*. Word goes Le Corbusier also would have offered his services for the reconstruction of Paris, and in Italy an open battle was fought for Mussolini's favor, who was invited to choose from among several variants of "genuine Fascist" architecture. The pseudo-contest for the House of the Republic and the Victory of Socialism Boulevard could have had other possible outcomes, too. Other projects were also submitted, some "avant-garde", others strictly modernist, others yet neoclassical with

Egyptian touches and Palladian statues perched on cornices — whose statues, Mr. Dinu Patriciu? Any of these versions would have been preferable to the one which was actually built, but Ms. Petrescu continuously modified the problem's data as she relentlessly upped, with every new version of the project, those hideous traits which she knew would please the Ceauşescu duo because their corrupt taste was thereby flattered. The final edifice can be already discerned in the initial scale model proposed by Ms. Petrescu. In the end, it came out much bigger, more adorned and infinitely more repulsive, but in nuce it was already there.

In their book entitled *The Stalinist Architecture* (London: King, 1992), Tarkhanov and Kavtaradze tell of cases of direct intervention from Stalin in architectural decisions — the re-designing of Moskva Hotel, the contest for the Palace of the Soviets and for the NKVD/KGB headquarters. Speer's Arch of Triumph or the Great Dome are not identical to Hitler's preliminary sketches, but we can retrace their development against the grain. In Nazi Germany, many of Hitler's acolytes commented on themes of architecture (Rosenberg, Schultze-Naumburg, Speer) or directly supervised the building of the edifices of power (Göring, Goebbels or Ley). Above all, as known, Hitler himself was an afficionado of gigantic architecture. At the antipode, we find Mussolini who allowed converted avant-garde architects (Terragni, Libera) next to neoclassicists such as Piacentini, Muzia (derived from the Milanese avant-garde) or Michelucci (re-converted to modernism after the war).

## *Pro Memoria*

There are statements about our urban environment which do not get all the stage light they deserve. They can define a personality, or shove it into the darkness without. I will try to give two qualitatively opposed examples of such "unnoticed" discourse.

215

The former comes from Mr. Alexandru Paleologu's allocution at a recent "Forum on the State of Culture" and says that:

> We witness a frightful degree of pollution of culture and civilization, along with disturbing phenomena of moral, social, and civil dishonor; (...) the Parliament, at least in part, has moved for the time being into a demoniacal and sinister hangar, in the worst taste possible, which compromises us worldwide. At least let us not have our Parliament there. For a century and a half, all of Romania's great orators, from Barbu Catargi to Alexandru Lahovary, to Maiorescu and Carp, spoke in the building on Metropolitan Hill. The true history of Romanian democracy is there. Abandoning it is an act of vandalism. And the presence of Parliament in that Kafkian building — you don't know to get in, you don't know how to come out — is an insult, an offense, a provocation and a dishonor.

I don't believe a more accurate definition of the current state of affairs concerning the House of the Republic can be given — or a more resounding slap in the face of Mr. Adrian Năstase, the very same one who had threatened to veto any project of the Bucharest 2000 contest which would have dared to shut the doors of "his" House to the Parliament. And no one dared. We will never know what solutions we might have had without this cheap, arbitrary act of momentary despotism. Instead we have an edifice which proves impossible to finish and to manage; we have melted plexiglass pouring down the heads of our elected from the height of dissolving cupolas; we have the same architect-in-chief of the project Ceaușescu employed; we have, to boot, a dizzying budget for the finishing of the totalitarian project.

The latter example comes from a book on *The Demolition of Văcărești Monastery* (Bucharest: Ed. Arta Grafică, 1997) by architect Gheorghe Leahu. In it we find a passage in which the former Patriarch Iustin defies Professor Dinu C. Giurescu, who had asked for his support to save the monastery. Such cruelty must never be forgotten; Iustin admonishes the Professor, scolding him for speaking like the hirelings of foreign radio stations; for opposing Ceaușescu's grandiose effort to build a new Bucharest; for defending a prison house, since Văcărești hadn't been a monastery for a hundred years (as if a House of God could ever cease to function). In the end, only a couple of insignificant little churches had been razed. What was all that fuss for? If what the book reports is true, may this Iustin be unforgiven and may he compear before the frightful judgment with the text of this shameful speech in hand.

## *Post-Modernism Every Bucharest Resident Can Understand*

One way to judge the city and architecture in general, from the post-modern perspective, it to value the co-existence of all strata and of all interventions into a site, even if they will have to be all present in a new house. This device of the "co-presence" has been used by Peter Eisenman in at least two projects: Wexner Center in Columbus, Ohio, and the intervention at La Villette, Paris, co-designed with Derrida. In the first case, the armory which had existed on that site is evoked in the architecture of the new house. In the second case, all the previous states of the site are simultaneously present and co-exist — with the same intensity — with the "new" stage.

An example is the already known project for Bucharest 2000 by von Gerkhan. From the beginning, we must say, however, that lacking an economic foundation, we can only discuss the merits of this project as a pleasant formal exercise, without basis in the reality of an execution. This basis was unfortunately missing even when the contest was launched (defying thus all financial logic) and the situation has not improved since. For the past three years City Hall has dragged its feet and has not yet approved the

217

functioning of the Bucharest 2000 Agency, while in the meantime many potential investors have vanished. Under the circumstances, a financial arrangement to get the project started becomes a distant dream. Of course, the project does have its weird side: for example, Unirii Plaza ought to be turned into a lake, but, if the state of the subway running underneath is any indication — it's flooded — maybe this would not be such a good idea after all. The same plaza is now marked, by the political and ecclesiastical hierarchies (united again as ten years ago in hurting the city) and against any common sense or experts' opinions, for the building of the Cathedral of the Nation.

But the sadness of these findings mustn't prevent us from judging this formalist exercise as such. Its blocks are superimposed geometrically on a site where formerly another street system and another architecture existed. For this reasons, these blocks are criss-crossed by a network of passageways lit from above, which copies the old street layout. The pre-existing structure is thus honored and celebrated by the new architecture, in which present and past co-exist. Another interesting example, proposed by HAX, Ltd., presupposed the co-presence of the old house — a ruin, but a political/symbolic ruin, casualty of the Revolution — and/in the Romanian Architects' Union new building, in the winning project of the contest organized by the Union for its new headquarters.

In what manner can the successive historical layers of a site be represented simultaneously into the substance of a new house? We must ask this question in all seriousness if we wish to keep out, at least from now on, the kitsch subproduction of inattentive architects who care neither about the inherent features of the site, as phenomenology advises, nor about its history, as the deconstructionists do. In addition, another question is whether or not we wish to impart any identity to the city, other than that of a city systematically destroyed and rebuilt. Perhaps instead of pouring concrete over the vestiges of Bucharest's old inns, we should consider the possibility of introverted buildings, at least in the historic center, with interior courtyards and atriums toward which the entire life of the house would be oriented, even if morphologically we will siphon the latter's expression from the Western typology. The essential condition would be to keep the atrium open to the public at least at street level and probably at the level of the mezzanine too. This could be a prerequisite for anybody who intended to build in the historic center and would be stipulated in the theme of all public contests for such edifices.

Bucharest's old inns, which were suppressed by the advance of French eclecticism, could thus come back to a new life, under the guises of glass-covered commercial galleries, of passageways criss-crossing a revitalized historic center, of atriums opening into individual buildings and deep courtyards into larger edifices, similar in type to those we find on Calea Victoriei's inter-bellum buildings. Here are semi-private spaces, saved from the street hubbub, one must of necessity cross before entering the building itself. At Duiliu Marcu's Utilities Building, he was paying homage, in his 1940 book of projects, to just such an interior courtyard for the use of the employees. The center of Bucharest offers many examples of "twin" buildings, flanking the entrance into an inner courtyard belonging to the respective ensemble. Regardless of their expression, which can be Neo-Romanian, Neo-Moorish or modernist, these ensembles joined through a semi-private space share a single perspective on the relationship between public and private space, which must not be understood in terms of mutual exclusion but, conversely, as a gradual transition from one into another, thereby less traumatizing. Very likely this wisdom should not be lost, in spite of the Oriental air of the typology (or, if we are reminded of communal living cvartals, in spite of their association with Stalinism). To this effect, we ought to look into the feasibility of creating such semi-public spaces inside every city block. Von Gerkhan's project creates Western blocks of this type — rarely used until now in Bucharest's urban texture — in the area around the House of the Republic. Clearly, because of the nature of the place where they would be created, these blocks would very likely need to ensure the privacy of their residents in other ways than those used in more "neutral" areas in terms of public life.

The arched cellars of the center could be rediscovered as types and used for restaurants, bars, clubs. Natural materials — wood, stone — could enter into fertile contrasts and dialogues with high-tech materials — glass and metal — as in the work of many great architects (Aalto, Siza, Wright, Ando, H. Fathi, Herzog & De Meuron etc.). Glass, so ubiquitous in today's architecture, can be used in a manner suggested by the merchant town — the windowed balcony — with an updated expression, as it has been used, for example, at the new BCR Main Building in Ghencea (Dorin Ștefan, DS Studio).

Renewal should not mean the slavish imitation of typologies and technologies already as a rule exhausted in the West. We need not necessarily repeat the errors of orthodox modernism, as Robert Venturi called it, but can find our own foundations for an architecture proper to the Capital, in which the present should echo the past, and the past pilot, from underneath the surface, the entire project. New methods for the investigation of architecture and urbanism do offer us this alternative path to the chance of being in step with our times without casting out the features, whether many or few, which particularize this city.

## IV. 2. National Character

### *What Is Really National?*

Searching for a national identity in architecture, Mincu had favored the architecture of the rural middle class in the hillside region of Wallachia (Muscel). From a regional architecture, this became thus representative of our entire architecture. Mincu's followers used the style of the Brâncoveanu period (1688-1714) and, hence, the architecture of monasteries as a source of inspiration — entirely different from Mincu's in matters of scale, layout, type of decoration and so on. Later, Joja celebrated the architecture of the merchant class in the XVIIth and XVIIIth centuries. Yet we have serious reasons to question the "national" character of any one of these architectures, to the exclusion of all others.

We are searching for essences at all cost. Thus sometimes the intermediary space (be it porch, veranda or atrium) with its symphony of light and shade, sometimes the style of a prince or another, sometimes an architecture socially and regionally circumscribed such as the peasant house is deemed essentially "Romanian". All of these attributes have at one time or another competed for the honor of being the one and only one representing "Romanian character", to the exclusion of all others from the monologue of power. But intermediary spaces appear in most architectures of the temperate climate zone, having its most renowned example in Japan. Kisho Kurokawa, the only one of the "monstres sacres" of architecture we were able to see in Bucharest (I was then a student of the Institute of Architecture in Bucharest), celebrated the *engawa*, the transition space between interior/exterior, an interval where the contraries could be reconciled.

Anchored in microclimates and regions of folk culture sufficiently autarchical, peasant houses differ substantially from Dobrogea to Maramureș. Any pretention of finding a single unifying character is thereby quelled. Other questions arise, too. How are we to regard the architecture of the Saxon and Hungarian minorities? How, that of the Turks, of the Slavs and so on? Must they be excluded from an image of the national character in architecture, on the grounds of their being minoritary, hence unrepresentative? Clearly what we have here is the effort to invent a national myth which in fact lacks empirical substance. The same diversity confronts us when we examine the architecture of churches. Contrasting with the exceptional unity of the Romanian language, the architecture of the Orthodox churches in the different regions of Romania varies widely (to say nothing of the architecture of non-Orthodox examples). Local echoes and imprints, simplified versions of the great styles — Gothic, Renaissance, neoclassic, Armenian and Georgian influences in Moldavia; Serbian edifices in Wallachia (Cozia Monastery, for example); pseudo-baroque steeples in the briefly Habsburgic province of Oltenia, Moslem influences in Dobrogea, the play of corsi/ricorsi between vernacular rural architecture and the urban one — here is the short version of the list of influences and styles creating Orthodox architecture in Romania, enough to give an idea of the confusion from which must be "saved" this seldom "Byzantine" (the name of another identitary myth) architecture. After the latest overdose of nationalism, we are — representatives of a small and marginal culture — once again stripped of identitary vestments. What next? New clothes and a new hairdo for the old myth? A new commercial synchronism, propelled by foreign technologies and materials?

## Sibiel

Not far from Sibiu, in a landscape from "Miorița", lies the village of Sibiel. I got there with a foreign delegation (the

222

Gulliver Group), at the invitation of the Romanian Cultural Foundation, having also organized — impeccably — the trip. Sibiel is probably an edifying example of the sad fate of Romanian agrotourism and, in general, of our fate in a future and nebulous Europe; they with their technology, we with our folklore, *sarmale** and girls.

Just outside the village four kids were waiting for us with the horses. In front of the church — the village folk, the four-man band and the local intelligentsia, all in traditional costumes. The guests stepped down right into steaming horse droppings and were presently invited to dance: horă, sîrbă, and other local dances, plus perinită (we were told that the girls of Sibiel are very wealthy). As passions were slaked and brotherhood set in motion, we entered the church after tasting bread, salt, brandy. The church, built in 1765, is a picturesque *camelostrich***: baroque Mittel-Europa on the outside, Hagia Sofia on the inside. The false dome discharged its weight directly upon the ground. On the last register near the pendentives were painted the popes until the Schism, in Orthodox vestments. Later, five layers of whitewash covered the fresco (probably for concordance with the Protestant exterior) which was rediscovered in 1965. On the other side of the graveyard, a collection of icons painted on glass was presented cheaply and poorly, without dating and without serious ordering criteria. Our guide from the Bruckental Museum had even discovered grounds for a "peasant feminism" in the form of an effeminate apostle at the Last Supper. Looking carefully, one would rather conclude it was a way to discern Judas among eleven beards.

Our hosts took us to lunch, distributing us around the village. We arrived in a typical courtyard. The gate itself was guarded by

---

* Cabbage rolls (t.n.)
** Fabulous animal in Dimitrie Cantemir's *Istoria Ieroglifică* of the XVIIIth century (t.n.)

a huge picture-poster. Rooms had been added around the courtyard, diving also across the gate, so that the cement yard was no more than a passageway to the garage and the latrine in the back. Inside, the fear of vacuum of our hostess — a powerful ex-store manager in Sibiu reconverted to authentic peasant — had decorated practically every square inch: plastic flowers, nylon curtains, family portraits, knick-knacks, color TV set and tape player emitting the wail of a folk band from Banat; a hysteria of useless objects of "beauty" forced to coexist and to tell the story of the owners' prosperity. Our hostess continued the local tradition and herself produced icons on glass, carved wooden spoons the size of Mr. Nicolae Porumbescu's buildings and other souvenirs from Sibiel. We ate Wiener schnitzel, potato salad/à la russe/boeuf and, of course, sarmale. For a grand finale, the foreigners danced in turn to the Slaves' Chorus from *Nabucco*, to "Little Shepherd with Three Hundred Sheep", "Kalinka", "Oci ciornîi"* and other melodies illustrating our folklore. The Apocalypse can also have picturesque disguises.


## *A Topos of Forbearance*

We lived in Tulcea in the Lippovan district, where my parents — in turn — headed an elementary school. On my way to high school, I passed the Catholic church, catching timid glimpses of its interior when the door was ajar; strange organ music could be heard and I'd see a Christ of gypsum in the half-shade. A little closer to the center, the Greek church followed: a towerless temple. The Cathedral of St. Nicolas right next to it had enough height. I knew the Greeks. A relative on my father's side belongs to the Greek community there: capable merchant, before as well as after

---

* In order: Romanian folk tune, Kazakh folk tune put to Stalinist words during WW II and Russian romance. (t.n.)

the Revolution; my aunt herself was Greek and a merchant's daughter: grains, ships, Sulina — Europolis! And in the center was the Bulgarian church, which had a clock and — strange and fanciful in Orthodoxy — a Romanesque nave, with, instead of the rosace, two windows like two tears of Jesus.

Very close by could be seen the synagogue — whose demolition, looming over it in the eighties, was avoided at the last moment, probably due to interventions from abroad, since one of the last Jews in Tulcea, a watch-maker whom I also knew well, died about that same time. My father had bought me my first watch from him — a Swiss-made Coresa of great marvel, and also a few bracelets for my mother: the watch-maker was selling everything he owned in preparation for his emigration to Israel. Babadag Street had to be "systematized"; the old houses were everywhere being razed and replaced by the blockish apartment buildings decorated with folk motifs. The obsession of rectifying the streets of Tulcea met face to face, though, with the opposition of the emigrated Jewry. In the same rather occult manner the Jewish cemetery escaped the fate many cemeteries of all denominations all over the country could not: that of being destroyed and turned into a no-man's land among the looming blocks of grey concrete (i.e. apartment buildings), taken over by Romanian and Gypsy children growing wild and weedy, unsupervised by proletarian parents working all shifts at the factories built by socialism.

Other times I took another route to high school, along the bluffs of the Danube. It was a poetic setting — river and birds, row boats with tarred ropes linking the bank with the cargo boats. For a young author, nothing could be more suitable to "creation", especially in the evenings. To promenade on the bluffs was to parade on the "corso"*. Changes in wardrobe or civil and social status were there displayed and commented upon, during lazy strolls borrowing their leisurely pace from the River. The bluffs

---

* Italian for town promenade, long adopted into Romanian usage (t.n.)

were not only the spine of the town, but also its site of maximum interest. It was the locale of social contacts, of promenades, of urban life. It had its special "zones"; high school and college students met at the "little graves", while the thugs had their headquarters in front of the Danubius Restaurant. At the two extremes — the exit toward the Old Market and the one towards Union Plaza — sat perpetually the retirees, putting all through the gossip grinder. Every gesture there became public and subject to censorship. Walking along the bluffs with somebody was equal to and more efficient than publishing bethrotal bans. Conversely, walking alone was the announcement of a drama; or, perhaps, an invitation. To stop walking on the bluffs meant an interior exile — or death. Unfortunately, market economy and cable television have cut down the activity and importance of the bluffs as a "social rheostat". The same probably holds true of any such public place anywhere in the country. Building the "civic center" anywhere but there was therefore an error. With the exception of Ceaușescu's "work visits" and of the few days of Revolution — which in Tulcea consisted of bringing in an ex-party leader of perestroykist convictions, Barbu Popescu, with an escort of hysterical dump trucks — the "civic center" is only a passageway.

En route to the bluffs, I passed — when we still lived by School 7 — near, and often through, the courtyard surrounding the Lippovan church. The funeral of an old woman neighbor whom all of us called Băbica, had troubled me exceedingly; the priest read to her uninterruptedly, until she was lain in her grave, from some large, ancient hour-books. In the same way that the Tibetans recited the Bardo Thodol into the ear of the deceased — a kind of instruction for the passage beyond — the dead woman was read to in a dead language. The priest had been chosen precisely because he was one of the few left who could still decipher the language of the old books — in private life, he was a truck driver.

For the rest, the Lippovan church was: painted in oil on the outside, adorned with crêpe paper on feast days, holding icons mounted in brass and silver within. Just barely were the faces and golden nimbs of the saints allowing themselves to be seen from the depths of their silver cocoons. The Lippovan women, wearing gowns and kerchiefs in delirious colors, walked stately behind their husbands, donned in Russian tunics, beards hanging down to their belts. They were the same fisherman folk who sold us roe and fish, asking us for "one more penny per pound if it moves".

Finally, right next to the Spiru Haret School was the great mosque in Tulcea, whose minaret no church steeple was allowed to surpass in height back in the old Ottoman days. The Turks, fanatics in Constantinople, became meek on the edges of the Empire, so that Orthodoxy had nothing to suffer from them in Dobrogea; on the contrary, churches and monasteries were steadily built. With modest means, perhaps, but all of Dobrogea is no different, a barren land of few resources. The tower of the mosque dominated the broad amphitheater through which the city offered itself to the Danube, and closed a promenade marked by sacred buildings which from the bluffs could be seen, in the order of the flow of the river, thus: first the church of the Heroes Cemetery, Popa Metru's church, whose parishioners we were too, then the Lippovan Church near the Old Market, the Cathedral of St. Nicholas in the center, the two Lippovan churches seated next to each other on Hora Hill and the minaret where the muezzin still uttered his calls to prayer at the time of my adolescence. We could hear his plaintiff tone from the classroom or, in the evening, from the terrace of the "Little Carnation", a sweets shop where one could eat the best rose ice cream in the world, whose recipe left this earth along with the Turk who used to prepare it. I had many Turkish and Tatar boys and girls in my classes; later on they married, granted, amongst themselves. Back then, however, these things did not concern us; I still dream sometimes about the baclava made by Serin's mother — a true... paradislam!

Architecture itself celebrated the same mutual forbearance; the pseudo-vernacular neoclassic cathedral harmonized with the

Ionic style of the Greek church, and, in turn, with the soft architecture of most of Tulcea's religious buildings. Where could the neoclassical style of the Orthodox architecture of Tulcea have come from? Was it a consequence of 1878, when Dobrogea was united to the Romanian Principalies, or had it preceded the political act, since Tulcea, like Sulina, lived the paradoxical double lives of provincial backwaters which at the same time were Europolises in tune with the times and with the world? The Catholic Gothic, in contrast, is barely sketched. Outside of the minaret, there are no daring verticals; the towers built by the Inquisition to spy on converted Jews who might have lit Sabbath fires could spring in Spain, but not in Tulcea: The city lived in peace, a collection of minorities in the margin of history, liven on braga*, tsatsiki**, votka and much fish.

Between the neoclassical style and middle-class eclecticism, Tulcea had inscribed its religious buildings. Countless others ought also to be mentioned: the Russian church, the Bulgarian, possessed of a clock tower, the Adventist, Evangelist and Baptist churches, the latter being the oldest Baptist church in the country. Each of these churches served as the center of a local community; ethnically homogenous, Tulcea's neighborhoods gravitated around their peaceful sacred centers. The Lippovans painted their churches toward the Monument of Independence green, like a house porch. Many churches had flower gardens among the graves of the parishioners departed to the world of the (more) just ones***. The Catholic had by far the best-looking courtyard, and later built a parish house to match it. Popa Metru (the Orthodox priest) also lived in an "eclectic" parish house, guarding the sleep of the heroes buried in his cemetery: Romanian, German, and Russian heroes of 1914 all together, later on called Nazis and, respectively, Soviet

---

* A Bulgarian soft drink (t.n.)

** Greek treat of roe, oil and lemon (t.n.)

*** "Lumea drepților", the world of the just ones, is a common Romanian way of referring to the dead (t.n.)

heroes. My mother, together with her pupils from the neighborhood school, put the same flowers on all their graves.

This model has become extinct. Even its physical contours have disappeared. Only our memory still recovers it, the memory of those who walked in this realm of normality. After the aluminum and iron-alloy factories were built, which taint the air even today and turn every sunset at Aegyssus into a socialist-realist landscape, ruin settled over the town. Block-like apartment buildings obstructed the natural amphitheater and promptly leaned over to one side as they sank in the mud of the bluffs. In an apartment building, you cannot be tolerant; you can only be rude. Uprooted Moldavians filled the place and the new proletarian districts. There's no longer service in Greek at the Greek church, nor in Bulgarian at the Bulgarian church. Neither the synagogue nor the mosque is open anymore today — for whom?

My grandfather — mother's adoptive father, a Bulgarian school teacher from Cerna — has died long ago. In my mother's village, the Ukrainean language of the "Hahol" folk I descend from is no longer spoken. My uncle, Zapp Zoltan, the most likable man in my family, I seldom see now: only at weddings and funerals. My aunt, daughter of a well-to-do Greek merchant family, has passed away, too. My father's brother was for years on end a school teacher in a village of Italian stone masons in the Măcin area (though the village called itself Greci — "Greeks"). Rîşnov*, where my paternal grandfather had come from, has been abandoned by its Saxon population** and is overrun by Gypsies; it is a ruin now, unfortunately.

Relatives and friends, speaking strange languages and thinking in strange ways, have modeled my being. The diverse and diffident architecture of all these places in the past is the space in

---

* Near Braşov (t.n.)

** German colonists from Saxony were placed on the southern border of Transylvania in the XII-XIIIth centuries (t.n.)

which my being nevertheless danced freely. As in a hologram, this architecture was recast in Tulcea — the remembered city, once real, with little churches on all of its seven (how else?) mounds; the city so mercilessly destructured by insiders and outsiders alike in only twenty years. Not by the Russians, Lippovans, Turks, Greeks, Jews and Romanians who had lived here together for generations, but by the rootless people brought here from anywhere, by the upstarts and the nationalists and proletarians multilateral socialism had forged overnight.

## *Church as Manifesto*

The wooden churches of Transylvania are often interpreted in an autochthonist key, as the themes of identitary nationalism are projected upon their destiny. To such ideologues, the Gothic style is a forbidden source, be it even secondary. This architecture is strictly rural and, untainted by the "allogenes" of the Transylvanian cities, it embodies, doesn't it, the ostracized and oppressed Romanian-ness (all the more steeled for all that) of the Romanian folk across the Carpathians. Interpretations of all sizes and values, more or less current (Dănuț, Cristache-Panait, Godea) have in common the effort to prove the "authenticity" of this architecture and the refusal to admit any "contamination" by the Transylvanian urban Gothic flame and/or that of Greek Catholicism.

As a consequence, we witness today an amusing identification; the wooden churches — those farthest removed from the Orthodox-Byzantine influence of all churches in Romanian territory — are regarded as archetypes of the Romanian Orthodox church by Romanian communities in Berna and Caracas; in the Bucharest satellite district of Titan and at Tekirghiol Monastery; even a famous architect between the wars, H. H. Georgescu, designed an updated version of a Maramureşian church for the Orthodox Romanian-American Church in Cleveland. Why does the wooden church act as a condenser of the affective memory, of the national and religious identity of expatriates, although it is rather the exception from the rule and being of the Orthodox sacred space?

Neo-Romanianism used the same device when celebrating vernacular architecture as a condenser of the national identity. Yet the diversity of this architecture, influenced by regional factors, by relief, by exterior contacts (in the case of religious architecture) could have been cause for more caution among the initiators of this trend. Mincu brought to Bucharest the Sub-Carpathian middle class house from Muscel. His followers, however, made up along the way — forced by the requirements of urban architecture — a gigantic collage-architecture. The Romanian village did not have hospitals, banks, city halls or cathedrals that could be imitated. This caused the confusion of the language; since no precedents for urban programs existed, other than the single-family house, monasteries were celebrated as sources. Their planimetric type appears at Mincu's Central Girls' School. The Neo-Romanian style preached the error that the national character of an architecture could be ubiquitous and homogenous throughout that abstract concept called national state. The error is immediately visible for example at the Orthodox Cathedral in Cluj, in its context. The Neo-Romanian style is inadequate, however, only in rapport with the sources through which it celebrates itself, having betrayed them through the exile in the urban posture of programs for which no precedents existed.


## Naming/Imitating Places

The name of a place or of a locality is seldom an accident, as it seems to many of its interpreters, or to those who all too easily change it. It describes an attribute either physical or symbolical of the place; it incorporates the name of its founder, real or legendary (București); it celebrates some famous son or daughter, or an event associated with the place. Settled in time, the name of a place tells something about its history, as is the case for example of the Plaza nowadays De Gaulle, formerly of the Aviators, formerly Stalin, formerly Hitler etc..... In a certain way, its name conditions the development of a place; what kind of a genius loci could haunt a street named Overhead Crane or Tool and Die Makers Street, as is called the alley I look at from my office window? And what logic can be found in the fury of changing the name of the People's Army Boulevard — a name more related, granted, to Ceaușescu's "military doctrine" than to the country's troops as they get mentioned in liturgies — into that of Iuliu Maniu* (killed in prison by the communist regime) although a street bearing the same name already exists downtown, when, not far from the Government, a street by the name of Filimon Sîrbu** continues to call itself thus?

Perhaps we should recall here the major role played by the overnight change of place names in confusing the mental map of Bucharest residents. You went to sleep on a street with the name of a saint and you woke up living on Morning Glories Street. Miraculously, Mother of the Lord Street*** survived until the end. Unification Plaza, rumor has it, was to have been Victoria, and, as Caragiale would say, viceversa. The French had done the same after the 1789 Revolution, when they rebaptised streets, squares and entire cities, intending to wipe off all past history of the place.

Another example which is worthy of mention is Dobrogea, one of the most serious and least cited cases of appropriation of a territory which was explicitely Romanianized, both by changing the ethnic componency through massive colonization and by changing toponymies. Entire villages moved to Dobrogea after 1878; my paternal grandfather, like most folk in his village, was from Rîșnov; his village was called Dorobanțu de Tulcea but had

* Leader of the historical National Peasant Christian Democrat Party before the Second World War (t.n.)

** Communist hero, died 1941 (t.n.)

*** Large causeway in Bucharest (t.n.)

been called formerly Deliorman. And indeed the forest was visible still at the edge of the village. If most pre-1878 names said something about the physical or ethnic attributes of a place, those into which these names were changed, and especially after 1945, were of political color. For the sake of their distinctive sonority, bear with me as I will quote some of these names whose strange sounds enchanted my Dobrogean childhood in Dorobanțu de Tulcea: Coiumpunari, Caraorman (Lippovan villages), Beștepe, Ceamurlia, Altîn-Tepe, Enisala, Murighiol, Sarinasuf (Russian Slavs), Slava Rusă și Cercheză, Nalbant, Hamcearca, Balabancea (Ukrainians), Greci (the village of Italian stone masons near Măcin), Cerna (Bulgarians).

Afterwards we had Făgărașu Nou, Lumina, Izvoarele, but mostly Dorobanțu, Bălcescu, and Kogălniceanu whose name appears twice, once in each of the two Dobrogean counties*. The names of places were changed into "Romanian" names brought from elsewhere in the country. The place was thus taken into possession by way of toponymy also. Then, in the 1970's, more and more workers, many from Moldavia, poured into the aluminum and iron alloy factories, poisoning what ought to have been a touristic pearl (although not for long; visually, however, they will still poison the Western horizon). For this reason, the Moldavian inflexion can be heard today in the speech of the folk in Tulcea; many of the ethnic neighborhoods have vanished as they were replaced by tall apartment buildings; the Turkish bazaar disappeared from downtown and took with it that Oriental charm of the city I can still remember from my grammar-school days.

In the exceptional book *Old Times in Bucharest,* Alexandru Predescu also tells us the stories of some long-forgotten names, from "Pricopoaia" to "Duca's Lot", and from "Bridge's Head" to "Scufa's Village", not to mention the famous "Malmaison"**. They were replaced by others and then by others yet. The process will never stop.

---

\* *i.e.,* Constanța and Tulcea (t.n.)

\*\* All of these are former place names in Bucharest; most of the places have changed names and faces several times in the interim (t.n.)

## *Silk Mesh + Marble = Heaven*

In the book of Wilfried Wang about architects Herzog and De Meuron — ascending stars on the sky of contemporary European architecture — there is a project of a Greek Orthodox church, put together for the 1981 Contest organized by Hochbauamt der Stadt Zurich. The church is made of two buildings, one inside the other. The outer building, made of glass and ceramic, contains the inner one, of transluscent marble from Pentelic — like a temple. The common icons are silk-mesh serigraphs applied directly onto the marble. Daylight passing through the glass of the outer layer lights them up, while at night lights are turned on between the two "boxes".

We are, comments W. Wang, in front of a "tatooed space", recalling the serigraphs of Jean Nouvel at the Paris Institute of the Arab World. There, an entire wall of smooth glass is inscribed with arabesques behind which are placed photo-diaphragms which can control the amount of light admitted into the building. Sadly, the diaphragms are not in use today, due to the negligence of the current occupants of the building.

Also… transparent is the reference to the Rare Books Collection at Yale University, designed by Skidmore, Owings and Merill. Its façade is made of transluscent panels of marble. Inside, one feels like Jonah in the belly of the fish. The veins of the marble are drawn against the dim light.

The Orthodox church in Zurich, quite vibrant in its conceptual simplicity, represents a possible answer given by contemporary architecture to the Orthodox church. Its sacred architecture is everywhere at an impasse. Not only communism arrested the development of this architecture. Neither Greece nor Cyprus has produced any alternative. While Catholic architecture, like the adjacent theological discourse, has constantly adapted itself, through aggiornamento, to the times, and produced even modern masterpieces (e.g. Oscar Niemayer's Cathedral of Brasilia), the

234

Orthodox church has chosen immobility. The fascination of the Byzantine model, belonging to a more felicitous period in history when the Orthodox church was greatly expanding, has calcified into the obsession of the "national model", probably at the same time that Orthodox churches became everywhere autocephalous.

For the Romanian Orthodox, any prestigious example predating 1800, from Voroneț to Hurez and from the wooden churches of Transylvania to Agapia or Cozia is "national" architecture. The problem is that in the end the differences amoung these architectures are much more dramatic than the unifying similarities. In planimetries and decoration, the role of various influences — Armenian, Russian and Georgian in Moldavia, Serbian in Wallachia, Central-European in Transylvania — is essential to the configuration of as many regional types.

From this moment on, the local example is in its turn decisive. In Constanța for example, there are pre-1877 Orthodox churches which resemble local vernacular architecture as well as the local mosques. They are more screwed into their context than any programmatic application of a "model" could have dictated. Just between Bucharest and the seaside, a host of churches have invented a spirit of the place of their own — restrained, neoclassical, of uncertain stylistic age. Genius loci, like the national character, are not necessarily geysers from which just-so architecture cut to the desired size will burst forth spontaneously. Blaga, descending from Spengler, believed in the existence of a sort of matrix which gave substance to the shapes, here, of divine wisdom. However, the "character" is often a conclusion drawn a posteriori, by interpreting already existing artifacts.

Neo-Romanian architecture and the 1930's offered a dramatic answer. The New St. Spiridon Church is an exemplary urban silhouette. Cașin enchants us today, sixty years after it was built, as its dome floats above the Herăstrău Lake. However, a single successful example of a new church — i.e. built in the last seven years — is more difficult to find. Of course, there are replicas and pastiches. Wooden churches are built where you least expect them, mostly in unsuitable places; now Titan, now Drumul Taberei, Berna or Caracas. Companies such as "Secrets of Wood Ltd." have à la carte menus for all clients.

Good projects do exist. Yet somewhere between the clergy and the architects a gap still persists. After having designed a few churches myself, I can bear witness that not many channels of communication are open, as prejudice obstructs most of them. Projects as complex as the church in Zurich designed be Herzog and De Meuron will not be seen too soon in Romania. The few new projects that have appeared lately essentialize traditional forms rather than conceive new approaches. What should be our starting point?

Constantin Joja, an exceptional name in Romanian architecture, designed in the early nineteen forties a Cathedral of the Nation of exceptional value. As long as the idea of building a Cathedral of the Nation is yet in the air, Joja's project should be, at last, executed. It interrupts for a moment the nostalgia of the Byzantine and the national obsession. Back then, Joja's project seemed inspired by Speer, the great German architect, and was therefore labeled as a Nazi project, especially as Joja himself sympathized with Legionnaire political ideals. Today, freed from the ideological label, this vibrant project could be finally built.

## Identity vs. Modernity?

The argument does not really need the question mark; Japanese architecture has already given one possible answer to the question posed by Paul Ricoeur concerning the apparently insoluble dilemma facing all countries where the process of modernization proceeded very rapidly (as was the case in Japan after WW II). This dilemma can be briefly stated in the following terms: a state can either choose to modernize itself, but then faces the loss of its national identity, whose foundation is almost always in the past (monuments, founding myths, traditional culture etc.) and its displacement, at least in part, by a "Californizing" subculture, or it can refuse to let go of its identity, with the risk of missing out on all chances to modernize, of isolating itself in folk lore, of becoming a picturesque and nostalgic ghetto and thereby turning its back on history.

One example is the Romanian culture in general, but above all its architecture. If the language is unitary, the architecture of the Romanian regions is diverse, and the sacred architecture even more so. For this very reason, Orthodox architecture which was also required to represent national themes — from the new church of the Sinaia Monastery to the cathedrals built in Transylvania and to the obsessive Cathedral of the Nation, idée fixe of both yesterday and today — found itself in an even more dramatic impasse than Neo-Romanian architecture itself. What is Romanian-ness and, assuming it can be defined, how could it be translated into buildings which would carry its unmistakable imprint?

What can we remark if we look at the Japanese case? In its fundamental data, the architecture of the Extreme Orient resembles, more than other architecture of the temperate climate, the architecture of the Romanian Sub-Carpathian regions, not so much in the sense of a formal identity as in that of the simultaneous presence, both there and here, of a few elements which, for our area, have been identified with sufficient accuracy by Constantin Joja.

These elements are:

a) *The temporary character* — the Temple of Ise is periodically rebuilt on one of two alternating sites after the same changeles model, so that while matter wears out, the concept lives on unscratched, as a celebration without end of the incorruptible world of ideas.

b) The predilection for (on even exclusive use of) *wood* imposes and/or serves ephemerality, in the same way that rice paper walls do — separating interior space in the manner observed by

Gottfried Semper in the abode of Oceania, i.e. the fabric that is and is not, that separates without isolating, without consistency and, above all, without permanence.

c) *The dimensional modesty and austerity* make the Japanese house an ambiguous space to a functionalist, since the use of the tatami (or, in the case of the Romanian peasant house, of the "laviță"*) does not impose a single defined use of the interior space, which thus remains at the stage of a *vague space*[50]. Finally,

d) *The intermediary space, engawa* or, respectively, the porch/veranda of the Romanian peasant house, is a feature so remarkable that it rose to fame not only within vernacular architecture but also within the "professional" architecture, for example that of Kisho Kurokawa or, in Romania, that of the Neo-Romanian architects, or, after WW II, of N. Porumbescu's buildings and of his followers, or, at the seaside, of C. Lăzărescu's team.

An entire philosophy of transition and mediation, descended from Blaga and Noica, emerged as being useful to the achievement of the ideal toward which Romanian architects aspired not long ago, that of coupling an architecture based on an explicit refusal of tradition — modernism — with the "national character", a false identitary notion tainted by the rhetoric of nationalist ideology. This ideal was a camelostrich which did not work, not because there were no precedents[51] to back it, but probably because the premises of this aesthetico-political project were totalitarian rather than democratic. Conversely, its promoters seemed to believe that it was possible to entirely re-invent a built environment, regardless of any prestigious precedents, which were even violently replaced, in the very name of the tradition they loudly proclaimed to celebrate.

There is one more thing I would like to bring up in this short commentary on Japanese architecture after the war. When architects like Kenzo Tange and Kisho Kurokawa became

---

* Bed/sitting boards running the length of the interior walls in old peasant house (t.n.)

internationally known — it was the post-brutalist epoch of pop culture and urban utopias — the philosophical basis of their work surprised and instantaneously won over the Western world. The philosophy of symbiosis, which underlies "metabolism" — the name of the style imposed by this second generation of post-war Japanese architects — was described in some of Kurokawa's books and inscribed his name among those of the exceptional theoreticians of architecture, as witness the eulogizing commentaries on his work and perspective to be found in many overviews and syntheses of the period[52].

This consistent philosophical foundation not only made possible the radical renewal of the expression of Japanese architecture, but also conferred it a distinct identity which sets it apart in the history of world architecture from the 1960's. There are post-modernists like Arata Isozaki, late modernists and deconstructionists in Japan, too. The manner in which their work relates to the local tradition (as is the case with the concrete, glass and, recently, wood minimalism of Tadao Ando) and even to specific attributes of the site (as does the work of Yamashita, inscribed into the chaotic delirium of Tokyo) makes the Japanese experience an exceptional example, of a quality of its own.

This is a very well-known matter to Romanian architects. Many or the works of "parallel architecture" stepping out of the official paradigm of the 1980's, produced by Zoltan Takacs, Viorel Simion, Petre Ciuță, all members of the team headed by Mac Popescu, against the spirit of those times and, of course, in their margin, were implicitly or explicitly (in the case of Z. Takacs) contaminated by the Japanese experience. The Romanian participation at international competitions, the mentions and prizes obtained there all prove the steadiness of this fascination. In 1996, I described the phenomenon of contemporary Romanian architecture in a book published in Japan[53] in the manner in which it seemed likeliest that the Japanese public would find this a familiar story: as co-presence of tradition with renewing impulses which continue, however, to be dichotomous.

The revelation which Kisho Kurokawa's visit to Romania in 1985 produced, concretized in an exhibition and a conference, seemed to justify those who proposed the Japanese model as a successful one, contrasting with the Romanian model at the time, of a fusion between old and new. Nevertheless, it will take at least another generation and especially, I must insist, a philosophical, theoretical grounding of the architectural discourse, before the profound meaning of this successful model can take root in our soil, too.


## *Firmitas, Soliditas, Venustas?*

When he wrote his books of architecture, whose sphere of activity he extended to mechanics and clock-making, Vitruvius believed that, of course, the Romans were the center of the earth. Because of their distance from Rome, the Barbarians either had blood that was too thin or, like the strings on a lyre, voices that were so. The houses, bridges and aqueducts of the Romans (let us not forget that Vitruvius worked at the water adductions of Rome before writing his books) had therefore to respect the attributes of central buildings; stability, solidity and, above all, beauty.

The Romans had met the architecture of late Greece: in its "flamboyant" Hellenistic period, when classical perfection had already been contaminated not only by Egypt (this being, perhaps, as of so many other arts, its source) but also by the encounters with the Orient and even with India. The Romans themselves, without being inventors, drove to their structural and formal apogee some of the original ideas of urban civilization, picked up from just about everywhere in the Empire: the city laid out to a pre-established plan of the Milesians, the classical orders (to which they added the composite), the arch and the dome of the Orient. These later on rose to all-time fame as a consequence of the prestige the Roman Empire conferred upon them.

There is a hypothesis that styles alternate following an oscillatory movement between the Mediterranean styles of the sedentary population — solar styles (i.e. Latin) and the Northern styles of the migratory populations — lunar styles (i.e. Germanic and, more recently, Anglo-Saxon). One of the critics of modernism, Alain Calquhoun, even goes so far as to talk about different modernities, which differ amongst them by their mode of celebrating racial origins. One of these would be the architecture of the troglodytes — those who promote the punctual structure, recalling the pilasters of the lake-dwellings of the lacustrine period; another would be that of the sedentary primitives, in love with the consistency and coherence of walls. The Romanesque, Renaissance, classicism and a good chunk of modernism would be thus "Latin". They remind one of the manner in which Le Corbusier-the-primitive traced, in the spirit of Descartes, the clearing in which he would install his dwelling, a device of high historic unlikeliness which Joseph Rykwert recalls, too, in his famous *On Adam's House in Paradise*; it was the only way, though, to make the crystalline geometry of modernity, in love with what is rational, white, Mediterranean, meet, across eons, its own origins.

All "Latin" styles respect the Vitruvian triad, and Roman architecture, whose imperial prestige nourished all of them, superseded the Greek temples in historic dignity for two millennia. The discovery of the fact that the Greek had painted their temples — in about the same manner in which Michael Graves had his dwarf-supported hotel in Disneyland painted — amplified the prestige of the Roman temples even more, since these marble edifices weren't about to let down the trust invested in them, upon which the entire neoclassicism had been built. In contrast, the Greeks could appear even rudimentary, with their "negligent" way of placing statues and temples, organically, into the landscape, without rigorously respecting as the later Roman administration always did, the symmetry, foundation of eurhythmics, because a spatially representable essence of the divine order.

Only later on would a number of leftist Latin modernists disparage the "schizophrenic" or "fascist" (Bruno Zevi) character of symmetry (which, deprived of significance, was no longer the Greek symmetria nor Vitruvius's), leaving it to Anglo-Saxon postmodernists such as Michael Graves to rediscover it as a positive principle of establishing order in an architectural composition.

"Fascist" symmetry owed its prestige to the thirties, when the architecture of the buildings of power in Italy, France, and also Romania, celebrated unanimously a classical architecture which was that of Vitruvius's Romans. By order of Mussolini and under the baton of architects like Marcello Piacentini, Italian cities traded in their mediaeval, irrational centers for ample, Cartesian spaces, veritable forums in which were celebrated, as in Brescia, the gods of the new empire: money (the bank tower), communications (the post office building), political power (the Fascist Party headquarters) and, perhaps, culture. In Bucharest, too, the vestiges of a similar project can be detected. In the 1930's, it aimed to monumentalize a city which for too long had been no more than a patriarchal backwater, beneath the dignity of the Kingdom of the Greater Romania.

The inheritance left by Vitruvius was questioned by post-War modernism but also, and especially, by deconstruction. Neither the stability, nor the definitive character of the house, nor even the traditional meanings of beauty were left unquestioned, and most of those questions, it is time we should mention it, came from the Anglo-Saxons, from the "North". In contrast, Le Corbusier, Oscar Niemayer and Lucio Costa continued to "Romanize" architecture, classicizing it. Today, after post-modernism and deconstruction — the former a collection of features beloved by the Romans, not the least of which is the spirit of collage; the latter clearly "Northern" in architecture — we are confronted with a fragmentary landscape, as if after a cataclysm. In what follows I will present the contemporary destiny of some post-"Latin" architectural ideas. They are practiced with predilection in the Latin countries, or prolong concepts which claim direct and explicit descendance from the Roman tradition. These ideas are today:

1. Transparence (with the essential contribution of Jean Nouvel);

2. Trust in the professional tradition illustrated by Vitruvius — from classicity to post-modernism — an urban tradition which has produced edifices and spaces endowed with civic attributes (Martorell & Bohigas, and, for different reasons, Tomas Taveira in Spain, Luigi Snozzi in Italy or Ruy Ohtake in Brazil);

3. Celebration of that genius loci of the vernacular and the preservation of the appetite for the sacred (Mario Botta in Switzerland, Alvaro Siza in Spain, Șerban Sturdza and Radu Mihăilescu in Romania).

1. **Transparence** appears to be the entrance into nirvana of the modern architecture fathered by Le Corbusier. An apotheosis of rationality, it was able to find a few non-Latin advocates such as Philip Johnson or the Soviet architects who, in the late 1940's, discovered glass as a new construction material, out of which even furniture and ambient elements for the lodgings of workers returning from war were made — the "Stalinite". Jean Nouvel, however, was the architect who pushed transparence to its conceptual limit. In works such as Fondation Cartier, the Défense tower and even the finalist project for Tête Défense, he questions the character of an artifact of architecture, which disappears before our very eyes. It is there, reason tells us more than our sight; often it is not perceived as we stare right through it; therefore it is quite difficult to accept it as a building. With Jean Nouvel, architecture stepped onto another ontic level, resembling, virtual reality rather than the common, physical reality accessible to the senses.

2. **Civic building** is the uninterrupted line connecting Roman preoccupations to appropriate, through architecture, newly conquered territories, and, for example, "les grands projects" of President Mitterand. Projects like the Voisin Plan for Paris and "Cité radieuse?", both belonging to Le Corbusier, also occurred

243

along the way. Civic building is a mode of rationalizing space, by eliminating all chance and administering thus the potential for order of a given site. The Roman descendence of the gardens of Versailles seems as obvious to me as their willfully contorted pendant, La Villette Park of Bernard Tschumi. French architecture in its entirety is placed under the sign of this dominating will to reason. The aspiration toward civic buildings and civic spaces, toward urbanity, could thence be exported as a Roman-Gallic paradigm; Chandigarh in India and Brasilia in Brazil are reflections of this same aspiration.

Lucio Costa and Oscar Niemayer's Brasilia is from many points of view a grand finale of architectural modernity. Certain obligatory commandments of modernism are on the one hand heavily stated, on the other parasitized by "mannerisms" which, as became more and more obvious in the first decades after WW II, were inherent to the architecture produced by this aesthetics. For this reason, as we see today at Chandigarh, classical longings, monumental metaphors and urbanistic segregation of functions combine to create a distopia: that of the control exerted upon human living by the space this living is constrained to use.

While Le Corbusier, this genial chameleon, had the grace to accept the interventions of the Indian users upon "his" city, and declared with dignity that "Life is always right," Oscar Niemayer, as proved by a recent documentary, does not for an instant distance himself from this peak of his career. The Utopia is claimed on behalf of a political "left" typical for the place and the time, in which the impetus of social reform was both driven and curbed by the dual revolutionary ideology. In the film, Niemayer explains unapologetically why a socially reforming project had to be imposed in order to modify the behavior of generic "man" through architecture. Yet, despite its leftist ideology, Brasilia preserves all the segregations of a class system, and even introduces — through manipulation of the urban structure — means to control and check any "superposition" among "ghettoes". If we follow closely the urban logic Lucio Costa had in mind, we can easily grasp the consequences of mixing wishful thinking and practical reality. Despite the unjustified absence of sidewalks — by which all walking becomes a risky undertaking (even houses are placed at intervals suited to the rhythm of the automobile rather than that of the pedestrian); despite the topsy-turviness of a city whose center functions outside of it, as "head" rather than "heart"; despite the impossibility to seriously support the translation of certain visual metaphors into the urban texture, without any logic but the symbolic one (bird? crucified Jesus? — for the plan, and alms box? — respectively, for the Parliamentary "saucers" downtown) Niemayer does not flinch. Le Corbusier or, more recently, Philip Johnson, grew along with their own conception about architecture and its socio-cultural role; conversely, to persevere in the utopian error, as does Niemayer, even when its collapse is evident all around, speaks volumes about the death of a myth which was born in the Renaissance and expired in modernist times: the myth of the demiurgical architect, who can — and even should — manipulate reality as he wishes and as the potent client for whom he works commands.

In the meantime, Niemayer has received the Pulitzer Prize for Architecture, being a prolific giant of the post-war epoch, even if, in comparison with Le Corbusier, he appears minor. His Casino in Pampulha has become a museum, because gambling was outlawed. The living city of Brasilia has spread "out of bounds", disregarding Costa's un-living rules. The sculptural-monumental-organic concrete shapes of Le Corbusier and of Niemayer made a career, in this order, in Romanian architecture too: in Cezar Lăzărescu's early projects for the Black Sea coast, in certain works of Nicolae Porumbescu or in the Tulcea Train Station, all of which are indebted to this vocabulary also used by Philip Johnson and Minoru Yamasaki in the U.S. However, the marriage between modernism and classicism was nowhere quite as successful as in the architecture of the inter-bellum as illustrated by Piacentini,

245

Terragni and Libera, by Troost and Speer, by Pope and Luytens, and even by Duiliu Marcu and Horia Creangă, for instance.

In the apartment buildings designed by Le Corbusier fires are lit; people sleep in reed tents on the terraces; the administrative buildings outside the city are either abandoned among weeds of badly managed. Brasilia fares much better, thanks to the perfusion, it seems, of politico-administrative life. A single unchanged element: the Cathedral, scenographically as dramatic as in the beginning. Churches were the most successful creations of this architect, perhaps because through them he could exorcize his predilection for the metaphors of power. The angels floating about in the cathedral, hanging from invisible wires, are in the end his only excuse.

However, few have noticed that the entire program of building civic centers throughout the cities of Romania, a program that went on for two decades between 1968-1989, is also a child, though illegitimate, of a fictional Le Corbusier, brought up a Roman and then enrolled in the Communist Party. Haunted by sources such as the concrete palaces of Chandigarh, the monastery of La Tourette and the inverted conch of Notre Dame de Ronchamp, Romanian city halls keep watch over deserted "forums", plazas only the Revolution of 1989 briefly filled up with a spirit somewhat equivalent to that of their Roman originals.

The tradition of edifying and arranging the centers and the public places of cities appears to be dying down. After the unsuccessful German experiments of the sixties and the gigantic failure of Eastern European projects à la the "House of the People" and the "New Civic Center" in Bucharest, its most hideous examples, the spaces in which people meet, negotiate, exchange ideas and/or goods and make momentous public decisions disappear in order to pass on, emasculated, into the realm of virtual space. The Internet and television are such surrogate substitutes, barely camouflaging the removal of the right to self-determination from the hands of the individual and of the community, an essential right plainly affirmed and valuated within the urban space by the agora and the forum through their very centrality.

3. **Regional identity**, whose celebration need not be "Roman", is probably the most fertile direction today and in the near future among Latin countries. This culture of the productive marginality, actually opposed to the urban direction presented above, is the very charm of certain works belonging to Spanish and Portuguese architects, to a Swiss architect from Ticino, to several colleagues from Timișoara and so on. These architects oppose the disfiguring uniformization promoted by the center of power of national states, by the industrialization of buildings and the globalization of architectural expression. In celebration of the vernacular, of the spirit of place, of natural materials, of the craftsman's spirit of production, these architects keep their distance from the capital cities, from the public prestige brought by impressive commands from political powers, from serial houses, and even from projects in which the clients are too wealthy.

I lack the necessary data which would allow me to draw a conclusion about a "quiddity" shared by all of the Latin architectures, beyond the themes shown above. There is undoubtedly a common reservoir, an "arché-tecture" shared by all those who claim to descend from the inheritance of the Roman Empire. It will continue to be a fixed star, a prestigious point of reference for all those who should wish to found their building discourse on something other than volatile theories.

# NOTES

1. The new large church at the Monastery of Sinaia, whose feast day is the Trinity, is not a church built anew and from the very beginning as a Neo-Romanian church. It belongs to the new precinct of the monastery, which also contains the seniorial manor which housed the royal family between 1871-1882 (i.e. until Peleș Palace was finished), and later on was turned into a museum. First built between 1842-1846 and then deteriorated, the large church was completely rebuilt between 1893-1903 after the plans of architect G. Mandrea. The architecture of the new version tries to reconcile the conspicuous typological differences between Moldavia and Wallachia, by having recourse to the Byzantine supra-model which predates them both. The result is an eclectic church, whose repertory does not belong to the classical style but to the architecture of churches in then Romanian territory. The buttresses (from the structural standpoint unnecessary) can be seen as reverences paid to the Moldavian Gothic, while most of the stylistic details go back to the style of the Brâncoveanu period. Over all these, brick and plaster are laid in simple arches around the steeples, and respectively in alternating simple and double arches, these latter ones finished up with a green ceramic console going around the entire church. A reference to the religious architecture of Wallachia, this play of alternating brick-stone or brick-plaster is not, however, in its "authentic" state, Byzantine-Serbo-Wallachian, such as can be seen at Cozia's sick ward, for example, or at the princiary church at Curtea de Argeș, merely a decorative element (as at Sinaia) but a wall-building method, recalled here only in the two small steeples above the narthex.

248

There are, in all, three steeples — another element of church architecture in the South — because the Trinity feast day demanded it. Also, there is a green ceramic girdle made of three "ropes" twisted at intervals, which once again recalls the unity of the trinity; but could also be, and was, read in a nationalist key, as a "symbol of the three Romanian provinces, Transylvania, Moldavia, Wallachia, all united in a single Romania". The votive picture inside the church is another occasion for ambiguous commentaries on the question of national identity. King Carol I leans here against a chipped stone column, "an allusion to the Kingdom of Romania, from whence Transylvania, Bassarabia and Bukovina were missing", an interpretation unsupported by the author's intentions. King Carol I, who no doubt had a large say in the becoming of this monastery — for example, he brought in electricity, Sinaia being one of the first monasteries in the country to enjoy this facility — is not known as an enthusiastic supporter of the ideals of unification. Neither before nor after the building of this church did he show himself as a partisan of the unification between his kingdom and Transylvania, although he did permit the cultural support of the Romanian population across the Carpathians, within the bounds, however, imposed by the secret alliance treaty he had signed and to which he was faithful. If the allusion to the architecture of Moldavia can be accepted as possible, no doubt all identification of the Holy Trinity with the triune nature of the future national state of Romania (constituted in any case after the King's death) is quite risqué (and in any case a posteriori).

The eclecticism of the church is also visible in the utilization of several types of crosses for its crown; one Greek — hence with equal arms — above the atrium, a Latin cross on each of the small steeples above the narthex, respectively a triune cross, of Slavic (or baroque, through the Slavic connection?) on the large steeple. Added to these crosses is the sun inscribed in the Latin cross surmounting the bell tower, and the cross called "Stephen the Great's" atop the old church. The description cannot be complete without mentioning the bell tower, built before the reconstruction of the large church (in 1892), itself a monumental commentary on the architecture of monasteries of the Brâncoveanu period, of which a faithful replica is here given, unlike the free interpretation which, later on, would be proposed by the church.

249

2. The Cathedral of Sibiu was built between 1902-1906. Architect Joseph Konner (of Budapest) won the contest also entered by architects from the Romanian Kingdom. The construction itself was entrusted to Joseph Schussing. The steeples, 58 meters (approx. 175 ft.) tall, are visible everywhere in the old city. The painting was partially executed by O. Smigelschi (the Pantocrator, the angels, the apostles and the altar screen), while the sculpture of the altar screen, by C. M. Balic of Bucharest, and the pews, by Emil Pătruș of Sibiu. As can be seen, the Cathedral is Central-European par excellence; in addition, the altar shrine was wrought in Wurtemberg, the chandelier, in Vienna, and the mosaics were done in München.

Built at the same time as the large church at the Monastery of Sinaia, the Cathedral of Sibiu illustrates another manner of interpreting tradition. The question of an architecture that should evince the "national character" could not exist in turn-of-the-century Transylvania. The absence of ample urban models belonging to the ethnic majority was complicated by the impossibility to investigate, in order to dress up a repertory of "Romanian" forms, all precedents, be they urban or rural, sacred or secular, mainly for political reasons. Moreover, there just weren't any Romanian architects in Transylvania who should programatically care about a "national" formal language in the way that Romanian architects, members of the National School in the Kingdom, did. The Cathedral of Sibiu is the work of a Hungarian architect, partially painted by a Romanian painter, decorated by Germans. Its source is St. Sophia. More than the large church at Sinaia, the Cathedral of Sibiu appears as the collective work of an eclectic and cosmopolitan social body.

The Orthodox church was not part of the privileged religious cults and, with the exception of a few wooden churches about which it is difficult to affirm that they be Orthodox of Greek Catholic without committing an act of interpretative hybris, it has not produced any kind of models which could be quoted as different from the architecture of the churches belonging to the other rites established in Transylvania. Perhaps only the unusual aspect of the rosace on the western tympanum, above the entrance, might recall the architecture of Budapest's and Vienna's train stations rather than Orthodox architecture. Made of clear glass, this semicircular sezession window is the mark of contemporaneity on an edifice whose primary model is St. Sophia, the archetype of Eastern

250

churches, and, on the level of decoration, Byzantine architecture. The reference to Byzantium appears to have been satisfying to all parties involved. Since the edifice was thus a "creation" of Justinian, it preceded the Schism and could not offend anybody — Catholic, Greek Catholic or Protestant. Also, the reference to St. Sophia eliminated all possible ethnic connotations. Finally, the Byzantine model was more worthy of a city belonging to a great monarchy than the mostly vernacular buildings, mostly small, which embodied Transylvanian Orthodoxy at the time.

3. "Romanian architecture is made without great concern for endurance, in the spirit of seasonal intermittence. Houses and churches grow and disappear, disappear and grow, like the ear of wheat which, harvested, is sown again, like the leaf which, as it falls, leaves behind it the latency of another leaf" (qtd. by Corneliu Bucur in *Transilvania* 1-2 (1995):63).

4. The Cathedral of Târgu Mureş was designed by Victor Vlad, Professor at the Polytechnic Institute of Timişoara, and built between 1925-34. The Greek-cross floor plan measures 48 metres (about 150 ft) on each side. The height of the steeple is 52 m (162 ft). The entire interior space of the church has a pronounced vertical silhouette; the steeple is not greatly detached from the rest of the church, as is common at many other cathedrals of the same period. With a total surface of 1300 square meters (12,000 sq, ft.), the church was painted by Nicolae Stoica in a manner which explains the role of this church as catalyst of the ethnic and religious revival in this area; for example, twelve medallions are painted that represent old Romanian churches from Transylvania — thus reaffirmed through this iconic presence.

5. It is difficult to decide if the model is the enclosed courtyard of the Orthodox monastery or the cloister of the Western one, celebrated in university spaces in Oxbridge or in France.

6. This construction device is in use even today in the vernacular architecture around Curtea de Argeş and Râmnicu Vîlcea.

7. According to the presentation in the church pronaos.

8. "Moral and spiritual requirements, in the first place, and practical and material ones, in the second place, which religious architecture must rigorously fulfill, have always represented the most delicate problems for architects. An aspect full of élan and of harmonious monumentality on

the level of aesthetics, combined with an endurance assumed and wished to be eternal, on the material and even spiritual level, can be achieved under certain special conditions of scale, namely on surfaces as capacious as can be" (*Arhitectura* 3-4 (1942): 9).

9. When Joja returned to his plea in favor of a fusion between modernism and autochthonism, his theoretical texts (either those in which Neo-Romanian architecture is analyzed or that in which the shade as vehicle of expressiveness is celebrated) however subtle no longer produced the same remarkable results. The extended series of porches prolonged horizontally and superposed vertically in order to form tall buildings, or the idea of using new materials that would imitate the old ones no longer had the force of his original solutions. Moreover, when his ideas were impounded by protochronism and by the nationalist ideology which reappeared after 1971 — along with those of N. Porumbescu — and when they were widely and uncritically preached in the schools of architecture, malignant deviations appeared; the prefabricated "national character" is only the best known of them. For a critique of Joja's views, I will refer the reader to my article in *Arhitectura* 1-2 (1990), which unfortunately appeared immediately after Joja's death, a circumstance which cut its chances of being properly received. Many of the arguments set forth there would need refining today, but I still subscribe to the opinion that the architect allowed himself to be manipulated in the context of the national-communist ideology of that epoch. In the end, however, his intervention on behalf of the villages which were being demolished at the time proved the independent thinking of this great architect and theoretician.

10. I've brought up the possibility of building this remarkable project in both *Dilema* ("The Cathedral of the Nation" issue of 1997) and *Libertatea* (5 February 1998). The only echo so far has come, in the same issue of *Dilema*, from His Holy Highness Bartolomeu Anania (Archbishop of Cluj), who stated that he was aware of this project and that it could be a basis for the execution of the Cathedral of the Nation.

11. This calls to mind Joja's explicit aversion toward roofs, which subverted his theories about national characteristics in architecture. Architecture, he claimed, inheres in what is under the roof, in the series of posts of the peasant-house porch, and not in the shape — determined exclusively by its function — of the roof topping it.

12. "Inside, especially, one will not be able to see all the space at a glance, as the excessively tall steeples will not be visible except from a point directly underneath them. This flaw appears in most old churches of both Moldavia and Wallachia, thereby excusing the project's shortcoming" (*Arhitectura*, 1942: 24).

13. "The author presents the plan of a modest Moldavian church, clearly separated in two equal parts — naos and pronaos — by means of a forcefully marked and for this reason awkward passageway, complete with massive rectangular pillars which obstruct the interior view" (Sp. Cegăneanu, 1942: 36).

14. The authors pursued "with thoroughness the main objective — the flawless functionality of the entire ensemble (...)" (Maicu, 1962, I; orig. ital.).

15. The discussion concerns one-bedroom apartments (cca 31 sq. m= 275 sq. ft.) representing 60% of the total number of apartments, two-bedroom apartments (37-42 sq.m = 333-380 sq.ft.) representing 35% of the total surface, and only 16 three-bedroom apartments and 36 studio apartments for a total of 5%. The justification of the typology of these apartments is quite interesting: "their design had as its starting point the idea that the *modern way of life* which reduces the activity of the cook to the quick preparation of semiprepared dishes and/or heating and serving ready-made ones, available today to our citizens through food markets, will no longer require a large kitchen but, in contrast, a small but well-equipped one. For this reason, the kitchens in these apartments have a *minimal surface* (cca. 4 sq.m.= 36 sq. ft.) (compare with the average 8 sq.m.= 72 sq.ft. per kitchen allowed in the 1980's, note mine) (...) bathrooms have *minimal sizes and are grouped around a prefabricated sanitary node*". Moreover, "a significant number of apartments was furnished with *modern furniture and delivered thus to the future residents*" (Maicu, 1962,; 8; in italics I have marked all the "modern" references that in part recall Khrushchev's speech). Notice the "educational" role given to architecture and furniture — to which were added the walk-in closets and built-in cabinets, appliances, Venetian blinds and so on — in modifying the traditional urban way of life.

16. Architects C. Moșinschi, D. Slavici and Gh. Gogulescu, see *Arhitectura R.P.P.* 10-11 (1958): 50-51. The discussion is not about one of the contest projects, but about another one which merely invokes the

principles of the contest-winning project as being equivalent to those of the project that was later executed.

17. With the additional remark that the published project has a still "Stalinist" colonnade on its ground floor and mezzanine, with arches in full cintre alternating with rectangular episodes, which is not to be found in the much sterner building actually built, with a superior part also quite different from the projected one.

18. Cezar Lăzărescu lectured on the theme of the current stage in the projecting activity at the Romanian Architect' Union on January 15-16, 1957, at the opening of an exhibition of "Balneo-climateric Constructions on the Black Sea Coast", after the trade publication *Arhitectura*, a year before, had featured the projects in many of its pages. Already then the ambiguous change in the vocabulary was quite distinct; on one hand there are picturesque classical projects such as the Rest Home for the Defense Ministry in Mamaia, by Irena and C. Ghițulescu, Adrian Corvătescu, described in extenso in *Arhitectura RPR* 1 (1957), which reminds one of Marcu and Cantacuzino; on the other hand, "purebred" modern projects had already appeared.

19. In urbanism, the enemy of the exhibition was the "capitalist urbanistic chaos", whose equivalent was represented by the Hansaviertel project of West Berlin — we learn from *Arhitectura RPR* 3 (1958) — as was, in fact, the entire Interbau project. Hansaviertel is a group of apartment buildings which were placed freely in the landscape of a West-Berlin park in the vicinity of the Brandenburg Gate, designed by 53 architects who at the moment were world-renowned.

20. "Folk architecture, as the architecture of the villages, is a product of peasant culture. The peasant has a mentality of his own, which is mirrored in all of his achievements, characterized by pragmatism and economy of means. These characteristics account for the fact that the peasant treats building problems without the romanticism of some city dwellers, whose expectations with regard to their houses concern very often a false stylistic décor" (Radu Crăiniceanu, "Case noi în Valea Jiului" (New Houses in Jiului Valley) *Arhitectura* 9 (1957)).

21. *Arhitectura* 3 (1957); 10.

22. The reaction against mainstream architecture can sometimes be read as a resistence against the majority and its tradition. "Are Le Corbusier's style and impact in Britain at all related, for example, to the

fact that his ancestors were Huguenot?", Linda Colley asks in "In the British Taste" (*Times Literary Supplement*. Nov. 10, 1995; 9). Although, it seems, the argument is distorted — Le Corbusier's ancestors were apparently Cathares and not Huguenot — it can probably be prolonged into the obsession of the marginal to defy the traditional center which it would conquer and/or remodel, as well as into the sectarian obstinacy to build alternative communities (twice utopian, urbanistically as well as geographically) in illuminist America and even in the U.S.S.R. after 1917.

23. To which J.L. Cohen, curator of the exhibition "Scenes of the World to Come — European Architecture and the American Challenge, 1893-1960" (Montreal June 14-Sept. 24, Edinburgh November 3-17, 1995), refers, I think abusively, as an expression of the "Americanization" of European architecture (namely, British), since it has enough conditioning coordinates of its own, so that we need not invent other genealogies and influences.

24. The author represented, it seems, the interests of the concrete makers; from this perspective, the formal history of the edifice, which claimed to be a manifesto of modernist renewal, receives a commercial tone.

25. See for more on this a few relatively recent studies on the plurality of modern voices, all equally justified: studies by Charles Jencks (*Modern Movements to Architecture*, 2nd ed. New York; Penguin, 1985), Colin St. John Wilson (*The Other Tradition of Modern Architecture — The Uncompleted Project,* Academy Editions, 1995), William J. R. Curtis (national voices and alternative discourses in *Modern Architecture since 1900*, Oxford; Phaidon, 1982), and Kenneth Frampton (*Modern Architecture — A Critical History*, 2nd ed. Thames and Hudson, 1992).

26. Essential to the period is Collin Rowe's work of 1978 entitled *Collage City*, an American replica of Rossi's book. The utopian idealism of modernity, its global visions proved naïve, Rowe believes, because the city has always been a collage, a juxtaposition of more or less haphazard fragments.

27. Which I have graphically formulated and explained first of all in my book, *Arhitectura și Puterea* (*Architecture and Power*).

28. Also in *Architecture and Power* I state that political power has few privileged spheres of action in architecture — central and local

administration buildings chief among them — without always penetrating what is (relatively) marginal with regard to the political discourse as affirmed in architecture. Sometimes dwellings, other times industrial architecture (although Stalinism wished to "classicize" the proletarian space, too) enjoy this marginality. The pressure of the "court" aesthetics is complete and inescapable in the superior sphere, but indirect, sporadical and peripheral in the inferior sphere, where islands of creative freedom can paradoxically survive. "Parallel architecture," as Radu Drăgan called it in the issue of *Arhitext* dedicated to the phenomenon in 1990, was a consequence of such odd breaches in the monolithic discourse of totalitarianism — an "enlightened" local despot, a friend in the Party nomenclature controlling licenses, pure chance or well-maneuvered chance.

This interpretation alters somewhat Groys' view concerning the underground continuity between avant-garde and the architecture of totalitarian regimes. The current production of architecture, from the infrastructure to social edifices, generally verifies the theory of the continuity, without having as explanation a Machiavellism of the political power but rather its indifference to expression, and, sometimes, the identity of functions requiring a similarity between formal solutions. In contrast, in the domain of official architecture ("the Furher's buildings" in Germany, the royal and governmental building in Romania during Carol II's reign, EUR and the Palace of the Soviets), the recoil is not only visible, but dramatic. Of course, we are confronted with a similar longing to rewrite (urban) reality from the ground up, but the aspect of these representative edifices of power is quite different from that of avant-garde buildings. One of the reasons, in the 1920's-1930's, was also that the avant-garde had not as yet succeeded in formulating its own credible versions of representative edifices. In addition, the theme of a justifying continuity could not achieve its full expression through an architecture of the voluntary rupture.

29. On the question of the several generations of Romanian architects we shall comment in a separate text. A comparison of the generations of the fifth, sixth, seventh decades, of their professors and of their rapport with the political pulsations could be clarifying in what concerns the architectural discourse itself.

30. See *Arhitectura* 3-4 (1940): 45, where, within the text of the review of the exhibition "Legionnaire Work in the Arts", we find the photograph of the splendid scale model of the Church of the Nation, by Constantin Jojea (sic) and, by the same architect, this time as co-author along with N. Goga, I. Pușchilă, V. Stănescu, the scale model of a Palace of Culture. The change in external source becomes obvious. If the Carol II style was indebted to Piacentini's "Fascist" architecture, Speer becomes the spiritus rector of "Legionnaire" architecture. Let us also remark in the same review the laudatory presentation of the second issue of the publication *Simetria*, dedicated to the question of the national identity of Romanian architecture, albeit obliquely.

31. About the confusion between vernacular (folk) and professional architecture which Joja occasionally commits, I have written extensively in *Arhitectura*, a text which also appeared in *Arhitectura și Puterea (Architecture and Power)*. The interested reader is referred to this source for a more amply supported critique of Joja's works.

32. "Defining an object through a measure which is its own, absolute and unique is a requirement of every natural creature, but also of every work of architecture. By its nature, every thing is the application of an idea which is only repeated in its general features" (Michelis, 1982: 208).

33. See for example the interview of Viorel Simion by Radu Drăgan in *Arhitectura* 6 (1987) 26-38, in which the name of Louis Kahn comes up over and over again.

34. But somewhere deep beneath the surface, many ancient and mediaeval cities developed "spontaneously" have "ideal" and/or sacred geometric designs as matrices. The Roman legacy, assimilated by the mediaeval cities which continued the imperial settlement, could be one of the causes. The nature of the foundation rites and their urban expression could also be factors. For those who study the architecture of Bucharest, it will probably come as a surprise to learn the conclusion of the late Dana Harhoiu, according to whose research the Capital is a much less chaotic city than we have been accustomed to believe. On the contrary, it would appear that there is a concentric development of the sacred sites around Metropolitan Hill which, joined with "the navel of the city" — the Old Church of St. George — and with the Monastery of Mihai Vodă, forms a triangular matrix of the city center. The bisectrix

257

of this angle is Calea Moșilor, the old commercial road entering the city from Moldavia.

35. Stories and anecdotes transmitted by those who were in effect characters in this drama simplify the question which, otherwise, could have lent itself to who-knows-what interpretative twists. The architect Jugurică, upon Ceaușescu's request that proposals for a new center of the city be presented, would have pulled out the plan conceived between the wars from the archives and would have shown this to Ceaușescu. Of course, the differences between the inter-bellum plan and the tragi-comical blunder which actually got built are themselves dramatic.

Oral history is useful in the study of the processes going on behind the totalitarian scene. Without it, one could easily fall in the trap of all kinds of apocalyptic interpretations, as is the one that sees the demolitions of the 1980's as a fatality which could not have been avoided since, in any case, and above ideologies, Arsenal Hill had been earmarked as site of a major edifice. This line of reasoning, needless to say, is internally vitiated.

36. The first apartment buildings on the Victoria Socialismului Blvd. appeared in the Unification Plaza front and were inspired, apparently upon Ceaușescu's very own suggestion, by the flamboyant building by Petre Antonescu in the Senate Square. Why was the building next to Antonescu's, Cucu's severe and imposing creation, not chosen? Could only the longing for decoration be the reason? We shall never know.

37. Anca Petrescu, pet architect of the Ceaușescu couple, boasted that she had "saved" the friezes of the Văcărești Monastery, by copying them in the ornamentation of the House of the Republic!

38. The interior floor plans of many apartments facing the boulevard are relatively independent of the rhythm of filled/hollow spaces in the façades. Interior walls can be found that coincide with the windows as well as many other such discrepancies between inside and outside.

39. "There was no ideology of a National-Socialist architecture... in the end, only the gigantic size mattered... The ideology was visible in the definition of the theme, but not in its style" (*The Spandau Diary*). And someplace else: "In architecture the only new thing was the definition of the command. When the order called for a large plaza that could accommodate parades, that had to have a certain length by a certain width, so that a number of several thousands or several tens of thousands,

258

or even hundreds of thousand, could march through, while seventy, eighty or even hundreds of thousands of people would watch them go by from the stands, naturally, then, this order of magnitude was determined by the political and ideological aspect" (qtd. in *Simetria*, Spring 1995; 113 14).

40. Part of the architecture after 1990 can be classified as pseudo-vernacular. Many architects have flattered the doubtful taste of their clients, the nouveaux riches. Certainly these architects would not wish to have their creations and their names in any way associated by posterity.

41.This text was written before the apparition of a McDonald's at Piaţa Unirii (Unification Plaza).

42. The southern gate bears the inscription "Southfork Ranch in Hermes Land", that is, we have stepped out of chaos and into a well-defined topos, a patch of land that has been saved from the generic "national territory", endowed with attributes of its own and a conspicuous identity: Hermes Land.

43. "The Earth is what, by its essence, closes. To pro-pose the earth means to lead it toward the Open, as being that which closes. The work fulfills the high fact of this pro-posal of the earth by that fact that of itself it re-poses into the earth" (Martin Heidegger apud. Michel Haar, 1998: 130).

44. "Every great work — plastic, musical, poetic — raises in the consistency of a singular earth a configuration (Gestalt) of 'truth', or of un-covered-ness" (Haar: 131).

45. A more detailed discussion is probably warranted as to how similar is the given site to the site called into being by the house or the bridge built on it. No doubt there is a certain potential quality in the site, making it eligible as ground for a house. Even if architects like Botta speak of the "building of the site", that is about preparing it to receive the work, and for this reason they are appreciated by Kenneth Frampton in his "Towards A Critical Regionalism" (1982), even if "The site does not always already exist before the bridge" (Heidegger "Building Dwelling Thinking": 185), I believe that we can justifiably propose the idea that *sites build potentially the buildings through which they will pro-pose themselves*, that the encounters occur not as the shaping and coagulation of an amorphous and "slippery" matter but, to paraphrase the Bible, half-way between an "earthly Jerusalem" (the site) and a "heavenly" one (the

ideal/imaginary, the project of the house). Not only do houses choose their site, but also the site should be able to choose the manner of the houses it grounds.

46. "But only a thing which is itself a place can order a settling" (Heidegger "BDT": 184).

47. This is not to say that hearing, for instance, is not in its turn a mode in which to experience the space of a building. In a conference delivered in January 1999 at the Institute of Architecture "Ion Mincu", Professor Liviu Dimitriu from USA Institute in New York spoke with passion about the attention paid by the architect of Vicenza, Carlo Scarpa, one of the pre-eminent names of "phenomenological" architecture, to sound in his architecture.

48. See the discussion of a "Communist Disneyland" in the competition of ideas for the House of the Republic (UAR, 1991), then immediately thereafter in *Arhitectura şi Puterea* (*Architecture and Power*, Agerfilm, Bucharest, 1992).

49. This is also the title of a recent book about his work; *Radical De-Construction*, New York; Princeton Architectural Press, 1997.

50. For an ampler discussion of the concept of vague space, I refer the reader to the article by the same title published through the kindness of Mr. Adrian Popescu in the magazine *Steaua* (*The Star*) 7-8 (1998); 96-9.

51. If we were only to recall Le Corbusier's late style, which remained, however, inimitable, as bear witness almost all attempts to copy it (Brasilia, Romanian civic centers) and which almost all failed, some lamentably (the same Romanian civic centers).

52. See for example in Charles Jencks and Karpf, eds. *Theories and Manifestoes of Contemporary Architecture*. London: Academy Editions, 1997 Kurokawa ("Metabolism in Architecture") as well as Arata Isozaky ("The Island Nation Aesthetic"), or the praise of metabolism by Kenneth Frampton in his synthesis *Modern Architecture − A Critical History*, London: Thames and Hudson, 1994 (Ist ed. 1980).

53. *581 Architects in the World*, Tokyo; Toto Shuppan, 1995; 242–5.

# BIBLIOGRAPHY

Antonescu, Petre. Biserici nouă — Proecte și schițe ("New Churches — Projects and Sketches"). Communication at the Romanian Academy, May 1, 1942. Bucharest: Bucovina Press, I.E. Torouțiu, 1943.

Blaga, Lucian. Case românești ("Romanian Houses"). *Cuvântul* 2 274 (1925): 1, qtd. in *Transilvania* 1-2 (1995): 61-2.

Chaunu, Pierre. *Civilizația Europei în Secolul Luminilor*, trans. fr. (*European Civilization in the Century of the Enlightenment*) 2 vols. Bucharest; Meridiane, 1986.

Ioan, Augustin. Fenomenul Joja ("Joja's Phenomenon"). *Arhitectura* 1-2 (1990)

*** *Arhitectura și puterea* (*Architecture and Power*). Bucharest: Agerfilm, 1992

*** *Celălalt modernism* (*The Other Modernism*). Bucharest: IAIM, 1995.

Ionescu, Grigore. Despre arhitectura religioasă la români ("On Romanian Religious Architecture"). *Arhitectura* 1-2 (1940): 6-25.

*** *Istoria arhitecturii pe teritorul României de-a lungul veacurilor* (*The History of Architecture within Romania's Territory*). Bucharest: Romanian Socialist Republic Academy Press, 1982.

Joja, Constantin, *Sensuri și valori regăsite (Rediscovered Meanings and Values)*. Bucharest: Eminescu, 1981.

*** *Actualitatea tradiției arhitecturale românești (Romanian Architectural Tradition Today)*. Bucharest: Ed. Tehnică, 1984.

*** *Arhitectura românească în context european (Romanian Architecture in the European Context)*. Bucharest: Ed. Tehnică, 1989.

Radu, Cezar, Restructurare, valoare și specific național în arta organizării spațiului ("Restructuring, Value and National Character in the Art of Organizing Space") in *Artă și convenție (Art and Convention)*. Bucharest: Ed. Științifică & Enciclopedică, 1989.

## Periodicals

Arhitectura 2-3 (1939), 1-2 (1940), 3-4 (1940), 3-4 (1942).
Secolul XX — Bucharest, 4-6 (1997).

PRINTED IN ROMANIA BY R.A. MONITORUL OFICIAL